W9-BGH-501

THE GILDED DOME

The Gilded Dome

THE U.S. SENATE AND CAMPAIGN FINANCE REFORM

By Greg D. Kubiak

UNIVERSITY OF OKLAHOMA PRESS : NORMAN AND LONDON

Library of Congress Cataloging-in-Publication Data

Kubiak, Greg D. (Greg Dale), 1960–
    The gilded dome : the U.S. Senate and campaign finance reform /
by Greg D. Kubiak.
        p.   cm.
    Includes index.
    ISBN: 0–8061–2621–3 (alk. paper)
    1. Campaign funds—United States.   2. Campaign funds—Law
and legislation—United States.   3. United States. Congress. Senate.   I. Title.
JK1991.K83   1994
324.7′8′0973—dc20   93–45027
                                                                              CIP

Book designed by Bill Cason

The paper in this book
meets the guidelines for
permanence and durability
of the Committee on Production Guidelines
for Book Longevity of the
Council on Library Resources, Inc.

1   2   3   4   5   6   7   8   9   10

To Mom and Dad,
for all their past support,
and to
Jeffrey, Stephen, Ryan,
Stephanie, Anna, and Annie,
for all their future dreams,
this book is dedicated.

Contents

Illustrations

Acknowledgments

I COULD NOT HAVE WRITTEN *The Gilded Dome* without the help, support, and encouragement of a number of people. Thus, I wish to say thank you to the University of Oklahoma Press, particularly Kimberly Wiar and my editor Mildred Logan, for their hard work and faith in first-time authors; Helen Alexander, my aunt and godmother, who assisted during my leave of absence with warm encouragement and important provisions; Bill Bailey, for proofreading, photography, faith, and friendship; David L. Boren, the hero of campaign reform, who gave me the background and his blessings for this book; Jamie Bowers and Karen Kay Speer, two of the best LCs and friends a Hill staffer could ever have, who helped me lubricate the slow-moving wheels of the legislative process; Taylor Bowlden, my friend who demonstrated that political disagreement and respect were not mutually exclusive on Capitol Hill; the late David Burr, my mentor, friend, and teacher, who encouraged my career, in whatever form it took; Pamela Brannon, fellow writer and cheerleader; former and current Boren staffers Cody Graves, Kellye Eversole, John Deeken, Dan Webber, and Beth Garrett, friends and fellow LAs; Mike Geissinger, a gifted and talented photographer, for use of his work in this book; Robert Hall III, who read through some rougher drafts of the manuscript; Brooks Jackson, renowned journalist and fellow author, who gave early encouragement for this project; Marty Lobel, my attorney and a valued adviser; David Mallery, for his motivation and bus ride pep talks and the chance to be inspired at his 1991 Westtown seminar; Susan Manes, for countless hours of lobbying me on the issue of campaign finance reform; Joyce McCray and the Council for American Private Education, for support during a critical leave of absence to complete the manuscript; my "family" at National City Christian Church in Washington; Frank Reiche, former FEC commissioner and election law expert, for his interview and visits; Laurie Sedlmayr, my former confidante from the Hill and great friend, who gave a crucial, final proofing of the entire manuscript between Anna's naps and feedings; Paul Somelofske, for proofing, artistic direction, and suggestions on references to "lawyers"; Patrick Turner, a superb legislative correspondent, a great proofreader, and a special friend; Laure Vaught, Denis Rischard, and Kim Ritchie, for unlimited friendship and encouragement; Charlie Ward, the "third Senator from Oklahoma," who steered me to Washington years ago; and my parents, Curtis and Pearl Kubiak, who have always given me their love and support.

Introduction

AS A CHIEF LEGISLATIVE ASSISTANT to a U.S. senator, David L. Boren, I had a unique view of our nation's Capitol. From a close vantage point, I participated in the legislative process and saw how political money and personalities of power had an influence on it. This story of Senate consideration of campaign finance reform legislation offers a view of a concealing and attractive Capitol, a view of a "gilded dome."

This book covers the seven-year struggle in Congress as members debated, delayed, and voted on legislation to curb their own appetite for money and its power. It is about personal experiences and observations, with a few biases about money in politics and the legislative process. It was not my intent to write an objective history of Senate action or inaction. That can be obtained from the *Congressional Record* and other library sources.

Although I state my remedy for reform of our unhealthy system of campaign finance in the last chapter, my purpose is not so much to vent political views. The challenge is for the reader to ponder his or her views of governmental power. From whom does that power come? From lobbyists, political action committees, the people? My view is that the way we allow our representative institutions of democracy at the national level to finance campaigns is corrupt. A system that puts a premium on money in politics is a system that puts style and delusion over substance and debate.

It is my hope that *The Gilded Dome* will shed light on just how our laws are made, our taxes collected, and our future as a nation formed: all are influenced by the unchecked power of money. In it, I take some shots at Republicans and some at Democrats. In other instances, I take aim at incumbent candidates on behalf of challengers whose prospects of success appear bleak. From time to time, bias toward the Senate over the House will be detected. I do not hesitate to identify heroes and heretics. The complex mosaic of personalities is further evidence that politics permeates all we do.

The material for this book comes from a number of sources, most of them static. With eight boxes packed with photocopies of personal files and about twelve feet of shelf space filled with binders, appointment calendars, telephone logs, books, congressional hearing records, and other material, I accumulated enough paper to create a simulation of the great fire of Chicago.

I also used other written sources for this project. In addition to news stories from the *Washington Post*, the *New York Times*, the *Wall Street Journal*, and *Roll Call* and other periodicals, I drew on such sources as Brooks Jackson's *Honest Graft* (New York: Alfred A. Knopf, Inc., 1988) and David Magleby and Candace Nelson's *The Money Chase* (Washington, D.C.: Brookings Institution, 1990).

Other sources were very dynamic—living people—in the form of written and spoken interviews. They included current and former congressional staffers and members of Congress, journalists, academics, lobbyists, lawyers, and even an occasional "ordinary" citizen. I should also note that while most of the quotations in conversations are taken directly from my notes from the time, I did make small changes to correct syntax.

The final source was my own memory. Between my 1990 departure from Senator Boren's office and the day the final draft of the manuscript went to the publisher, the legislative battle over campaign finance reform was kept fresh and vivid. I could not escape my desire to tell this story as daily media reports, news articles, professional challenges, and dinner conversations reminded me that money plays too big a role in the governance of this nation.

If the subject of this book were revenge, it might have entailed a plot with grotesque mass murders. If the subject of this book were romance, it would have developed into a steamy, X-rated novel. But *The Gilded Dome* is a book on money, power, and government. You will read of political action committees buying access to Congress, not of a murder weapon discovered with blood and flesh fragments. Instead of a wife discovering her husband's affair, you will hear a congressional aide reveal that a $5,000 fund-raising dinner "bought" his boss's vote on a banking amendment.

Do not read this book as the genealogical bloodline of "S. 1806," "S. 2," or "S. 137." Do not get caught up in the parliamentary wrangling without following the human story of personal leadership, human interactions, and individual frailties. A review of how Congress works is as much a study of personal dynamics as it is of flow charts on "How a bill becomes a law."

Certain terms of the trade were unavoidable in writing this book. They are as follows: "PAC," political action committee; "LA," legislative assistant, the aide assigned specific legislative issues on a Congressional staff; "the *Post*," the *Washington Post*; "CFR," campaign finance reform; "both sides of the aisle," "aisle" refers to the passage that separates Democrats from Republicans in congressional chambers, thus "both sides" refers to that which is "bipartisan" in Congress; "inside the beltway," "beltway" refers to I-495 circling the District of Columbia and is used to describe the mentality of the press, pundits, and politicians in Washington, as opposed to the regular views espoused in "middle America"; "the bill," any of the versions of legislation by Senator Boren given above.

The Gilded Dome is not fiction. It is about the electoral system and the government that we pay for and expect to protect us. When the government becomes the protected, instead of the protectors, something needs to be said. Even more, something needs to be done. But first you must read the book.

GREG D. KUBIAK

Washington, D.C.

THE GILDED DOME

CHAPTER ONE

The Gilded Dome

*gild·ed   (gil'dəd), adj.   1: covered or highlighted with
gold   2: having a pleasing, fine appearance that
conceals . . . ; superficially attractive*

THE U.S. CAPITOL BUILDING, with its gleaming white
dome, is perhaps the most vivid symbol of democratic governance the world has ever known. More clearly than our Constitution, our Declaration of Independence, our Bill of Rights, or any
other document of democracy, the splendid architectural lines
provide an almost divine symbol of freedom for our nation.

The original Virginia sandstone used to build the home of the
U.S. Congress was hauled in over three and a half decades to
construct the early portions of the Capitol building beginning in
1793. As the growing republic added states to the Union, a
cornerstone was laid in 1851 to add two wings with larger
chambers to accommodate the Senate and the House of Representatives. Pres. Millard Fillmore and a team of architects
expressed concern that the existing wood and copper dome
would be overshadowed by the wider, longer Capitol building.
Thus plans were developed to have a grand, cast iron shell nearly
twice as high encapsulate the Bullfinch dome, which was constructed in a classical, Old World style.

Thomas Walter was the architect selected to design the new
structure. He studied the domes of several cathedrals including St.

3

Paul's of London, St. Peter's of Rome, and St. Isaac's of St. Petersburg, Russia, which proved to be the best model because of its ironwork. According to the U.S. Capitol Historical Society, construction took ten years, from 1855 to 1865. In the society's videotape tour of the Capitol, commemorating the Congress's Bicentennial, Cornelius Heine narrates, "There is not just one dome in the Capitol but two domes, an inner dome and an outer dome. They are held together by a great skeleton of cast iron—thirty-six principal members . . . [with] 5,000 tons of cast iron."

Few Americans realize this international symbol of their freedom is actually a facade that hides the original dome, rebuilt after the British burned the Capitol in 1814. Even with all its magnificent white splendor, it is but a gilded dome concealing what is underneath. In the same sense, few Americans realize what goes on day to day beneath the roof of the Capitol as their elected leaders go about the business of governing the nation. In its third century of housing the Congress, the building itself may be stronger than the representative government quartered there.

Many of us have the perception that members of Congress represent us by casting votes on the chamber floors, working in committee hearings on various issues, and protecting "truth, liberty, and the American way" through stirring oratory, much the way James Stewart did in the film *Mr. Smith Goes to Washington*. Yet underneath the pleasing and concealing dome, a very different world exists.

WE THE PEOPLE

Perhaps the most basic principle within our system of government—a principle that has kept the United States functioning through civil and world wars, economic depressions, and various government scandals—is that each branch of government has oversight and constraints placed on it by another branch. Moveover, the citizens of the United States theoretically have the ultimate say in government because we have the power to vote.

Yet what oversight do we as electors of the government

exercise beyond our vote? Who really has the most say in not just how members of Congress vote but what they vote on? Who sets the legislative agenda? Congress? Political consultants? Lobbyists? The Democratic and Republican party leaders? Political action committees? The people? These are valid questions for every citizen of a democratic society, not just students of civics and political science or political activists.

As a holder of a bachelor's degree in political science, I read the texts, heard the lectures, and examined the constructs of the legislative process. As a legislative assistant to a U.S. senator, I saw a much different world in which that process works. I saw the use and abuse of legislative rules, the importance of legislative leadership, and the power of individual motivation. These traits relate more to human psychology than they do to civics.

The Gilded Dome is meant to be a citizen's guided tour through the halls of Congress as it does its legislative work. For the student of political science, it is a real-life look at the legislative process. For the journalist or government watchdog, it is a trenchant behind-the-scenes analysis of a personal process. But more important, for the voter/taxpayer/citizen, it is a leveler of Congress. It is to serve as a reminder that Congress is still the people's branch of government, no better and no worse than the people who send its members to Washington.

Like any element of society, Congress must be governed by rules. When those rules get broken, bent, or outdated, they should be exposed and changed. Everyone who is affected by decisions made by Congress has an interest in how Congress makes its decisions. This book describes congressional decision making as it relates to a bill on campaign finance reform.

When we read about congressional action in the newspapers or hear on the evening news about a bill being passed, we get a false impression of the legislative branch of our federal government. Not all of its work can be neatly packaged in ninety seconds on the networks or in a five-paragraph news wire story. While I do not intend to bash Congress for its collective inability to get results on issues of importance to the everyday lives of citizens, it is important to realize that congressional action does not equal a democratic product. In fact, most congressional action is best defined by volumes of bills introduced, speeches made, press conferences held, studies commissioned, investigations launched, or action threatened. Surprisingly little of Congress's valuable energy is used to generate actual legislation that gets enacted.

In the 101st Congress, from the beginning of 1989 through adjournment in October 1990, a total of 11,824 bills and resolutions were introduced in the House and Senate. That works out to almost twenty-one bills each day that each branch of the Congress was in session. However, in 1989, only 240 of those measures became law, 410 in 1990. The rules of Congress purposely slow down the path of some bills on their way to the law books. Most bills do require thoughtful consideration, and, I believe for the most part, we can thank our forefathers for a legislative system that operates very slowly.

To isolate behavior and get the truest sense of how the process works, what single issue offers the most incisive view of how Congress really operates? I assert that there is one legislative issue that not only affects the deep, personal interest of nearly every senator but also stands as an illustration of the ethical character of the institution itself—campaign finance reform. It is one issue on which all members believe themselves to be experts.

Senate and House candidates must abide by the laws governing campaign finance. Voters are limited to selecting candidates who campaign within those legal and financial boundaries. Citizens are affected by elected officials who accept our votes and public trusts. All of us, then, should look beneath the gilded dome covering our Congress and review the outdated legal and ethical boundaries governing our electoral process.

MONEY: THE MOTHER'S MILK OF POLITICS

In 1992, members of the U.S. Senate received an annual salary of just over $125,000. Yet the cost of running a successful race for election to that body averaged $4 million. Senators running for reelection must raise roughly $12,000 each week during each year of their six-year term to amass an adequate campaign war chest. To the average American, such funds must surely seem extravagant and such a fund-raising capacity, exhaustive.

Even after being adjusted for inflation, the four Senate election (six-year) cycles between 1982 and 1988 saw an increase in the cost of winning a seat in the U.S. Senate—from 51 percent to 166 percent. In other words, when the seven elections from 1976 to 1988 were calculated by what the winning candidate spent (in 1976 dollars) to get elected, the results were as follows: the 1982 elections cost 100 percent more than in 1976; the 1984 elections cost 51 percent more than the 1978 elections; the 1986 elections cost 166 percent more than the 1980 elections; and the 1988 elections cost 54 percent more than 1982 spending.

Moreover, money follows power. On February 11, 1986, the *Wall Street Journal* ran a story entitled "Some Ways and Means Members Saw a Surge in Contributions during Tax Overhaul Battle." The piece, written by Brooks Jackson and Jeff Birnhaum, looked at individuals on the tax-writing committee, such as Rep. Wyche Fowler (D-Ga.). Fowler, who had only a 27 percent approval score from the pro-business barometer of the U.S. Chamber of Commerce (and, conversely, a 67% approval from the AFL-CIO), raised over $57,000 in one day from Texas contributors affiliated with Quintana Petroleum Corporation of Houston at an event arranged by a Washington business lobbyist. Interested in tax provisions favorable to the drilling industry, Fowler, like others, received immense financial support from interests unaccustomed to contributing to liberal Democrats. (Over 40% of Fowler's 1985 receipts in his bid to unseat Sen. Mack Mattingly [R] in the 1986 race came from PACs.) Then Congressman Judd Gregg (R-N.H.) told the *Wall Street Journal* that being on a prestigious, influential committee was "like night and day, being on the Science Committee before and being on Ways and Means now," in terms of raising money.

Indeed, ABC's "20/20" reported in the midst of the markup of that tax bill that then Senate Finance Committee Chairman

Bob Packwood (R-Ore.) was the top recipient of political action committee (PAC) money the previous year. Out of $966,016 in PAC money, $344,326 came from the insurance industry, $105,700 came from the banking/finance industry, and another $93,565 came from labor unions; all had a substantial stake in the tax bill.

A public interest lobbyist, Fred Wertheimer of Common Cause, told "20/20,"

The system legalizes buying influence. . . . When I give you, a member of Congress, a substantial amount of money, we both know that you've accepted money from me and you know I have something in mind. . . . They [PACs] are buying a lot more than access. But even if that was all they were buying, what kind of system do we have, where you get access to your representative if you can put up a bunch of money?

People with money are ready, if not eager, to fill with money the outstretched hands of incumbents who come to them months, even years, before their elections. PACs are the most obvious, visible, and powerful force in providing money. And they do it for a reason.

In a 1985 interview about PACs, Tom Baker of the National Association of Home Builders, one of the largest such committees, told CBS News why contributions to incumbents were good investments. "We want access. We want to be able to get in the door and be heard."

But newspaper columnist Mark Shields reverses the viewfinder. In a 1991 column, he explained that PACs are not the principal villain in the corrupt system. "PACs . . . are frequently victims of leagalized extortion at the hands of incumbents who sit on congressional committees, the decisions of which can directly affect the fate, fortune, and future of the PAC's membership. Failure to contribute carries with it the risk of loss of access to the fund raiser/lawmaker and no chance to please your members' taste."

PAC's, which numbered 4,170 in 1990, became "the ultimate whipping boy in the debate over reform," according to a May

1990 advertisement in the *National Journal*. The ad, placed by the National Association of Business PACs (NABPAC), was part of a public campaign to remind Congress and the public that—a result of a previous reform bill—PACs "have stimulated millions of Americans to become involved in our political system."

PACs cover a wide range of occupational and special interests, a spectrum beyond the categories of animal, vegetable, and mineral. There are committees for avocado farmers, Native Americans, rum distillers, Walt Disney employees, right-to-life advocates, sellers of Avon products, Ohio psychologists, and Veterans of Foreign Wars. Individually, they represent no threat to democracy.

But what has been their collective effect on congressional behavior and electoral competition? Whereas in the 1974 election cycle, PAC contributions only made up about 17 percent of a House member's receipts, twelve years later that figure doubled to 34 percent. The actual dollar amount contributions of PACs to Congress grew from $12.5 million in 1974 to $149.9 million in 1990, nearly a 1,200 percent increase.

Such facts might not indicate cause for major concern to those who believe an open system of government must allow for political activism in the form of financial assistance. However, if the system is truly "open," why is the staggeringly disproportionate share of that $149.9 million—a ratio of 11 to 1—going to incumbents?

The answer lies in the fact that special, monied interests—PACs, lobbyists, political fund raisers, and wealthy individuals—want "more than just good government" in return for their contribution, as a Senate leader once said. Some may want an appointment, say, ten minutes with the senator, to discuss a tax provision. Some may want a vote against a nomination in the committee of a senator. Some may just want an "insurance policy" of sorts, the ability to see the member of Congress when they need him or her. People who give a $25 donation to a political candidate's bean supper fund-raising event may want "good government." However, people who write a $1,000 check to a congressman's campaign committee probably want access.

Over the course of several years as a Senate aide, I came to discover that for many in Congress, raising money is seen as a sport. The strategy, the hunt, the catch, and the victory are immensely enjoyable, as though it were sportfishing or a baseball game.

Former Sen. Rudy Boschwitz was the quintessential fund raiser for sport. He thrived on harvesting the mother's milk of politics. He prided himself on raising $7.1 million for his campaign in 1984. His Republican colleagues must have been proud of him, too, because they selected him to serve as their chairman of the Republican Senatorial Campaign Committee (RSCC) the next year, an opportunity to have a bigger pond in which to fish. The native of the state of ten thousand lakes served as the leading opponent of legislation to put limits on political action committee funds.

In fact, money was always on Boschwitz's mind, mixed with a little humor. While conversing with another senator in a markup session in the Senate Agriculture Committee, Boschwitz passed his colleague a note to commend his staff person. The note said, "The woman (your ass't) needs more $ (as I have written you before)— Maybe I can arrange a PAC contribution—Anonymous." Drawn on the bottom of the page was Boschwitz's trademark signature, a huge smiling face, like the yellow ones on buttons or inserts that instruct, "Have a Nice Day!" Whoever said senators don't have a sense of humor? But the laughing and fund raising stopped for Boschwitz in 1990, when he lost his reelection to first-time office seeker Paul Wellstone by a 52 to 48 percent margin.

Members of Congress like Boschwitz, who was the only Senate incumbent defeated in the 1990 elections, partly as a result of his image as a big money candidate, personify the view that money is the mother's milk of politics.

"The Dinner Bought the Vote"

PACs, journalists, or even members of Congress cannot indict the system as effectively as those who see it broadly and objectively on a day-to-day basis. After I left my job in the Senate, I surveyed several current staff members on Capitol Hill who are in high-level legislative positions. Some of the confidential stories from my former colleagues tell how awful the power of money can be.

One aide talked of helping a congressman's fund-raising efforts during office hours, in violation of congressional ethics rules. "He would have me call specific individuals and ask outright if they would buy tickets to a fund raiser. Other times when he was needing money, I would make the rounds asking for honoraria. The companies seem to expect this as a means of doing business."

Another staffer boasted of making a routine decision about signing a letter with several of his boss's colleagues. A farm interest group sought several senators to send a letter to the secretary of the Department of Agriculture protesting a new policy adversely affecting markets of the commodity group. The agriculture LA noted that the affected industry's PAC "hasn't yet ponied up in the boss's campaign fund." The LA decided he would not even show the senator the group's request. Staff have that power.

One newly elected senator reportedly had her campaign committee issue lapel pins to contributors after her 1992 election victory, allowing the senator and staff members to easily identify campaign contributors who visited the Washington office. The committee went so far as to issue particular gems to be inlaid in the pin, denoting the donor's level of financial support. Such a system saves the supporter the embarrassment of actually telling the senator or staff member that he or she gave money to the campaign. The badge of proof is evident.

Another House aide expressed his disappointment in seeing his boss "take part in a $5,000 dinner in D.C. with two other congressmen," after which "his vote switched 180 degrees the next day on a banking issue [with] no constituent input." Disgustedly, the aide concluded, "The dinner bought the vote."

One Hill office implemented a systematically coded rolodex for a senator to keep track of lobbyists and organizations with PACs to denote who or which were contributors to the senator's reelection efforts. With such a system, it would be far easier to decide who would receive an appointment with the senator when such requests were made.

Still other staffers were instructed to make lists of interest groups and PACs that could best be targeted for requests for contributions and honoraria. Such an activity is a common occurrence in many, if not most, Hill offices, despite the broad ethics and campaign laws that restrict political activity in congressional offices.

Such examples, only a scratch on the surface, expose a system in need of analysis at the least and massive overhaul at the most. The words of retiring senators decrying the "money chase" for campaign dollars may roll off the ears of voters as the protests of old-fashioned politicians exiting an electronically sophisticated world. But increasingly, Congress and the citizens it represents, believe something must be done to clean up the system.

CAMPAIGN FINANCE REFORM

Campaign finance reform (CFR) was debated in the Senate from 1985 to 1992. This debate encompassed discussions on PAC reform, spending limits, public financing, "soft money," independent expenditures, and a constitutional amendment limiting campaign spending. No one segment of the congressional election finance system could be isolated to represent the problems in the law.

The Senate realized that if it changed the law dealing with PACs, it would have to address the increasing practice of informally organizing wealthy individuals to contribute to elections. If it disallowed contributions by PACs to candidates, they might increasingly utilize their First Amendment rights to engage in "independent expenditures." Or if the Senate did not constrain newly discovered loopholes in political party finances, money deterred through spending limits could be funneled through national parties to affect federal elections.

This explains the "pop-up" theory in the study of campaign finance. The assumption is that if one stops the flow of political money through one legal avenue, it will find a way to flow through another and pop up somewhere else.

If years of staffing the battle of campaign finance reform taught me one thing, it was that it must be viewed as more than a one-dimensional issue. Some senators saw it as a purely partisan debate. Republicans assumed Democrats wanted only to strengthen their hold on control of Congress with revision of the law. For some, that was true. Democrats assumed Republican resistance was to preserve individual seats in Congress. For some, that was true.

Several opponents of campaign spending limits, a ban on political action committees, and other reforms argued that millions and millions of dollars each year are spend to market such consumer items as bottled water, cosmetics, and dog food. So why worry about how much is spent on something as important as democracy? Still others contended that the volume of money from disclosed, limited sources was a healthy, free-enterprise show of political support for a candidate. They pointed out repeatedly that arbitrary limits on political access gained with money was an imposition of the government over the governed and that competition would thus be stifled.

The 1990 Illinois Senate race pitted Republican Congresswoman Lynn Martin against incumbent Democrat Paul Simon. NBC's "Today" show looked at that race in an April 26 news report that told the audience "raising money is the single most important thing candidate Lynn Martin does." Reporter Lisa Myers showed that despite a quarter-million-dollar fund raiser featuring First Lady Barbara Bush and an earlier $700,000 fund raiser with Pres. George Bush, Martin would still have to raise $21,912 a day (or $913 an hour) to be competitive in an election against the Democratic incumbent.

Simon already had raised twice what he spent in his election just six years earlier, stating, as he pointed at the reporter's camera, that "the main reason is that television camera, right there." He complained that television advertising costs in the Chicago market doubled in his first term in the Senate. How else could he defend his record and promote his candidacy if not over the airwaves? A longtime supporter of spending limits and public financing of congressional campaigns, Simon gave special insight into why limits should be placed on campaign dollars. In the interview, he illustrated his rationale with the following scenario.

"If I get into a hotel, say, at midnight, and there are twenty phone calls waiting for me—nineteen from people whose name I don't recognize and the twentieth from someone who gave me a $1,000 campaign contribution, at midnight, I'm not going to make twenty phone calls. I might make one. Which one do you think I make?"

A balanced view of this issue would recognize that reform of the campaign finance system must be considered from both an ethical and a competitive standpoint. Both candidates in the Illinois race raised issues that indict the system of campaign finance. The rationales for reform are both idealistic and realistic.

Ethical Reform

Simon's scenario offers very real insight into the ethical pressures on persons in positions of public trust who, to be effective candidates, must raise large amounts of money in today's campaigns. It is human nature that a candidate would first return the calls of contributors over anonymous constituents. Not doing so could likely be the end of a candidacy.

It is an ethical dilemma. Without money, one cannot seek office in today's expensive campaigns. And if a candidate takes too much money from special interests, his or her ethical conduct can be called into question. But if donors are neglected, they stop contributing to one's campaigns.

This dilemma constituted the first line of reasoning in the battle to reform campaign finance laws. But slowly, this ethical quagmire expanded to view the quality of life and work in the Senate. Earlier in the year of the Simon-Martin race, Senator Boren noted in a speech to the National Press Club that "the very schedule of Congress itself is driven not by policy issues, not by these changes in the world. The schedule is driven by political fund raising."

Any system of political competition that involves the pursuit of campaign money is subject to the confusion that the funds sought may become the *end* instead of the *means* to a campaign. For in the absence of those means, there is an absence of political competition.

Competitive Reform

Martin freely admitted in that preelection interview that she was frightened and intimidated when consultants told her of the money she would need to raise to challenge Simon. What is the use of having an open electoral system if in all practicality, potential challengers are discouraged from running because they can only afford a minimum level of visibility.

Martin was deterred from addressing the issue of Senator Simon's record. One reason could have been the constant barrage of fund-raising demands. Sure, she could make her pitch *against* Simon and *for* her candidacy at all those fund-raising banquets, barbecues, and receptions. But such an audience is too small and too limited. Further, the media's coverage of her speeches at those fund raisers and rallies was out of her control. What she and all candidates want is the necessary money to get "their" message to the electorate, which means paid television advertising. Otherwise, one risks unflattering or inadequate news coverage of one's candidacy and issues, or having the opponent define one through negative ads.

So to enjoy the luxury of controlling one's own candidacy, it takes money. That expensive undertaking brings us back to the first issue of ethics: do you risk selling out your political soul in exchange for those necessary dollars?

At issue, therefore, is not just how much it costs to run for the Senate but from whom the money comes. After fruitless years of filibuster, posturing, ethics investigations, and behind-the-scenes negotiations, Congress eventually passed a reform bill, only after they felt certain it would be vetoed. The underlying rationale that is given by political analysts as to why campaign reform has not yet been passed is simple: what incentive do those who vote on it have to change it, if that same system put them in office?

PERSONAL AND SPECIAL INTERESTS

Each of the one hundred members of the Senate, with the occasional exception of one or two appointed to fill a vacancy because of death or resignation, is elected by the people of his or her state after a long and exhausting campaign. This has been the case since the adoption of the 17th amendment in 1913, which provides for direct election by the people. While most candidates leave the day-to-day operations of a campaign to consultants, fund raisers, paid campaign staff, and volunteers, it is safe to say that they consider themselves to be virtual experts in the field, due to their personal interest in their own career.

Proponents of campaign finance reform, in their own way, have said, "Congress is becoming a 'closed shop' company and needs some healthy competition." The argument went that through government intervention, Congress would be more accessible to the common citizen and thus a more responsive institution. Yet the jobs and the livelihood of members of Congress would be in jeopardy if changes in campaign finance laws were made. Senators seemed to be saying, "If I got elected, everything must be fine." Like any person, a senator has a natural, special interest in keeping his or her job.

Congress does not fare well in any political analysis of the public's opinion of their own member's performance. Pollsters and political scientists constantly recite this fact. But it tells us nothing. The collective stalemate so common to Congress is typical in any committee or organization in which human nature prevails in a search for consensus over confrontation. Congress is no exception. Further, electors of public officials are reluctant to admit to electing a bad or weak officeholder, as such a misjudgment reflects poorly on the voter. In 1960, despite the historically narrow margin of victory John Kennedy had in that election, a much larger number of voters polled months later said they voted for the president.

The persistent low level of public esteem for Congress seems to revolve around money, ethics, and the constant campaign. The candidacy of Ross Perot and the appeal of Bill Clinton for "change" in Washington uniquely connected with 1992 voters. So any serious review of the systemic problems afflicting Congress must look at our officeholders' relationship to money. Any effort to reform congressional campaigns must contend with special and personal interests.

These interests are not just those of members of Congress and candidates for office. They are the interests of the PACs we assume will be curtailed by new rules of the game and broadcasters expected to abide by new political advertising rules. Those who will be affected most significantly will be the voters, who are expected to get a clearer picture of politics from any new set of rules. Still, no one takes those rules more seriously and more personally than the officeholders, who typically want to be reelected.

In their defense, some Hill veterans probably feel like a tenured college professor who is told that a new faculty member will be interviewed and possibly placed in the professor's job, upsetting the established tradition of job security. While Congress was never meant to be a tenured position, anyone would be leery of new rules that bolster competitors.

Sen. William Proxmire (D-Wisc.), who retired from the Senate at the end of 1988, was long noted not only for his "golden fleece awards" aimed at government waste but also for his "myth of the day" floor statements. One such speech was delivered on September 26, 1986, on campaign finance reform.

The myth was cleared stated: "We dare not tamper with the campaign finance laws because of the law of unintended consequences." In keeping with his style of asking rhetorical questions on the Senate floor, Proxmire inquired, "What are the real reasons that Congress refuses to reform campaign financing? I believe there are two: political advantage and incumbency." He continued, "Every change must pass Congress, which is, by definition, composed of incumbents. And incumbents are leery of any change which might benefit a challenger. . . . The people are ahead of the politicians. The people believe that the present system is little better than legalized influence peddling. They are right. We should be representing the people and not a political party or an incumbent."

In an interview after his retirement from the Senate, I asked Proxmire if he felt special interest money could be linked to the costly multibillion-dollar savings and loans bailout? He told me, "I am convinced that PAC contributions and individual contributions of savings and loan officials persuaded members of the Banking Committee in the Senate, which I chaired, to support weaker regulation responsible for the S&L debacle."

Clearly, if you believe that big campaign money affects government policy and government policy affects taxpayers, then it is in the interest of all taxpayers that the rules affecting big campaign money be changed. Otherwise, taxpayers will continue to pay for big policy mistakes like the S&L bailout.

MOTIVATION TO CHANGE

In stinging oratory about the conduct of Senate Democrats after the controversial nomination of Robert Bork to the Supreme Court, Republican Sen. Alan Simpson of Wyoming charged in a speech on the Senate floor that the Congress only responds to the symbols of "emotion, fear, guilt, or racism." In his disgust for the special interest campaign against Bork, Simpson argued that it is these four devices that push the Congress to act. His point, broadly interpreted, is that Congress wrongfully acts on variable winds of popular will, which can be misguided, instead of exercising their balanced judgments.

In a short but action-filled five years on Capitol Hill, it was also my observation that Congress rarely acts on a national issue until and unless it is surrounded by public outcry, emotion, or fear. It is my further observation that "special interests," in many forms and through numerous avenues, run the Congress to a larger degree than ever before and in a way that is unhealthy for a democratic form of government. In such a situation, we have the makings for the kind of stalemate and confrontation on important issues that was polished in the 1980s and that are being recognized as "government in gridlock" in the 1990s.

Such was the case with campaign finance reform in 1985, when a reform-minded, conservative Democratic senator from Oklahoma decided to force the issue out in the open with a bill to severely limit what PACs could give to House and Senate candidates. There was no discernible public opinion on the bill, only a slight hint of public disgust with the role of special interests in Washington. Bills of this nature were introduced from time to time but not with the sort of dedication that that senator gave the legislation when he decided to take the bill directly to the Senate floor as a nongermane amendment in October 1985.

A review of the steps taken to get this bill to the floor of the "world's most deliberative body," as the Senate is regarded, would be a mere mechanical restatement of actions within the parliamentary scope of the Congress. The real story is the struggle to make ninety nine other senators face reform proposals and why it was such a struggle. This reform crusade is more a series of human stories than it is a saga of process and logistics.

The legislative process and our democratic system of government cannot be understood without a basic understanding of human nature. Broadly, "political science" may better be understood as the combined studies of human psychology and government, with emphasis on the psychology. A former governor and presidential candidate summed it up best in an interview: "Personal preservation is a natural and fundamental instinct, and political preservation is not much different."

POLITICS PERMEATES ALL WE DO

A basic premise of this book is that "politics" permeates all that we do. It is not limited to presidential and city council campaigns but exists in all professional and personal settings.

Politics surrounds the simplest of social exchanges and everyday quid pro quos. It is seen when a young associate with a downtown law firm—who is a frequent racquetball partner with a senior attorney—gets an office with a window while a more senior associate does not. It occurs when the son of athletic boosters gets more playing time on the basketball court than he might if his parents were not club donors.

Politics is the science of actions of politic persons who use shrewd, expedient, discreet, or delicate actions or words to influence or accomplish their ends. Often employed in perhaps unintentional schemes to gain influence, while not in the form of a direct bribe, is money. The story of campaign finance reform illustrates the resistance of changing the law and the money it regulates, as well as power and the human behavior that clings to it. The influence of money is one issue. The pursuit of it is quite another.

Congressman Barney Frank, a Massachusetts Democrat and maverick reformer, said, "We're the only people in the world who are expected to accept thousands and thousands of dollars and *not* be influenced by them." But the motivation to have financial security in a campaign speaks to another human reality. Money in election campaigns and society-at-large is viewed as a factor of success. Money for a campaign is perceived as an essential means to a desirable end—being an elected member of Congress.

Thus, those whose names we face in the voting booth in a biennial ritual of democracy are our most vital link to government. The rules that regulate whom we choose in that process are perhaps the most essential and elemental to our democracy. If they are flawed in design or practice, our government will bear those scars. If we the people are ignorant of those flaws, we must educate ourselves and work to effect change. The notion of "term limitations" in the Constitution jumps the gun on a people's right to choose. Political debate and competition have always been the saving grace of democracy. If we see a non-responsive attitude from elected officials, we have the tools to discharge them from their duties without limiting our future choices with the immovable pillar of a constitutional amendment.

We can accept that politics will surely permeate the discussions on what role money plays in who is elected and how they perform when they are in office. We can accept that money's role in the electoral process is a given that affects ethical behavior and competitive realities. But more than just political speeches, press accounts, and public interest studies, a process occurs in the debate of how to change those rules. It begins in the long, dark corridors of the Capitol.

IN THE SHADOWS

The work of Congress is seen in more than just the existence of the House of Representatives and the Senate. It is carried out by legions of staff, research by the Library of Congress, sophisticated computer and mass mailing systems, a separate police force, the operation of tour guides through the Capitol, and a $100 million printing office. In 1989, the legislative branch cost taxpayers $2,269,842,000.

Hidden in the shadows beneath the gilded dome that houses Congress are staff members. There are ten thousand legislative, administrative, and support staff persons—more than twice the population of my hometown, Spencer, Oklahoma. A typical staff of a senator will range from 25 to 45 professionals, depending on the population of the senator's state. Each senator has discretion to staff his or her office with a block of money budgeted for staff salaries. Further, those aides will be divided between the Washington, D.C. office, and two or more state offices.

The hierarchy of a senate staff is really quite simple. There is the senator, whose autonomy from any central regulations on setting up his or her personal office is guaranteed. Next in line is an administrative assistant (AA) or a chief of staff, whose job it is to run the office as general manager. An AA is usually the chief political contact for the senator, the manager of personnel, and the general office administrator. The AA will typically depend on an office manager to handle the office budget, personnel files, and other daily administrative chores.

In my former office, we thought of our organization of thirty-three people in the following categories: Press, Scheduling, Administrative, State Offices, and Legislative. This is how our average staff broke down (with overall duties):

Administrative: administrative assistant, office manager, computer/systems operator, assistant systems operator (the latter two worked with the in-house computer system that coordinated our massive correspondence output)

Press: press secretary, assistant press secretary, and/or communications director (their function was media relations, coordinating press interviews and appearances, and drafting opinion pieces or certain speech notes)

Scheduling: executive assistant, personal secretary, and staff assistant (these people coordinated the senator's office appointments, state appearances, and travel arrangements, arranged the senator's wife's official schedule, and coordinated honoraria speeches and many other affairs for the Senator)

State Offices: caseworkers (handled individual constituent's requests for assistance with federal agencies), field representatives (traveled to various areas of the state to represent the senator, hear area concerns, assist local leaders with federal projects, and maintain contact with key supporters of the senator), and the office manager in each of three state offices

Legislative: legislative assistants (LAs; assigned various legislative issues to study and advise the senator on), legislative correspondents (LCs; assigned to two LAs to respond to letters on legislative issues to constituents), and the chief legislative assistant or legislative director (coordinated the work of the LAs in addition to handling certain legislative issues).

From 1983 to 1990, I held three of the jobs listed above. I got a taste for politics when I was a field representative in Oklahoma City for a year and a half. I then specialized in a variety of policy issues in Washington as a legislative assistant. And for the last two years of my tenure, I held the job of chief legislative assistant, my personal pinnacle of congressional work. From that vantage point, I was able to work with very talented LAs and LCs and to see that there was not another job on Capitol Hill I would rather have.

From my position, as one of hundreds of staffers in the shadows, I worked on an issue that strikes at the heart of our democracy—the electoral process. I was awed by the beauty of the Capitol and its dome, visible from my cramped Russell Senate Office Building desk. Before I left my service there, I contemplated the history reflected around that gleaming white roof.

As the Capitol dome was being built, this nation was thrown into the midst of the Civil War that nearly severed the Union, leaving deep scars on our battlefields and our history. Construction was halted in that first summer of 1861 by the chief of the Army Corps of Engineers. However, Pres. Abraham Lincoln insisted that construction continue. He reportedly said, "If the people see the Capitol going on, it is a sign that we intend the Union shall go on."

From much younger, idealistic days, I viewed our Capitol and our country as being built on a strong base. The Union has endured, as has the Capitol's dome. But the caustic effects of monied power have corroded the public trust that serves as the real foundation of democracy.

CHAPTER TWO

"A Boy, a Bicycle, and a Broom"

One day you'll realize that the people capable of running the country are too smart to get into politics.

JAMES UNGER, IN "HERMAN"

OKLAHOMA'S STATE FAIR is always a big event. As the sultry southwestern summer days turn cooler, the annual festive folk-way marking the end of a season is celebrated in the Sooner State. From prize-winning homegrown vegetables to the display of the new model automobiles to the carnival rides and games of chance on the Midway, the State Fair has something for everyone. It is the one opportunity each year for one million paying visitors (over a 10-day period) to see and experience all that a proud state and a proud people have to offer.

The 1973 State Fair was to a preteenager from Oklahoma what China must have been to Marco Polo. With my dad in tow, I adventured through the crowded "Made in Oklahoma" building after a rather disappointing view of a "motorcycle mania show" on the Midway. We had made the last big weave through the exhibits when I asked Dad to wait so I could get another look at an odd political booth up the last row.

Here was a display proclaiming a new face in the race for governor in 1974. To a 12-year-old, that was an eternity away.

Why would a candidate want to start running for office so early? I had not heard my dad discuss the governor's race during that time-honored weekly social event, "coffee and doughnut hour," after church on Sundays. Surely if this were a serious candidate in a serious campaign, it would be brought up for discussion at that freewheeling political round table.

As I had a growing interest in politics, having already written to Pres. Richard Nixon and received a response from the White House, I decided I had nothing to lose by going to the booth for some information. While not paying great attention to political party or issues at the time of my hasty visit to the booth, I did notice the name, rank, and political symbol of the candidate. He was David L. Boren, a state representative from Seminole, and his trademark was a broom, an old-fashioned, corn-straw, house broom, with which to sweep out the "old guard" politics and clean up government.

Some time after the fair, having examined and discarded all the free literature on tourism in Green Country, Oklahoma, and on new cars that I would not even be able to drive for another three and a half years, I came to the brochure by the Boren for Governor Committee. On the back of the brochure was a coupon asking not just for my monetary contribution to help Boren's campaign but for volunteers as well. Having nothing better to do in my spare time between seventh-grade studies and raising chickens, I thought politics would be an ideal pastime. I signed up.

Besides, perhaps it would afford me the opportunity to fight injustice in the form of my least favorite chore—feeding and watering the chickens, harvesting their eggs, and (every four months or so) shoveling out the manure from the coop. The dual and ironic injustice I felt in doing this task was that profits derived from the sale of eggs went directly to my mother, who in turn used the proceeds to pay for piano lessons for her youngest son. The fact was, I hated those piano lessons just as much as I hated shoveling the manure from the chicken coop triannually. Even if my entry into partisan electioneering did not spare me this inhumanity in 1973, it would be a nice delusion.

STEP ONE: CAMPAIGN VOLUNTEER

In the first week of September 1974, I was sent some campaign material from the Boren campaign in a small manila envelope with three ten-cent stamps guaranteeing its third-class delivery to me in Spencer. The contents were limited to four or five brochures, a few *Clean Sweep* tabloid-type newspapers, five buttons, three hand signs, and about as many bumper stickers. This was hardly what I expected. Did the campaign want my help or not? Here I was, a young, energetic volunteer, and they sent me a mere handful of materials.

Taking matters into my own hands, I convinced my oldest brother to drive me to the campaign headquarters one day to pick up more materials that I could distribute. So off we went to the Boren headquarters in Oklahoma City in his 1959 white Chevy Biscayne (the kind with side fins larger than the counters in beer taverns). The office was just about a mile from the State Capitol. It had a slanted window in front with "Boren for Governor" written as large as a billboard.

Once inside, we discovered my future friend and confidante, Ann Dubler, Representative Boren's longtime secretary, sitting, smoking a cigarette, and lunching on a cold can of Coca-Cola and a Snickers candy bar while stuffing envelopes to one of a hundred different groups of registered voters in the state. Conservative and skeptical of the young campaigner, she gave me a small supply of tabloids for distribution.

More than ten years before I moved to Washington, D.C., as a legislative assistant to U.S. Senator Boren, where I avoided breaking any Senate rules or standards of ethics, I now confess to having broken at least a couple of postal and utility company regulations as a volunteer campaigner. Not knowing any better, I stuffed bumper stickers, buttons stuck through index cards, and those *Clean Sweep* tabloids in mailboxes and nailed 8″ by 10″ Boren from Governor signs on telephone poles and private fence posts. I was never caught, and Boren was elected governor.

. My more personal involvement with politics and Boren's

career in government service began in July 1978. It was between my junior and senior years of high school, when my early summer days were devoted to working out with a Universal weight set at my high school football locker room with rock music cranked on the stereo—and wishing I had a summer job.

My father, who was a marketing representative for Mobil Oil Corporation in Oklahoma, knew a service station operator who ran a station on Interstate 40 just east of Oklahoma City. The owner, an interested observer of politics, gave my dad an invitation to a reception honoring Governor and Mrs. David L. Boren on July 16. The Sunday afternoon get-together was to be in the Congress Room of the Lincoln Plaza Forum, a hotel just north of the State Capitol. The invitation was shared with my father because of my interest in Boren's gubernatorial campaign four years earlier. So that July afternoon, my dad and I went to the reception.

A 17-year-old, I was probably a little out of place. But there we were, standing in a slow receiving line to meet the governor and his wife, Molly Shi Boren. I do not remember a great deal about the party, other than my dad embarrassing me by trying to tell the governor that I had campaigned for him four years earlier with homemade signs. The governor responded with a reminiscent nod followed by a pat. "Yes, Yes, I remember. Thanks for all your help!" Of course, I would later learn the poor man had no recollection of such efforts, nor should I expect him to.

This reception marked the first time I actually spoke to David Boren, despite his telling numerous, impressionable, young Washington interns in my presence that he first met me as I rode my bicycle up to his 1974 campaign headquarters seeking campaign materials and his request for my "endorsement." However, the most memorable thing about the event was not that I got to meet the governor but that I had a warm visit with his campaign staffer, John Bode.

Bode, whose background included being president of the University of Oklahoma student government, coordinated the governor's campaign staff and Youth for Boren Corps. As his new duties included enlisting youthful volunteers, he used the opportunity to approach me.

"Hello, my name's John Bode, with the governor's campaign."

"Hi, I'm Greg Kubiak," I replied.

"So where are you in school? Do you go to college?" John inquired.

Sensing the beard on my face darkening and thickening with this instant assumption of age and maturity, I quickly but humbly responded that I was between by junior and senior years in high school.

"Well, we need to get you involved in the campaign."

That is all I needed to hear to jump start my idled interest. The following Monday, I hopped in my dad's 1968 blue, 6-cylinder Ford pickup and headed for the Boren for Senate state headquarters on North Lincoln Boulevard in Oklahoma City. On entering, the first person I saw, occupying a prestigious front office in the one-story office/warehouse, was Rob Pyron, the governor's press secretary, whom I recognized from television. Across the building in a smoke-filled office was Dubler, the governor's campaign treasurer and general keeper. She looked little different from when I saw her four years earlier in the gubernatorial campaign headquarters south of the Capitol. And finally, wandering in the back of the office amid sawdust and yard signs was the only really familiar face, John Bode.

Even Bode was somewhat surprised to see me so soon after that all-too-familiar cocktail party promise to "be in touch soon." He greeted me, and we small-talked for a short while before I was put to work.

I was in the back end of the headquarters stapling yard signs to wooden stakes that morning when Pyron's telephone rang with an urgent call. The governor was calling to report that his chief opponent had made some comments about his campaign during a press conference that morning. Reference was apparently made to Boren's previous campaign, which featured the broom symbolizing a clean sweep of government and reform. The candidate half-mocked the governor for losing his broom. The U.S. Senate campaign quickly began to heat up on that July morning. After hanging up with the governor, I overheard Pyron exclaim to the campaign staff, "The broom is back!"

My first real campaign job that required more than fourth-grade training was to actually purchase the first two brooms to be used in that 1978 campaign. Bode took me to Dubler's office. She had just finished calling the Target discount store for an exact price (including sales tax) of the brooms. Then as reluctantly as any tight-fisted campaign treasurer in the world, she wrote a check for something over $5. I went in the pickup to get the brooms.

My timing in volunteering for Boren's first Senate campaign was advantageous. Two days later, the governor was to travel from the Capitol to north central Oklahoma on a two-day campaign swing. The campaign staff wanted visibility of the reform broom that Boren proposed to sweep into Washington and needed a Youth for Boren volunteer to carry it. I was the most accessible to be recruited for the duty.

The morning of July 19, I met a campaign aide at the governor's mansion, where we had coffee with Boren. We soon left to campaign on the town squares of three Oklahoma communities, followed by a Highway Patrol security guard. It was a remarkable experience for a teenager not accustomed to such a presence of power. And I had never seen such beauty in a home where people actually still lived as I saw in the governor's mansion. With due diligence, at each tour through Blackwell, Newkirk, and Tonkawa, I proudly held high the broom I bought two days earlier, with its white on blue Boren for U.S. Senate sign stapled on both sides.

Boren was very pleasant and down-to-earth. Even then, of course, I knew he would be somewhat guarded in front of a high school student whom he did not really know. However, before the long day ended, Boren asked the aide where he had arranged for us to stay the night in Tulsa.

"The Camelot," the aide replied.

"What, you're kidding! We can't stay there. It's run by [campaign opponent and state Senator Gene] Stipe people!" the

Governor exclaimed. "You just don't know what kind of tricks they'll pull."

Judging that it would be too risky to change the reservation and offend the hotel operators, the aide settled the governor's anxiety, and we went to the Camelot. But the lesson of not underestimating your opponents would forever be etched in my mind by Boren's reaction.

Boren was sworn in to the U.S. Senate in 1979 after winning his primary, runoff, and general elections. The following year, just before Ronald Reagan was nominated to face Pres. Jimmy Carter in the 1980 elections, Senator Boren offered me an internship in his Washington office. In those brief six weeks on Capitol Hill, I gained more insights into the honor of public service, the importance of political leadership, and the life under the gilded dome.

ON-THE-ROAD JOB INTERVIEW

I was busy my final year at the University of Oklahoma (OU) with work as student government president. Between meetings on campus security, parking, and tuition increases, I had been invited to have lunch with Senator Boren's field representative, Pete Glavas, in early January 1983. I really never got acquainted with Glavas through my consistent contact with Boren's office, but I knew that he was destined to play a major role in the senator's reelection efforts in the coming year.

Glavas told me of all the early fund raising that they were planning—in the form of "county salutes." The impetus for these tributes and fund-raising events was not to be from those counties and the resident supporters, as I expected, but from Glavas, the senator, and my old OU student government friend and mentor-turned-Boren-staffer, Cody Graves.

However, the point of the lunch with Glavas was not so much to give me the exciting details of how a government staffer was plotting the reelection efforts of a senator but rather to tell me that Boren wanted me to be a part of the team. Glavas explained, all too briefly, that the way he and the senator saw the new structure, Glavas would eventually be the full-time fund-raising campaign manager, and I would take Glavas's current position in the Oklahoma City office. While this did not constitute a job offer, I expected one to come.

Not long after our lunch, I received a friendly telephone call from Charlie Ward, the senator's administrative assistant in Washington. Ward had been a chief aide to Speaker of the House Carl Albert and a great friend to me when I was an eighteen-year-old intern in summer 1980. Though I expected to be offered the job then, the offer would come from Boren himself.

Weeks later, on a cold, snow-threatening Friday afternoon, I received a call in my Ellison Hall office from Graves, who in a flustered, whispered voice asked, "Where are you?"

I replied, "Right here, why?"

"The senator's here at the office and was expecting to see you," Graves said. "Didn't Pete call you?"

Not wanting to indict Glavas for an obvious mistake that could foil what I expected to be a formal job-offering conversation with Senator Boren, or wanting to admit to forgetting something I had not been informed of, I merely said, "Well, I don't think so, but I'll get to the city as quick as I can."

As Boren was due to leave the downtown office soon, that would not do. Graves put me on hold for a short time, then came back on the line. "He's got an interview at Channel 9, and then he's going to see his dad at Baptist Hospital. Why don't you just meet us at the TV station."

Nervous and hiding my anger, I agreed. "I'll get there as soon as I can."

I gathered a couple of items from my desk and flew out of the office, telling my secretary, "Cancel my afternoon appointment, and have a good weekend. I'm off to meet with Senator Boren in Oklahoma City."

Pushing my little 1968 Ford Mustang as fast as I could up Interstate 35, I got to the Kelly Avenue exit off the Northwest Expressway in Oklahoma City just 30 minutes after my depar-

ture from Norman. Suddenly, I saw Graves furiously waving at
me as he slowed his southbound car to meet my northbound blue
streak. By the time I looked in my rearview mirror to make sure
it was Graves, I saw the rotund Senator Boren extracting himself
from Graves's white Honda.

Quickly, I made a U-turn around a construction area fifty
yards beyond the senator and crept along the road's shoulder not
knowing what was going on. Without explanation or fanfare,
Boren approached my car and hopped in.

"Hello, how are you? We finished up at Channel 9 so thought
we would just run into you on the way."

Still shocked at the sudden meeting, I merely greeted the
senator with, "Hello, how are you?"

"Why don't you just follow Cody to Baptist Hospital. I'm
going to go see Daddy, and we can visit on our way," Boren said.

Visit we did, in sort of a moving job interview. I learned very
quickly that senators know how to improvise. No mention was
made of the scheduling snafu. Boren got to the point. Would I be
a field representative at a starting salary of $20,000? I accepted.

LESSON ONE: FUND RAISING

After agreeing to take the job of field representative to start May
31, 1983, I was invited to accompany the senator to two regional
meetings of Boren supporters in the western part of the state in
April. I remembered Glavas having mentioned these fund-rais-
ing/supporter rallies around the state to begin the 1984 campaign
at our lunch.

It seemed to me at the time to be a little early to worry about
raising campaign funds, especially since Boren enjoyed very
high popularity with no Republican in sight to run against him.
But I was new to the team and just learning. I was anxious to see
what my new job would be like.

I met Graves in Norman, and we left to meet the senator's wife,
Molly, at the Oklahoma City airport on the evening of April 8.
We were then to drive to Enid, eighty miles to the north, and

meet the senator and Glavas. The five of us would spend the night at the Holiday Inn, paid for by the campaign, and be ready for the first meeting the next day.

The senator and Mrs. Boren greeted arriving guests more like family at a holiday reunion than supporters at a political rally. Glavas and Graves also hobnobbed, introducing me to as many random bankers, farmers, newspaper publishers, and retirees as they could. These would be the constituents and supporters with whom I would work for the next year and a half.

The meeting started with a lunch at a popular home-cooking restaurant in the wheat and cattle community. We were joined at the restaurant by Dubler, who drove in from her home in Shawnee. She would be on hand to collect any early campaign contributions that would be made that day.

After enjoying the meal, Boren announced why he had called his friends together. Fund-raising goals were set county by county based on the earlier receipts of two statewide campaigns. These figures were shared with guests who lived in those counties. The plan was really quite simple. Supporters in each county would help coordinate a "salute" to the senator for his service to Oklahoma. The public, political event would be advertised in area newspapers and would be geared to a large audience. But if that event could not generate enough donations to meet the fund-raising goal, the community supporters would be asked to set up another, more private event, such as a reception in a home, where a more direct fund-raising hit could be made.

The senator closed the rally/luncheon/meeting with inspiring oratory reminding his supporters why he belonged in Washington. With his appeal for their financial and strategic political support came his vowed commitment to work on their behalf in the Senate. His efforts for tax fairness, support of the farmer, reform of Congress, and fiscal responsibility could not progress if he were troubled by a tough race for reelection.

Only with an early start—by a year and a half—could he raise the contributions from individuals necessary to run a strong race. He and his lieutenants reminded these supporters that his commitment to public service was not being compromised by a reliance on political action committee funds. He was their senator, not the special interests' senator. Several who took the instruction and county goal sheets wasted no time in writing checks to "Oklahomans for Boren." They believed this man and were convinced to help him continue his crusade for political reform. The second stop in southwestern Oklahoma was a repeat of the Enid experience: strong support and commitment to Boren, his broom, and his political strategy.

I returned to Norman that night with mixed emotions. While I knew the political realities of running for office, raising money, and public service, my new job presented me with dilemmas — on the one hand, promoting the work of an officeholder unhampered by special interest money, and on the other, promoting the candidacy of a politician in need of campaign funds. But for now, I would not question the duality.

While I was in my second full week on Boren's Oklahoma City staff, planning campaign trips to the western part of the state, the senator was in Washington introducing a bill. His June 8 speech about S. 1433 warned of "the danger to the political process . . . which hastens the day when members of Congress will no longer depend upon individual contributions from their home states for their election efforts. Instead, they will be primarily dependent upon political action committees."

My first six months as a full-time field representative and part-time campaign fund raiser were successful. And the statewide fund-raising strategy was going well, too. A December 16, 1983, paper was assembled to document fund-raising figures on a county-by-county basis compared to the 1978 election numbers. In the 1978 race, Boren amassed $708,626 from 3,151 donors. By year's end, we had raised $863,019 from 3,968 donors. The 1984 goal was to raise $1,171,800. We may have had no opponent, but we were already winning the fund-raising game.

My 20-county area, a Republican region, had raised only $24,003 from 219 contributors in the 1978 campaign. By June 10 of the election year, nine of my twenty counties had raised their goals, and in the total area, 500 contributors gave $49,340, just $10,000 shy of the $59,700 goal.

One fund-raising effort was undertaken by a physician friend of Senator Boren's. A mid-August salute was held to honor the Boren's in Beaver, the county seat of Beaver County in Oklahoma's panhandle. Dr. William G. Harvey, Jr., a respected community leader, felt that a public fund-raising event would not be wise in this Republican heartland. Instead, he invited supporters to the public reception and followed up with a fund-raising letter, sent three weeks later, on September 8, 1983. In it, Harvey explained that Boren was a key senator in the fight to repeal the 10 percent withholding tax on savings accounts, the effort to exempt royalty owners from the windfall profits tax, and legislation to abolish inheritance tax between husband and wife. Further, he explained that Boren did not receive political action committee or special interest group money, only money from individuals interested in good government and grass-roots involvement. With that letter from Harvey, Beaver County made its fund-raising goal.

Another fund-raising effort two months later was more of a direct—and typical—scenario. Boren and I traveled to Washita County on December 5, where we first went to the home of a banker for a fund-raising reception. The invitation to that evening's 5:00 to 6:30 P.M. event was a bit more direct than the Beaver letter.

We hope you will come and visit with the senator personally and then encourage him to continue his public service with a financial contribution. Your individual contribution is needed since Senator Boren does not accept financial support from political action committees, labor unions, or other organized groups.

After a successful, private, money-raising event, the senator went on to make a speech to the Cordell Chamber of Commerce in a "public" salute. After his address, the senator received the mayor's key to Cordell (which doubled as a bottle cap opener). Another successful salute and fund raiser.

GETTING INTO MY WORK

I did a great deal more than help David Boren's political career through fund raising. I helped his public career through service to his constituents. After all, that is the official task of a state office aide.

In fact, there are ways in which to measure the efforts of congressmen on behalf of their constituents, mostly in the form of casework. When a veteran has a delay in settling a claims dispute with the Department of Veterans Affairs, he may write to his congressman for help. The same is true for a city applying for assistance from a federal agency, or a small business owner who feels the Environmental Protection Agency is driving the business toward bankruptcy in a waste disposal dispute. Members of Congress sometimes act as brokers in settling conflicts or speeding up consideration by slow-moving federal agencies.

In its first year of operation in 1979, Boren's Oklahoma City office helped with such complaints and projects 1,030 times. By 1984, that number grew to 2,570. Such contacts and cases included the ABCs of the federal bureaucracy—the BIA, CHAMPUS, EPA, FAA, FHA, HUD, IRS, OPM, USPS, SBA, and VA. Ann Dubler alone handled 320 cases in 1984 dealing with disputes with the Social Security Administration. Of the 67 that I handled in 1984, half were with the FDIC, the Federal Deposit Insurance Corporation.

Rarely does such casework get the attention of the public. I can recall only one significant case for which Boren received a high-visibility "thank you" for the work of his office. It involved a Polish mother's request for a visa so she could visit her son. The Sunday *Oklahoman* ran a June 1984 story with a picture of the happy reunion of Maciej and Irena Chopjecka.

My work as a field representative was very active. After a busy summer and fall of planning the fund-raising county salutes for the senator and a constant stream of casework and federal project coordination, I started to focus on a particular banking casework situation. My accidental assignment to the project started my interest in legislative work in Washington.

Boren was to speak to the Oklahoma Farmers Union banquet on February 13, 1984. I was to accompany Boren to Stillwater that night for some speeches the next day. Glavas had asked that I meet him and the senator before the banquet speech in a room at the Lincoln Plaza Hotel. A contingent of diverse individuals was meeting with Boren about their yearlong problems with the FDIC. They referred to themselves as the "Uninsured Depositors of Penn Square Bank."

Penn Square Bank was declared insolvent and closed by the comptroller of the currency in July 1982. Unlike most banking closures before it, the FDIC, named as receiver, did a "deposit payoff," that is, it paid off the insured ($100,000) depositors and settled claims and sold assets to recover its loss. Any institutional investors, business, church, or individual who had an account in excess of the insurance level was out of luck. While the transaction of closure—as opposed to merger or sale to another bank—was questioned at the time, no one knew that the uninsured depositors would be so long without a bigger return on their money.

So the casual meeting with Boren was requested by the depositors to complain about FDIC practices of disposal of assets, share rumors about their mismanagement of the receivership, and seek his help in getting some answers. As Boren was pressed to get to the speech before the farmers group, he had to end the meeting. In doing so, he introduced them to me, saying I would be glad to work with them on the continuing problems with the FDIC.

I did continue to serve as Boren's semiofficial liaison with this strong and influential group of depositors. I became so secure and comfortable with my field representative job that I closed on a house in Norman on May 21. I really began to enjoy my job: a few projects, a little big of policy, and a little bit of politics.

An interesting side trip developed for me in late July 1984. I was to attend a Dallas fund raiser with the senator, then accompany him to Louisiana for a breakfast fund raiser the next morning. We had a private jet provided by one of many wealthy businessmen/contributors which took us from Dallas to New Orleans and on to Washington, where I would spend a few days, at Boren's invitation and initiative. It was a thrilling itinerary, for which I gave up attending my father's retirement party.

After the small Dallas fund-raiser/dinner high in the skyline office suites of a financier and Democratic fund raiser, Boren got word of an early vote in the Senate the next morning. Thus, plans of the breakfast with oil men in Louisiana would have to be canceled, and we lifted off from Love Field in Dallas for Dulles International in Washington instead. Flying in the comfort of a $5 million English passenger jet with a three-man crew, we landed after 2:00 A.M. Boren and I shared a cab into Arlington, where I was deposited at a hotel and he went on to his townhouse a couple of miles away. Only a few hours later, I was met by Boren and Charlie Ward, to drive to the office.

For me, that day in the Washington office was mostly made up of visiting with LAs whom I talked with constantly by telephone from the state office. But as I sat in Boren's personal office late in the afternoon, his press secretary, Barbara Webb, came in to discuss a big news story that just broke. The Continental Bank of Illinois had collapsed.

In the absence of Boren's banking LA, Webb came in to give him some facts of the deal, after which she could get a statement for the Oklahoma press addressing the implications of such a bailout to a state ravaged by the Penn Square Bank closing two years before. With the two of us in his office, Boren began to construct the statement, and Webb wrote down his words.

"The FDIC was faced with the fact that if it allowed the Continental Illinois Bank to collapse, it would have had a devastating domino effect on the entire national economy."

His first sentence was clear and gave the broad scope needed to be conveyed.

"Collapse of Continental Illinois would have had a particularly harsh impact on Oklahoma."

This second line came more slowly. He looked at me and

asked, "Since I don't know enough about what this will mean, I don't want to just give them [the FDIC] carte blanche approval for this bailout, especially since it was a different approach than Penn Square. Greg, what do you think?"

Not expecting to be called on to help make a policy statement on the agency I had been battling on behalf of Penn Square depositors, I did agree that the harsh regulators could not be let off the hook for this multibillion-dollar bailout. I responded, "I think what you need to say is, 'While it's clear that Continental had to be saved, it raises the policy question of whether a double standard is being applied to large banks as opposed to smaller ones like in Oklahoma.'"

Boren jumped in, "That's good, that's good. Barbara, did you get that?" Boren, Webb, and I spoke my lines out loud again before Boren took on his baritone statement-making voice and said, "Let's say, 'While it is clear that it was necessary to save the Chicago bank, the action taken again raises the policy question of whether a double standard is being applied to large banks as opposed to smaller ones in states like Oklahoma.'"

Webb read the full statement back and returned to her office to type up and telecopy the release to the press. It was an exciting and defining moment in my Senate work. I was concerned about the little guy in the big world of money and power. And double standards were no friend of mine or of Boren's. The brief encounter helped me see more clearly what my interest was in government and where my energy was best expended to act on it.

My work with the Penn Square project continued for the next several months but shifted from in-state hand holding to cause advocacy. In the wake of the federal bailout of the Continental Bank, I faxed Boren a draft of a "Dear Colleague" letter to go to selected senators from states with credit unions that lost funds in Penn Square. This was a big shift in the kind of work done by a field representative; it joined casework with federal banking policy and practice.

Even though such a letter would normally be drafted by the Washington staff, I had never given working in Washington much thought. I knew that Glavas and Graves were destined to depart for the Capitol after the elections, assuming Boren held onto his more than 45 percent lead over his challenger and won reelection. One LA was to return to the state to work as a field representative, and one was to leave the staff. Thus two positions would be open for Glavas and Graves to fill. Although I did not realize it then, another LA would depart after the election, and his position would be open.

Three and a half weeks before the November election, I was to accompany Boren to Longview, Texas, to meet his children, Carrie and Dan, and attend the OU-Texas football game in Dallas. However, thunderstorms and logistics required that we drive rather than fly in a private plane. This meant many hours in my car—from Seminole to Longview (to spend the night) to pick up the kids, drive to Dallas, go to the game, go to dinner, return to Longview, and drive the senator back to Seminole. Little did I know he would use the opportunity to try to talk me into coming to Washington after the elections.

Our big adventure started when I met the senator in his hometown where a film crew was taping a campaign commercial in the local drugstore. We did not get on the road until very late in the evening. But Boren wasted no time in bringing up the subject of my becoming an LA. He had actually mentioned it before this trip, but I put it out of my mind, intimidated by the prospect of leaving Oklahoma. Now he became more serious.

"You know, Greg," Boren said, "my second term will be a lot different from this first. I'll be more focused on national legislation and less on firming up my base in the state. It's where the action will be."

In time, I felt the senator was sincere in his desire that I move. He had known of my involvement with his first statewide campaign. He met me in his first campaign for the Senate when I was an idealistic high school junior. He had seen my genuine interest in government as an intern on his staff in 1980. And he felt my concern for the unfair treatment of Oklahomans at the hands of a federal agency. He had confidence in me. Why shouldn't I?

The November elections saw David Boren win an impressive, record-breaking victory to a second term in the Senate. His statewide percentage was 76 percent, bolstered by the aggregate percentage of 78 percent in my twenty western counties. With the election decided, it was time for me to decide whether to join his staff in Washington.

Despite the warnings of friends, the comfort of my newly purchased home in Norman, and the fear of a new job setting, I let the senator talk me into moving to Washington, D.C. Washington was where the action would be for me.

So on December 4, 1984, Graves and I drove out of Oklahoma City in light snow flurries—he with his car pulling a U-Haul trailer and me in a 14-foot moving truck with what must have been a measley six-cylinder engine. It took us three days to reach Washington. We had arranged to rent a townhouse apartment just three blocks from the Capitol building with a legislative correspondent who also worked in Boren's office. On December 7, I started work as a legislative assistant in the Russell Senate Office Building.

"WHAT DO YOU DO IN WASHINGTON?"

A brief job description does not begin to cover all of an LA's duties. Besides responding to mail and telephone calls, legislative research and initiative, constituent response and outreach, parliamentary knowledge, policy expertise and legislative coalition building, an LA spends much of his or her time in meetings.

A big part of an LA's job is to see that constituents' letters are answered. No member of Congress would be in office for very long if he or she did not respond to the mail.

That task is made easier with the assistance of legislative correspondents. Had it not been for my LCs—Helen Weinstein, Patrick Turner, John Deeken, Jamie Bowers, and Karen Kay Speer—I would never have had the time to devote to proactive legislative issues.

Most of the time, an explanation of the "dual duties" of a member of Congress includes a dissertation on the responsibilities of "legislation" and "constituent service." But the volume of mail would almost require an additional duty listing. The chore includes more than just responding to people writing about their views on gun control or capital punishment or funding of the Star Wars strategic defense initiative. They all deserve to have their views heard and to seek out their congressman's position as well. And there are more than the casework letters about lost Social Security checks. Often other claims are brought to a congressman's attention.

For example, a woman once wrote to Senator Boren that she had been "the wife of John F. Kennedy" and then the "wife of Lyndon B. Johnson." She complained that she did not have her "properties, money, etc., from these marriages" and that she did not kow who had them. It all boiled down to the fact that "insurance company representatives" told her she would "need a claim number to file for insurance," and she did not have one. Even after speaking to "over 100 lawyers during the years after leaving the White House," she had gotten nowhere and had to turn to the senator for help. Unfortunately, I could not find her insurance claim number either.

There was also a letter from the Circumcision Prevention Society in Houston. It advised the senator of the group's goal: to halt the procedure that underlies "all of the violence in America." (They enclosed a complimentary bumper sticker reading, "Child Abuse Begins with Circumcision.") Many writers were very creative. A person from Santa Barbara, California, sent a festive Christmas theme postcard in mid-February 1985 urging the defeat of the nomination of Edwin Meese for attorney general. As the "justice" LA, this fell into my mailbox.

One final letter from my files deserves an honorable mention. A man wrote in February 1987, "I am pleased to inform you [Senator Boren] that I have decided to make myself available for elevation to the office of President." He was kind enough to include a one-page position paper that contained the following statements, among others: "Nicaragua—give them statehood," "Palestine—let me draw the boundaries," "Mexico—help with the debt by buying Baja California," and "Crime—legalize drugs." that's as far as I read.

POLITICS ON THE FRONT LINE

Personal dilemmas are common not just to elected officials but to us all. Choices concerning career and family can become more of a tangle of high-speed highways than meandering pathways. The allure of elective office creates the twinkle of ambition in the eyes of politicians.

All of us are faced with vocational choices from time to time, but most of us never have to make such public choices as running for public office. A small business secretary who wants to become the office manager in a twelve-person operation can keep her ambition a private matter between her and her boss. An esteemed educator can be assured of privacy as a candidate for a college presidency within a small search committee that vows confidentiality. If they are not chosen for the job, they can move on with pride intact. A candidate for public office is not merely running on principles and issues but for a job. Losing is public. While there are many obvious rewards to serving in elective office, getting there involves many risks—personal and professional.

Most politicians I know look at election results much like a fourth grader would consider a class election—as a popularity contest. After his 1984 reelection, Boren instructed his press secretary to issue a two-page press release trumpeting the "history-making record" of his 76 percent tally: "the highest percentage of votes ever received in a U.S. Senate, gubernatorial, or presidential race in Oklahoma." Of 2,354 precincts, Boren carried all but 6. Thereafter, it became a staff joke as to the punishment we would suffer when Boren found a way to blame one or more of us for the loss in those few precincts.

A continual, not-so-bluntly-stated belief held by many of my family and friends in Oklahoma was that I would some day run for office. (My father's Aunt Vernie is confinced that some day I will be governor.) With my interest and involvement in student government in high school and college, it was no secret that aside from having good leadership, speaking, and "people" skills, I liked politics on the front line. However, seven years on a senator's staff taught many things. The answer to my greatest supporters and future campaign volunteers became pat: "The more I'm in politics, the more I'd rather someone else be up front." I could accomplish a lot behind the scenes. The personal dilemma became real for me in June 1986. I was asked to run for the Oklahoma State Legislature.

During the 1986 Memorial Day congressional recess, I decided to take a trip back to Oklahoma. It was to be a trip to not only do official business for the senator by meeting with banking and education leaders but to follow up on some advice I had been getting to think seriously about a race for the state senate. The incumbent senator for the district that included my Norman home was a law school classmate of Boren's and a longtime veteran of the state senate. Many people within the university community at OU were concerned about his inability to get better support for higher education. One executive officer of the university described him simply: Senator Lee Cate was "lazy."

One of the best people I have ever known—a mentor, a friend, a father figure, and a teacher—was David Burr, Vice President of University Affairs at OU. I had grown close to him and his family since entering the university in 1979 when I was a freshman in the president's Leadership Class. I had worked in Burr's office as a student legislative assistant during my sophomore and junior years. He had hoped that I would return to Oklahoma and travel my own path, most likely in politics. Burr had talked to me about the weakening Democratic support Cate was facing and encouraged me to feel out the political environment in Norman.

I first decided to see what Cate's standing was with two of his Cleveland County colleagues in the House, Representatives Carolyn Thompson and Nancy Virtue. I had made plans to go to the State Capitol the next day, just to stop by and visit.

Thompson was a friend and member of my church. Our compatriot, Kathy Heiple, was constantly plotting Carolyn's and my marriage. Carolyn was always supportive of my returning to Oklahoma to run for office. However, despite the wide opening, she did not discuss that opportunity in terms of running against Cate in 1986.

Nancy Virtue was a good friend, too. She lived just a mile up the road from my home. At my house warming party two years earlier, to the delight of my other friends and family, she came by with two bright orange campaign yard signs for me to put in my new lawn. Nancy and I had a nice visit—we discussed the state budget figures for education or some such issue—but she seemed very distant. Even her answers to my questions about her reelection campaign were short and unfocused. Like Carolyn, Nancy made no mention of Lee Cate's standing or the need to have a Democrat challenge him to keep the seat from going to a more aggressive Republican candidate. I left her office feeling relief but disappointment. While the biggest career decision seemed to have passed me by, it was probably for the best.

MEANWHILE, BACK IN WASHINGTON

By the next week, I was back in Washington, busy with events, meetings, and thoughts that did not allow me to focus on the decision I had made to stay in a U.S. senator's office and out of state senate race. The reasons not to be a candidate in the race were reaffirmed. After all, I was twenty-five years old, living in Washington, D.C., for the past year and a half. Even though my legal and voting residence was in Norman, I had only lived there six months before leaving the state. Although Oklahoma was not a state during the Civil War, the term "carpetbagger" had real meaning.

On the first Monday morning back in the office, we had an afternoon staff meeting that thrust me back into the world of legislative work. Two days later, I had a high-level meeting with staffers whose senators were cosponsors of one of Boren's biggest bills at the time. The most significant event to take my mind off the domeless Oklahoma State Capitol and affix it to my working in the shadows of the gilded dome occurred the next evening. I had been invited to speak before an evening class at the American University law school in D.C. The class of about thirty-five law students was studying regulatory process, and that evening's focus was federal election law. After a brief lecture to students my own age or older on Boren's legislative goals to change election laws, I answered questions on a panel with Federal Election Commission (FEC) Commissioner Thomas Josefiak and an election law attorney from San. Francisco. In addition to the satisfaction of presenting a college lecture as an expert from the field, I was rewarded with an honorarium check for $150 (a nice allowance for an underpaid $28,980-a-year staffer).

However, word soon came to me from Oklahoma that my political future there was still a possibility. I learned that though the senate seat would not be wise to pursue, the state house seat held by Virtue was coming open. She surprisingly decided not to run for reelection.

Carolyn Thompson called me soon after learning from Nancy that she would not run again. Carolyn was direct and somewhat impatient. As a self-appointed broker, she told me the news and gave me forty-eight hours to decide. She would set wheels in motion to stop other potential candidates. Otherwise, the race would draw all kinds of competition if a Democratic party-sanctioned candidate were not identified. David Burr called as well. He asked if I would allow him to inquire of some individuals how they might help me financially. I granted him the latitude to express my interest to business leaders in Norman and report back to me.

A third call came from Cal Hobson, a state representative from Noble, just south of Norman. I knew Hobson well from my student government days at OU as a friend supportive of limiting tuition increases for students. He was my keynote speaker at a statewide conference of student government leaders that I initiated at OU in 1983.

Hobson encouraged me to run. He said Boren's help would be a great boost and that I could count on help from him, Thompson, and the house speaker. He said that I not also count on his financial help. "I can help you get lots of PAC money, too." I suddenly realized I had spent my entire professional career working for a politician devoted to limiting the financial influence of PACs on a national level. Now, without realizing the role I played on Boren's staff with that legislation, someone was offering to help me exploit the PAC game.

I did not want to appear so naïve as to sound surprised by that. I just had not thought enough about my own principles to reject the offer on the spot. I thanked Hobson and told him my decision would be made soon. It was a difficult time. Between the support and advice from my parents and friends, I had to ask myself one question, "Where can I make the most significant contribution in public service right now?"

I decided to stay in Washington. Being a foot soldier in the U.S. Senate was a larger and more significant place for me in 1986 than the state budget battles I would fight from the back bench of the Oklahoma House of Representatives. My role on the congressional staff is nicely summarized by a quote from the commercially popular 1991 comedy, *King Ralph*. In an important scene, Willingham, a character played by Peter O'Toole, says to the soon-to-self-depose king of England (John Goodman), "It's easier to whisper advice from cover than to risk its merit at the point of attack."

CHAPTER THREE

"Let's Throw Some Bombshells"

*Societies are renewed . . . by people who believe in something,
care about something, stand for something.*

—*JOHN W. GARDNER*

AFTER A PRODUCTIVE AUGUST congressional recess mixed
with work and relaxation, Senator Boren assembled a meeting of
his legislative assistants on a Friday afternoon, September 13,
1985. He was anxious to get an aggressive legislative program
underway and use this part of his second term to become a
national legislator. After his overwhelming reelection in 1984, he
had made the assertion to me on more than a few occasions,
"What good is having political capital, if you don't expend it on
what you think is right?"

THE PAC BILL

Boren's six legislative assistants gathered around the conference
table in his Russell Senate Office Building suite, which resembled the Oval Office with its overstuffed couches facing each
other in front of a nonworking marble fireplace. We began to
discuss what opportunities lay ahead in the traditional areas of
tax breaks for the energy industry and new agriculture programs

and benefits for farmers. I had just chimed in with an update on the work I had been doing on legislation concerning the Penn Square Bank debacle that had been sent to Sen. Jake Garn's (R-Utah) banking committee when Boren shifted the conversation to a lesser-known legislative effort.

"Whatever happened to my PAC bill?" the senator asked.

"Well, Senator, I think our legislative fellow, Mike, had done some more research on it," I replied. I was referring to Mike Sharp, a six-month research fellow and graduate student we had been loaned from the University of Oklahoma's Carl Albert Congressional Studies Center. "But he's gone now, so I don't think . . ."

The senator quickly interrupted. "Well, I think this issue should be on the national agenda!" And without taking a breath, he continued, "Now remind me what it does exactly?"

"As I recall, it sets aggregate PAC limits on what Senate members can accept, based on the number of congressional districts in the state and a flat $75,000 for House members. But Mike was really doing the stuff for Dave, and . . ."

Boren jumped in again. "Greg, get what work Mike did on it, and let's get ready to just take it out there to the floor. I'd like to go ahead and try to get a vote on it as an amendment. I think it's time that the Senate focuses on campaign reform. I'm ready to just throw some bombshells! I don't care if I only get fifteen votes!"

After a few more housekeeping items, the lengthy legislative strategy meeting was adjourned late in the afternoon.

Actually, Boren's interest and action on the issue of campaign finance reform predated my coming to Washington to work as a legislative assistant. I had been on his staff in Oklahoma City all of ten days when on June 8, 1983, he issued a statement on his introduction of the Campaign Finance Reform Amendment to the 1983 bill he had sponsored with two House members which would limit contributions that candidates for Congress could receive from political action committees. The two House Democrats were fellow Oklahoman Mike Synar and Beryl Anthony of Arkansas.

Besides noting the typical and familiar statistics of PAC growth and strength, Boren made the comment that only 17 percent of all firms with more than $100 million in assets had registered PACs, that "we are just beginning to see the growth of PACs and the amount of money they can pump into campaigns." His statement pointed out that by the end of 1982, the FEC showed 3,371 registered PACs who gave $83.1 million in the 1982 election cycle.

Boren stated in 1983 that "the danger to the political process lies in this trend which hastens the day when members of Congress will no longer depend on individual contributions from their home states for their election efforts" and instead will depend on PACs "directed and led by people outside of their home states." He was concerned that Congress was "becoming addicted to the quick cash available from a PAC located in Washington and less dependent on financing from home" and that "this out-of-state money machine" discourages "new people with fresh ideas from getting involved in politics."

While those words are not terribly prophetic, they were similar to ones used years later by Republicans to promote their narrower legislation to eliminate PACs and address the problem of large, out-of-state contributions to candidates.

FINDING THE FILES

I was not able or motivated to find Sharp's files on the campaign finance reform issue until the next Monday. The legislative staff had seen and heard the senator make grand proclamations about his intended actions on an issue only to have our work sit in his in-box with suggestions for action growing old and outdated. Sharp, who worked with our chief legislative assistant, Dave Holliday, left the office several weeks earlier. Eventually I was able to find his files and materials.

It seems that before Sharp left, he actually had the old bill from the 98th Congress, S. 1443, redrafted and introduced in early January. I assumed that Boren was going to be angry. He did not even act like he knew his bill had been introduced, but there was a copy of it, with his signature in the upper right-hand corner of the first page, indicating it was to be introduced and printed in the *Congressional Record*. Sure enough, the files had a copy of S. 297 and a signed "Dear Colleague" letter asking for every senator to join as a co-sponsor.

I had been a legislative assistant for the senator for a mere ten months, yet it seemed to me he would have remembered that he had already introduced the bill. But this is a good indication of what kind of diverse pressures are on members of Congress. Boren was a Rhodes Scholar and the brightest, most popular politician in Oklahoma, but he was so busy that he forgot he had introduced the bill. Of course, I did know Boren well enough to know that that would not matter. He sounded like he really wanted to push the thing as a floor amendment to any legislative vehicle he could.

He had some experience with this process, as he made use of the Senate rules to hold up the nomination of Edwin Meese so as to get consideration of emergency agriculture legislation. In the February filibuster, Boren was not at all opposed to Meese becoming head of the Justice Department under President Reagan. As a member of the minority party, he was determined to use the rules to his advantage to hold up a nomination the majority party wanted very badly and to release his stranglehold on it only when the Republicans yielded to provide assistance for struggling farmers.

After my quick investigation into the work that Sharp did on Boren's PAC reform amendment, I was ready to put together a memorandum for the senator. Typically, there was never the time or convenience to have a face-to-face conversation with Boren on an hourly or daily basis, so the "one-pager" memo became a staple of Hill life. Sure, you could catch him on his way to a committee markup or hearing or speech, but he was always too busy being briefed about what was happening in the next five or ten minutes. It was not a good idea—nor was it efficient—to try to get answers to questions or pass along information in any way other than written memos.

My first memo on the issue of Boren's campaign finance reform efforts first included lots of figures: 1982 campaign expenditures were $342 million, $83.6 million of which came from PACs, equaling 24.4 percent cumulatively given by PACs to all congressional candidates. For whatever reason, however, my focus indicated some ambivalence about his previous bill's goals. The legislation called for an aggregate limit on what candidates could receive from PACs. In my memo I asked, "Would an aggregate limit on total PAC money be unconstitutional—by virtue of the *Buckley v. Valeo* Supreme Court decision which found that personal and total money spent limitations in elections are unconstitutional?" (I also encouraged him to consider "equalizing" the amount individuals and PACs can give, say, $2,500 per election. In retrospect, that was actually bad policy advice. But Boren liked the idea because many of his own contributors would be able to contribute at the higher limit.)

Boren's quick response to my questions and comments indicated that he was not interested in an armchair debate with a twenty-four-year-old staff member on points of constitutional law. Instead, he wanted to move forward. He said, "Don't you think our approach is OK because it doesn't limit what a particular PAC can give in total? It limits what a candidate can receive from PACs." On a copy of the *Buckley v. Valeo* decision that I provided him, he turned to page 3 of the syllabus, circled a phrase, and wrote that limitations were protected by the decision. He continued, "Let's go with our original bill but raise it [the minimum limit] to $100,000 on House + $25,000 where [there is a] runoff and also raise individual's limit to $2,500 and PACs to $2,500." Despite my final appeal on the memo and later changes and questions, Boren said, "Go ahead and draft this way."

At that time, I got the legislation redrafted through the Senate Legislative Counsel's office, a nonpartisan support office that does the actual drafting of legislative language for senators. But refinements and changes were so common that I put the text of the amendment in my own computer at the office, so that when changes were to be made, I could do it myself. In a period of about three weeks, I learned more about legislation and how laws are written than in four years of college as a political science major. I had never really grasped the idea that all of our laws are written somewhere. Our bill was to amend Title 2 of the U.S. Code, the federal catalog of laws, entitled "The Congress."

THE SENATE FLOOR

I received the Senator's final approval on the substance of his bill by September 27, less than two weeks after he stated his intent to move the amendment. In a mèmo clarifying the $100,000 PAC limit for House races and a December 31, 1986, effective date, Boren, showing concern for substance and strategy, said, "OK, let's go for it." But always quick to add others to the fight, the fun, and the cause, he added, "Will [Warren] Rudman [R-N.H.] or [Lawton] Chiles [D-Fla.] cosponsor?"

Our legislative director, Blythe Thomas, and I found a potential vehicle to carry our nongermane amendment: S.J.Res. 77, the "Compact of Free Association." The Senate loosely allows for amendments to be considered on just about any "authorizing" piece of legislation, without a hard and fast rule that holds it to a test of germaneness. This meant that a bill negotiated by the Pentagon and the State Department with the Marshall Islands as a settlement of claims for nuclear testing many years earlier would serve our purposes very well, especially because it was due to be passed by October 1.

We had to clear a final hurdle before going to the Senate floor. If we were going to offer a nongermane amendment, we had to make sure we knew the Senate rules. With unnecessary prompting from the senator, Thomas and I made an appointment to see Bob Dove, parliamentarian of the Senate. Little did I know then that Thomas, a self-proclaimed school board mother-turned-congressional aide, was as nervous about this meeting as I was.

Thomas, a Republican, had worked for Sen. Henry Bellmon and his 1980 replacement, Don Nickles, before jumping the GOP ship to work for Boren. I always felt comfortable with Thomas because of her motherly gentleness, coupled with her ability to smoke, drink, and cuss with the best of us yellow-dog Oklahoma Democrats. She had only been on the Boren staff since February 1985, taking Holliday's place when he transferred to the Senate Intelligence Committee.

It was necessary for Thomas and me to sit down briefly with Dove to discuss our options under the Senate rules to ensure that we could get a straight up-or-down vote. What we did not want to happen was to offer a nongermane amendment to some authorization bill only to see another senator object or make some motion that the parliamentarian would uphold. Nor did we want it to have a second degree amendment offered which would gut the bill of its purpose. Finally, we did not want to have anyone move that the legislation is in another committee's jurisdiction and thus should be sent there for appropriate consideration. All of these possibilities were a threat—some we could not protect against—but our brief encounter with Dove answered many of our questions about Senate legislative process.

The night before our trip to the Senate floor I suggested to Boren that we give fair warning of our intentions with a "Dear Colleague" letter. These impersonal letters, starting with the salutation "Dear Colleague," go to all members of the Senate (or House, if you serve in that body). They typically are to inform members of legislation you have introduced or plan to introduce or to make any other pertinent announcement. Usually, the letter is simply given to the Senate Service Department, which copies, folds, stuffs, and delivers it to every senator in twenty-four to forty-eight hours. We did not have that much time. The night before the Senate was to consider the bill, we put together a letter that consisted of two paragraphs;

Dear Colleague,
    I am considering offering my bill to limit Political Action Committee (PAC) contributions as an amendment to the pending Compact for Free Associations, which is now on the Senate floor. As it has implications for all members during their election cycles, I wanted to call it to your attention before it comes up on the floor. It would not

affect the 1986 elections but would take effect for the 1988 election cycle. I have attached a copy of my statement introducing the bill which explains it.

It is an attempt at a moderate and responsible approach to a serious development which threatens the integrity of the election process. If you should have questions or would like to cosponsor the amendment, please have your staff member call Greg Kubiak in my office at 224-0148.

Sincerely,
David L. Boren
United States Senator

The compact's October 1 deadline passed, but October 2 came as a day like any other in the U.S. Senate. With pressing business, Majority Leader Robert Dole of Kansas was getting ready to seek quick action on the Compact of Free Association. It was not to be an issue that was controversial. In fact, he probably thought it could pass without a roll call vote. However, it was time to go to the Capitol to announce our intentions. Boren and I traveled the quarter mile underground from our Russell building offices to the Senate floor on the second floor of the Capitol. That north half of the Capitol, in the early autumn shadow of the gilded dome, was about to hear the first shot in a long battle, a battle that continues today.

I had never been on the Senate floor before that day. I remember being awed by an awareness of the history made there when I stumbled about, getting my floor privilege pass, pinning it to my Senate ID, and following Boren into the chamber. Despite my preoccupation of the moment, I heard fragments of Boren's whispered conversation: "Never walk in front of a senator while he's addressing the chair." And he asked, "Have you got the amendment?"

Boren was seated at his desk and motioned to a page to fetch a chair for me to be placed next to his. In previous months, I saw staffers, usually older, sit in those armless, straight-back black chairs, never knowing whether I would have a chance to be so close to that power and influence. The page brought the seat and I sat down nervously, waiting for the moment of attack.

Boren went to Dole to whisper to him that he had an amendment. He obviously had to tell the majority leader the nature of the amendment and that an amendment on PAC limits was not germane to the measure that would "provide compensation to the natives of Bikini as a result of the nuclear test conducted by our country."

After caucusing with other senators and making mental notes to himself, Dole asked for the Senate's approval to move on to S.J.Res. 77. Dole spoke in stern tones, "I am not unmindful of amendments that could be offered to that legislation. I know that the distinguished senator from Utah [Mr. Hatch] has an amendment. I understand that one or both senators from South Carolina have an amendment on textile legislation, and I understand that Senator Hart has an amendment. The senator from Oklahoma has one relative to Micronesia."

Boren quickly rose to respond, "It refers to political action. It has some reference to Micronesia."

The stern-faced Dole, half-humorously, half-angrily, inquired, "Do they have a PAC?"

Boren replied, "I do not know." Dole ignored a catfight and went on.

That was it. The amendment was filed. Boren turned to me and said, "Well, we've got it in, but nothing's going to happen today." I felt like a thoroughbred, nervous with sweat at Churchill Downs for the Kentucky Derby, who had been stopped at the gate because the contest was postponed by the starter.

I noticed Sen. Gary Hart at his desk behind us. I was struck in the presence of a 1984 presidential candidate whom I had supported as a county delegate in Cleveland County, Oklahoma. Hart leaned forward over his desk toward Boren and asked, "What's your amendment about?"

"It would limit PACs in a congressional election," Boren replied, not thinking Hart was terribly interested.

Hart pressed further, "What would it do?"

"It's along the lines of the Obey-Railsback bill that the House passed in '79 to put an aggregate limit on elections based on the size of the state," Boren said.

After some additional whispers I could not hear very well, Hart said, "Put me on as a cosponsor."

I was thrilled. My heart was racing. We had gotten our first cosponsor without having to ask.

But before my heart could return to a normal rate, the senate minority leader, Robert C. Byrd of West Virginia, eyes casting a cold, steely glare, approached Boren and said, "David, Senator Mitchell and I and others want to see you in my office about this rather quickly." Byrd, in atypical senatorial discourtesy, turned and left the floor, expecting Boren to be close behind.

Boren gave me a skeptical and somewhat frightened look and left without saying anything. As I could not remain on the floor without being at my senator's elbow, I politely and respectfully left the chamber. After waiting for at least forty-five minutes in the Senate reception room, an ornate, public space just off the Senate floor, I saw Boren. He seemed surprised that I was still hanging around. He looked a bit haggard as I asked, "Where have you been?"

"I've been with Senators Byrd, Mitchell, Bentsen, and Ford this whole time," Boren responded. "I feel like I've been wrestling with a bunch of bears!" Although Boren was prone to exaggeration, I sensed his underlying seriousness and felt sympathy for what must have been a tough meeting.

Boren was subjected to opposition and concern from the Senate minority leader, the ranking member of the Rules Committee, and the former and current chairmen of the Democratic Senatorial Campaign Committee. He explained to me that those senators felt he was "putting our guys on the spot." Though not stated as directly, it meant that Democrats were improving their abilities at PAC fund raising so did not want to compromise that good relationship by supporting limits on PACs. At the same time, they wanted to be known as the party of clean, good government not manipulated by special interests, so a vote against campaign reform would look bad.

Though I was not present, it was obviously a time when Boren pressed the Senate Democratic leadership to rise above the politics of money and work with him. Before he left that confrontational meeting, he even had Sen. George Mitchell (D-Me.) explaining the need to broaden his legislation, to at least include language to close the "bundling" loophole—a way Republicans found to evade the spirit of the law on contribution limits.

We both left the Capitol on an emotionless walk back to the office. We had not won, and we had not lost, but we certainly got a lot of attention very, very quickly. Since the amendment was filed and the die was cast, I turned my energies to strategy, since that was clearly Boren's focus right now. What we now needed were friends.

TIME FOR STRATEGY

The next day, I asked Boren in another quick staff meeting with LAs if I should try to get in touch with some interest groups to support the amendment. Not knowing which groups would be the most likely to help our cause, I mentioned to Boren groups like the League of Women Voters.

Boren said, "Yes, give them a call, tell them what we're doing, and call Common Cause, too. This should be on their agenda, too."

I made a call to Common Cause on Friday, October 4. The staffer I talked to was Jane Metzinger, who was eager to talk with me soon. In fact, we set a meeting for 10:00 A.M. the next workday, Monday the 7th.

In that meeting, held in a corner of our cramped reception room, I explained to Metzinger and her two colleagues from Common Cause that we just did not have much conference space. After she introduced me to her office mates, she described Common Cause's history and background with the issue of campaign finance reform. Finally, I informed her of what our amendment did, which she already seemed to know.

Common Cause was a major player in the reforms coming out of Watergate. While public financing of presidential campaigns had been deliberated well before the public scandal of the early 1970s, spending limits were established for congressional elections as well in the Federal Election Campaign Act of 1974. However, the Supreme Court's decision in *Buckley v. Valeo* overturned that portion of the law as an inhibition of free speech. The reading from the court was that spending limits could only be voluntary. And a voluntary system would not work very well without the incentive of public financing like that which existed in the presidential system.

I assured Metzinger that Boren had no interest in pursuing an agenda to refight the battle Common Cause lost to the Supreme Court nine years earlier. Respectfully, I suggested that such reforms were not a practicality with a Republican Senate or with a conservative like Boren. Instead, I appealed to the group's interest in curtailing the most obvious problem with the system: political action committee funds. Metzinger left to report to her superiors at Common Cause. And I reported my efforts to Boren.

That evening, I talked about my day's activity to a good friend on Sen. Wendell Ford's staff, Elizabeth Wilson. I was her guest that evening on a Potomac River cruise on a boat chartered by one of the maritime associations with a strong lobbying reputation. The "booze cruise"—as such lobbying ventures are dubbed—was set up for Ford's staff, as similar outings were for other congressional offices. The lobbying organization provided food, drink, and a boat to take a slow, leisurely float from the Washington Marina in Southwest D.C. to just above Mount Vernon, George Washington's home south of Alexandria, Virginia.

The irony of the evening was not lost on me at the time as I described to Wilson my desire for help on this amendment from groups like Common Cause. Although she worked for one of the senators who took Boren to the woodshed days earlier, Wilson was sympathetic to the need to reform PACs. While she agreed that I needed help from outside groups, she also said that I had better be cautious of what senators like her boss could do for, or against, the effort. She told me one cannot fight for "truth, justice, and the American way" on one's own and win. It is necessary to have allies inside and outside the Senate. But still I knew that if we were right, a populist issue like PAC reform would catch on and force senators to support us.

I remembered the other irony of the evening, well after the buzz from flowing bourbon wore off, that the boat trip to win favor with Senate staffers was sponsored by a group that earned disdain from my boss. In his 1978 runoff election for the Senate, Boren ran television ads against his opponent for accepting PAC funds from out-of-state lobbying groups, while the names of PACs scrolled down the screen. The question was asked, "Why does a seafarers union want to help Representative Ed Edmondson get elected to the U.S. Senate?" The answer, of course, was the same reason they spent hundreds of dollars for a floating party for Senate staffers—influence. I knew then that if most Americans saw the way these lobbyists were trying to gain influence over impressionable, thirsty, and powerful staffers, as well as the way PACs bought influence with members of Congress through political contributions, they would force drastic changes in the system.

The next day, I contacted the League of Women Voters. I let Boren know that "the buy [with the League] is discussing it with his people and will get back to me later," to which Boren responded a confident, "Good." Little did I know it would be nearly two years later before the league would officially support our legislation.

In my memo that day, October 8, I let the senator know that I had visited with Common Cause and that they were interested and might very well help us. I also warned him of some unseemly behavior by certain staff on the Rules Committee. I had learned that certain individuals had informed major PACs about the legislation and Boren's intent to push for a floor vote. Boren, never one to be spooked by a gathering storm of opposition, merely told me to "be sure and draft our amendment so it's not subject to further amendment."

The other part of the memo was to let the senator know that I had contacted the staff of four other potentially supportive

senators: Nancy Kassebaum of Kansas, Chiles of Florida, Proxmire of Wisconsin, and Rudman of New Hampshire. At that early
stage, however, the staff could only assure me that "they were
looking at it." Ten days later, in an October 18 memo, I advised
Boren that I had discussions with six offices in the hope of
getting cosponsors. I encouraged him to help in the effort more
personally by talking to these members. Boren agreed to call or
talk to Rudman, Kassebaum, and Chiles. As Dole was reluctant
to allow our legislative vehicle to come back to the floor, we had
this time to find supporters before making our next move.

The strategy of having good legislative language proved to be
elusive. The bill originally had three provisions: an aggregate
limit on PAC contributions to House candidates set at $100,000
(plus $25,000 extra in case of a runoff); an aggregate limit for
Senate candidates set from $100,000 to $750,000 depending on
the number of congressional districts in the state; and an effective date of December 31, 1986, affecting the 1988 election cycle.
Boren liked it.

The biggest challenge became to expand the very limited bill.
The discussion Boren had with Byrd and the other senators
proved that a straightforward, aggregate PAC limit was not going
to go over well. Senators were worried that PACs would put their
extra resources into independent expenditures, and Senator
Mitchell, the chairman of the Democratic Senatorial Campaign
Committee, was particularly worried about the newly discovered
loophole called "bundling," through which one senator netted
nearly $200,000 with the help of only one PAC.

Boren's response to such expansions of the limited bill was,
"Not sure." Actually, looking back, I can understand his initial
reluctance for two reasons. One, I was not clear with him about
how the law could be remedied to stop bundling. For Boren,
counting contributions toward an aggregate PAC limit was as
important as counting the contribution against the individual
PAC limit. As long as PAC influence was limited, it did not
matter to Boren.

The second reason was probably political. Rep. Jim Jones (D-

Okla.) benefited from the loophole as reported in a national news story. Jones was running for the U.S. Senate against Boren's Republican colleague, Nickles. Oklahoma Democrats might think that Boren, who had somewhat strained relations with Jones, was adding this provision to try to make it look as though he was taking bad money.

To help clarify the issue, I wrote another memo three days later devoted solely to the subject of "conduit contributions." After again explaining the abusive nature of this loophole, I asked the rhetorical question, "Do you favor having this kind of back door PAC influence?" Boren responded was a definite "NO." The antibundling language would be added to the legislation.

The strategy to develop a strong set of allies and good legislative language that cornered senators into supporting us would not be enough to prepare for battle. The composition of a good, solid script would have gone nowhere had it not been for a strong director to oversee the production.

STATE OF THE SENATE

I learned very early on that senators are very busy. Senate days are filled with breakfast speeches to trade associations, pictures with visiting high school student groups on the Capitol steps, committee hearings, meetings with constituent groups, ad hoc conferences with senators on a joint project, time in the office to make calls to federal agency heads and state political leaders, time to develop legislative positions from staff memos and input, going over their weekend schedules for visits to their home states—all of which is interrupted by the occasional but persistent need to dash to the Senate floor to vote.

All members of congress have great demands on their time. Community leaders in their state or district expect access to them either in person or on the telephone. Lobbyists or trade associations who represent industry or workers back home expect access. PACs or interested money brokers who fund their campaigns certainly expect access. And last but not least, constituents who send them to Washington to represent them with their vote expect access.

Some members utilize time better than others; some have more pressing leadership responsibilities or more diverse constituents to represent; still others do not mind getting up out of a group meeting with constituents to say, "I've enjoyed this time to meet together, but I now have to represent our state on the Agriculture Committee. Please continue to meet with my top staffer on this issue, and we'll help anyway we can." That is all that has to be said, but few can do it.

Staffing is the saving grace of the Senate — as well as a curse. Back in the days of billion-dollar total federal budgets and a limited national government role in the daily lives of citizens, senators could get by with one secretary and maybe one aide, to open the mail, answer telephones, troubleshoot, and do a little research on legislation. Today, however, there is tremendous federal involvement in transportation, the environment, space travel, health care, tax policy, worker safety, education programs, the war on drugs, civil rights, and medical research. That is because before the turn of the century, the complex issues of mass transit, acid rain, the space shuttle, Medicare, IRAs, asbestos abatement, Head Start, crack cocaine, affirmative action, and AIDS did not exist. And these are just a few of the hundreds of *domestic* issues.

There is no way that a member of Congress can be expected to know and understand the intricacies of past or present federal policies spanning $2 trillion worth of spending — much less the wisdom of certain future policies. Thus, within any organization dealing with diverse, complex tasks, comes the need to bureaucratize and specialize. Because of the scope and magnitude of today's issues, senators also must pick and choose the scope of issues they wish to be focus on. As a seventh-year, minority party senator, who did not sit on the Senate committee with jurisdiction over campaign finance laws, I knew in 1985 that Boren was not well suited to be a leader for this cause. He sat on the Agriculture Committee, a plum spot for an Oklahoman, as well as Finance, the highly coveted tax-writing committee.

Further, Boren had just won an unusual eight-year appointment to the Senate Select Committee on Intelligence. At the time, I was uneasy about the excitement he expressed at this appointment. I saw it as not only a committee most Oklahomans would not appreciate but also, even if he nobly served on the panel, as a committee whose work would probably be top secret and could not be discussed or publicly released. Most political experts would agree that foreign policy can get you defeated, but it never gets you elected.

But it seemed in that September staff meeting that Boren really wanted to invest some energy in the reform agenda. As Boren gave me the assignment to work on campaign finance reform issues on his staff, I was determined to help make him a reformer. To do so, I figured he must publicly — and within the Senate — do three things: (1) distinguish himself as knowledgeable about the issue, (2) show himself determined to push his reform package, and (3) be energetic and stay interested to see it through.

WHERE'S THE PASSION?

Senator Boren showed a distinctive determination with his October 2 stand on the Senate floor. And I knew he was certainly more than able to grasp the technical aspects of campaign finance law. Further, he seemed to be willing to answer my memo questions, talk to senators, and encourage my outreach to groups like Common Cause. There is, however, another factor that makes or breaks leadership reputations through the legislative process, passion.

This fourth ingredient in legislative success is harder to quantify and detect. But history could show us several instances in which passion and belief in a cause brought many a bill out of sleepy committee hearing rooms. Personal conviction often means more to moving legislation than does committee jurisdiction. Committee chairmen have to address legislation by virtue of content. Legislative crusaders push measures out of personal motivation. But members of Congress who crusade for or against something to which they are personally committed are very powerful.

There are many tools senators may employ in trying to influence legislation: personal speeches, testimony, nongermane amendments, op/ed columns, staff and research resources, personal time studying the issue, personal telephone calls, and conversations with those involved in the issue. But after subtracting time for sleeping, eating, family and personal matters, travel, press interviews, position development, social engagements, photo opportunities, constituents, meetings, speeches, and obligatory time to manage a staff of thirty-five, there is very, very little time left. What percentage of time a senator gives to really learning, reading, and discussing a particular legislative issue tells how much he cares about that issue. More than even their time management decisions, their personal experience will demonstrate their passion about an issue.

Boren's populist roots came through each and every time he would tell three different stories that related to his passion for campaign finance reform. One was told by David Boren the citizen, one by Boren the politician, and one by Boren the teacher. As the staffer who followed him for five years to nearly every Washington speech (and many in Oklahoma) he ever made on the subject, every press conference or interview, every meeting with constituents or lobbyists, and every speech on the Senate floor, I could almost recite in my sleep the stories Boren related about his determination to rein in special interest money in congressional elections.

One story was that while governor of Oklahoma, Boren had a meeting with a group of bankers one day. It was a casual meeting, after which a banker from the southeastern part of the state came up privately to Boren and said, "Governor, we appreciate your help for the bankers and all you've done for folks down my way, but isn't there something we can do about our state senator, Joe Smith [not his real name]. He's been up here in the Capitol so long, we think he's forgotten about us. Every time we think we've got someone to run against him, he's able to raise the money to scare 'em off."

Governor Boren then asked the banker, "Joe, are you a member of the Oklahoma Bankers Association?"

The banker responded, "Why, yes."

Governor Boren asked, "Do you give money to the association political action committee?"

Joe said, "I sure do."

Governor Boren said, "Well, Joe, did you know that your money went to help reelect Senator Smith in the last two elections because the bankers' PAC gives him campaign contributions?"

Senator Boren would then make the rhetorical statement to his audience, "I wouldn't delegate to someone else or some committee somewhere my right to vote in an election. Why would I delegate my right to contribute to an election campaign?"

Boren the politician told another story about political action committees that speaks to his passion about the electoral process. Prior to U.S. Senate elections, the Democratic Senatorial Campaign Committee—like its Republican counterpart—sponsors a "campaign school" for the candidates and incumbents running the next year. Boren attended the 1983 session as he was up for reelection the following year. This seminar, set in southern Maryland, was to focus on campaign techniques, strategies, and advice for candidates. Many of the speakers were fresh off the Senate campaign trail from the 1982 election. Boren often recalled the taste of reality he and his wife got from this experience.

"We were basically told how to play the PAC game," told Boren. He recalled the advice of a political consultant in one session: "What you have to do is go out and get yourself a poll that says you've got good name ID [identification] and are unlikely to have a hard time getting reelected." Boren went on to relate the rest of the advice with this illustration:

If you're on the banking committee, you go to the bankers PAC, show them the poll, warn then that major banking legislation could be considered in the committee, and say, "I hope you'll get on board. As you can see, this poll shows I'm going to be around here for a while so I want to be sure of your support with an early contribution to my campaign." Then you go down the street to the savings and loan PAC and say, "You know, the bankers PAC has helped me out, and I hope you will, too. They've got competing views with yours so you better get on board." Then you get word to the insurance industry groups that the bankers and the S&L's are helping your campaign. Before you know it, the insurance PACs will be more than anxious to pony up to the bar. Then you give the securities industry PACs a chance, and on, and on, and on.

Boren admitted on more than one occasion, "By the time Molly and I left, we absolutely felt dirty." He reported that one campaign consultant who helped an incumbent senator get re-elected in 1982 boasted about getting "nearly all of [their] money from PACs in Washington." That senator could afford a fully paid campaign staff without the hassle of volunteers and a virtually total media campaign with just a few rides in parades. This particularly troubled Boren, who prefers personal campaigns of pressing the flesh, seeing people and depending on in-state donations.

That incumbent senator was Quentin Burdick. I always wondered how the people of North Dakota felt about Burdick. In his waning days of Senate service before his death in September 1992, his real value to his people was solid seniority and an aggressive staff. But in many respects, that is all it takes to bring home the bacon.

Burdick, reelected in 1988 at age eighty, was referred to by a journalist as "one of the Senate's kings of pork." In an October 7, 1991, column, Jack Anderson disclosed that North Dakota State University football fans would have an easier trip to the Fargodome stadium thanks to a $500,000 mile of road supposedly used to connect U.S. Department of Agriculture laboratories on the campus. Burdick chaired the appropriations subcommittee overseeing Department of Agriculture spending. It's all in a day's work for a staffer who has the patronage of the chairman to see to it that funds go to projects of the chairman's state, by writing it into the bill or a committee report. No senator wanting hard-earned projects funded with the chairman's help will risk raising red flags on the chairman's local projects. Under the gilded dome, there is no reward for scrimping.

The final story I most often associate with the passion Boren felt for the issue developed much later than 1985. It actually was told first on the Senate floor in 1987. The oddest part of the story is that it was delivered before it was experienced.

In desperation for a catchy paragraph for an opinion piece I was drafting for Boren to run in the *Washington Post*, I needed a line to illustrate the danger of inaction on a reform bill to future generations. Then it hit me. What better example for a former college professor like Boren than students. In writing the draft, I started with 1976, the bicentennial of independence, when the cost of winning a seat in the U.S. Senate was $600,000. In current terms, 1986, the price tag had grown to over $3 million. My draft op/ed piece read, "If current trends continue, 12 years from now, when this year's graduating high school students are eligible to run for the Senate, the average cost could easily be $15 million."

Boren liked the illustration and the opinion piece, which ran in the *Post* on June 30, 1987. Later, I became so convinced of the illustration's power that I drafted a floor speech in which Boren would relate that he met with some high school seniors who discussed current issues with him. Concluding the session, Boren supposedly asks the question, "How many of you seniors might like to get into government service some day?" Several hands go up.

"How many of you think you may want to run for the U.S. Senate some day?" Again, several hands go up.

Finally, Boren would ask, "Now, how many of you will be able to raise the average of $15 million it will take twelve years from now to get elected when you're old enough to run for the Senate?" Dejected and forlorn, no student puts up a hand.

This was the only time literary license and ethical use of illustration have collided so violently in my experience with the senator. But I can successfully report that Boren did have such a session with a group of high school students that did get such a result—albeit, after the fact.

Each of these three stories demonstrated to me that Boren did care about the issue of campaign reform. He showed no sympathy for an uninformed PAC donor who "delegated" his monetary vote with a campaign contribution. He was disgusted by a seminar on modern PAC fund raising. And he worried that the next generation would be turned off on public service—not wanting to auction themselves off to serve in Congress.

Boren did not like what PACs represented to the system of campaign finance. In his heart, he wanted to do something about it.

SPEAKING OF PACS

Within a couple of days of our assault on the floor, I had calls from the PACs of the National Association of Manufacuters (NAM, one of the biggest pro-business PACs), the American Medical Association (AMA), and the Oklahoma State Medical Association (OSMA). It was obvious to me at the time that the lobbyists at the AMA got on the phone to the OSMA in Oklahoma City to tell them to put some pressure on Boren to abandon this PAC reform idea.

Robert Baker, the OSMA political action committee manager, called me to get information about the senator's intentions concerning the PAC amendment. I recall being torn about that call, as I had known Baker at the University of Oklahoma. Until then, I had not thought about the PAC managers in Oklahoma who would be upset with the senator for his campaign finance reform views. While I wanted to trust Baker, I knew that whatever I said would be related to the top officials at the national AMA, who would continue to plot with the rest of the PAC community.

However, Baker told me sometime later, after I left the senator's staff, that "the AMA and the OSMA believe that politics is local and therefore left this matter [contacting Boren directly to oppose the legislation] to us to handle as we chose." He admitted to using the PAC's "influence with other congressmen on this issue" to oppose campaign reform.

My distrust of the PAC community came through early in a memo to Boren dated October 21. I warned him,

> Some of the people on the Rules Committee are trying to get a copy of the amendment from me. Of course, they're probably the same people who contacted the National Association of Manufacturers, the American Medical Association, and the other major PACs. I think it unhealthy to be cooperating with the people who are trying to stab you in the back. Your thoughts?

I obviously feared that it was Boren and me against the world. For the next three weeks after announcing the amendment on the floor, I had taken calls from lobbyists for the NAM and the AMA as well as from former Oklahoman David Johnson, a researcher at the Democratic Senatorial Campaign Committee. Judging from the kind of questions folks asked me about the amendment and the senator's intentions, I knew they were working for the opposition. Boren responded, "Tell them it's not finalized."

The U.S. Chamber of Commerce is perhaps the most respected and feared pro-business forum in Washington. As the counter-vailing force to do battle against the labor unions, the Chamber is looked to on business-related issues. There wasn't a snowball's chance in hell (with the Republican-controlled Senate) of getting legislation taken seriously on the Hill if the Chamber was not supportive, or at least unopposed, if it affected a major sector of business. Probably no sitting member of Congress today has not spoken to a chamber of commerce in his or her district or state. The Chamber does not need money for influence. It already has power.

The Chamber took early opposition to the Boren PAC bill. In an October 30 letter to the "Members of the United States Senate," the Chamber stated its strong opposition "to this measure as an unwarranted intrusion on the rights of individuals to participate in the political process through PACs." It went on to argue that "individuals will be prohibited from contributing through their PACs to candidates who share their philosophy." Yet they admitted that something was amiss in the process by claiming that "any limit on campaign contributions naturally favors incumbents by denying challengers access to crucial funding sources." Their letter concluded by stating that "organized political activity is healthy and shows that enough individuals are motivated to form a group dedicated to certain goals."

It would be much later before the Chamber would speak out on how those goals should be realized. Cynics like me knew already that many PACs would play the game of hedging their bets by contributing to both sides in an election. That way, close elections were no risk to PACs who wanted to pick a winner.

The American Bankers Association in a December 2 telegram to all Senators likewise made an interesting observation: "[The ABA] is as concerned about escalating campaign costs as are other members of the public . . . [but this bill would] limit the receipts of campaign contributions from only one source, political action committees. It will not diminish the role of money in political campaigns." That letter from Edward Yingling, executive director of government relations for the bankers, seems to suggest that the ABA would support broader legislation to get at overall campaign spending. However, years later they would be silent on the question.

A Dow Chemical employee PAC based in Freeport, Texas, first saluted Boren for his pro-business stands by stating that "if you did accept them, our employee PAC would very likely offer such a contribution." But the PAC chairman wrote in a November 22 letter that he respected the fact that Boren chose not to accept their money. He went on to say that he doubted "that any support or lack of support by our employee PAC would have any appreciable effect on your decision [to offer the PAC amendment]" and that if it did, "we could not support any candidate who would sacrifice his principles and convictions in return for a contribution from us."

This was one of those letters I had to read twice to discover its meaning. Was he offering a contribution if Boren would drop the amendment? Was he offended that Boren was offering the amendment? Or did he admire Boren for offering an amendment that he believed in even though the writer did not?

Business PACs were not the only ones to declare opposition. A few think tanks got into the game, too. David Denholm, president of the Public Service Research Council (PSRC), which had an advisory board that included conservatives like Senators Orrin Hatch (R-Utah) and Jesse Helms (R-N.C.) and Representatives Mickey Edwards (R-Okla.) and Stan Parris (R-Va.), wrote to the Senate as well. Denholm did not stop with his opposition to "a desperate attempt on the part of the elitists to change the rules of the game to restore their once preponderant position of power" but went further in urging the repeal of the current Federal Elections Campaign Act. I guess Denholm preferred the days of $100,000 ambassadorships, bags of money, and true corruption. Yet the PSRC was quick to point out that "so long as a single decision by Congress can cost the average American taxpayer hundreds, even thousands of dollars," they should be able to contribute uncontrollably to influence that policymaking.

A good insight into Boren's response to such arguments was summed up in a letter we put together to a Norman, Oklahoma, constituent.

I am concerned that the more incumbent members of Congress and challengers are dependent on "special interest" money to fund their campaigns, the more we will be kept from our national goals. . . . Clearly, the national consensus on the two most important domestic issues the Congress should address are the need to balance the budget and reform the tax code. This is the message I was given in my campaign for reelection in 1984. . . . However, when the monied PACs come to lobby the Congress, . . . it is not the overriding national interest that they promote. Rather it is to preserve one or two particular programs in the budget with appropriations or one or two "loopholes" in the tax code. The yearlong stalemate on both a comprehensive budget resolution and tax reform bill are evidence enough for that.

Clearly, Boren was right as late 1985 brought the country the need for the Gramm-Rudman legislation to impose draconian budget discipline on Congress.

GIRDING FOR BATTLE

Great coaches of sports are fond of saying that the best offense is a good defense. Such a precept is as true in legislative strategy as it is in football. The best strategy for Boren in his fight for campaign reform in the 99th Congress was to team up with Arizona Senator Barry Goldwater.

As a result of Boren's bipartisan nature, not to mention his amiable manner, he had developed a great mutual respect with Goldwater. The outspoken Republican went so far as to tell a national media reporter that the Democrats would be wise to look at David Boren for their presidential nomination in 1984. The comment earned Boren a kind editorial in the state's ultraconservative newspaper, the *Daily Oklahoman*.

The greatest prize of that early strategy was captured in a personal conversation in which Boren asked Goldwater to join him in the fight for combating PACs with this bombshell amendment. Goldwater agreed. Goldwater had sponsored arguably unconstitutional measures before, such as limiting campaign time, placing spending limits in congressional races that flew in the face of the *Buckley* decision, and even outlawing PACs. But this would be a moderate attempt at reform legislation.

The first discussions with Goldwater's office began when I talked to his staffer two days after we announced the amendment. It was a delicate conversation with Terry Emerson, Goldwater's top aide, in which I tried to inform him of our intentions with the amendment and the bipartisan nature of its impact. In an October 24 conversation, Emerson said that not only would Goldwater cosponsor the amendment and freestanding legislation but he would be willing to sign on to a "Dear Colleague" with Boren and other senators urging support for the measure.

After thanking Emerson, I asked if he could look at a "Dear Colleague" draft that afternoon. I wanted to get the letter out that day. He expressed a little concern at the urgency of the request but agreed to give it top priority. I sent the draft of the letter to Emerson—with a space for Hart's and Goldwater's signatures as well—for him to look over with his senator, revise, and approve. At this point, I was on top of the world. A Boren-Goldwater combination was beautiful. A respected Republican would put our automatic opposition in a tough position to fight the amendment on the Senate floor. However, my heart nearly stopped late that afternoon when I received a hand-delivered envelope from Goldwater's office with big letters on the front reading, "RUSH, ELECTION AMENDMENT DRAFT." I feared that Goldwater balked after Emerson talked him out of supporting the amendment or that other enemy Republicans got hold of the language and would try to get Goldwater to add things to the simple approach.

Yet inside was a note to me from Emerson on the "Dear Colleague" draft which read, "Greg, My suggested changes. T. E." The changes were not substantial. Every reference to "bill" was changed to "amendment." Changes were made in the letter to make it clearer and a little more hard-hitting. The final letter read as follows:

We will be offering a revised and more comprehensive bill which will limit political action committee (PAC) contributions, as an amendment to the pending Compact of Free Association, S.J.Res. 77. In the election cycle just completed, 163 members of Congress relied on PAC contributions for over half their campaign expenditures. PACs have obviously contributed to the astronomical leap in campaign finances. In the Senate alone, the average cost of a winning campaign in only the last 8 years has jumped from around $609,000 to well over $2.9 million—an increase of 385%!

The letter went on to point out the five essential parts of the amendment: (1) set limits on total PAC contributions; (2) lower the PAC contribution limit from $5,000 to $3,000 and raise the individual limit from $1,000 to $1,500; (3) close the current loophole for "conduit contributions" whereby PACs get individuals to contribute money to candidates through the PAC; (4) require a disclaimer on media advertisements paid for by PACs as an independent expenditure; and (5) allow a candidate victimized by an independent expenditure to get "equal time" from a broadcast station to combat it.

Hart quickly agreed to sign the letter as well. We had the signatures of two former presidential candidates and respected senators next to Boren's name on the letter. What more could we ask for?

Apparently, Boren's personal lobbying with senators was more effective than the staff-to-staff approach, especially when it came to Carl Levin (D-Mich.) and Kassebaum (R-Kan.). So on that pivotal day, October 24, I got approval to make space not only for Hart's and Goldwater's signatures on the "Dear Colleague" but for two other senators as well. I could not have imagined greater equity. Two were Democrats, and two were Republicans. Two were highly recognized presidential contenders—one in 1964, the other in 1984. Levin was a nontraditional liberal, more of a government watchdog than a Great Society leftover. Kassebaum, daughter of 1936 presidential candidate Al Landon, not only was a respected Republican, woman, and conservative-to-moderate but was also close to Senator Dole. That would prove to be beneficial. So we had stature, balance, and respect.

Sensing the potential firestorm of partisan concern by Democrats that was sure to develop, Boren and I felt that I should draft a "Dear Democratic Colleague" to get a special message to members on our side of the aisle. Without some strategy, the experience of Boren wrestling with the Senate Democratic "bears" would seem a mere warmup match before a real fight. The letter went out the day after the Boren-Goldwater-Hart-Kassebaum-Levin letter, October 25. It stated, in part,

As I indicated in an earlier letter, I have worked on a bipartisan proposal to address the problem posed by the undue influence of political action committees and special interests on campaign financing. This effort was a concern strongly supported in the 1984 National Democratic platform.

Campaign reform, because of the historical and traditional values of our party, is an idea I sincerely believe should be especially embraced by the Democratic party. Because of concern voiced by some of our

Democratic colleagues, I have made changes in my original proposal in an attempt to satisfy these concerns.

In all, that letter contained words derived from "Democrat" a total of six times. We were still worried about a family feud that might develop and felt we needed more converts to the cause. The plan was to introduce the amendment as a freestanding bill also, so it could be printed and distributed more easily, as well as to provide the opportunity for a press conference that centered on something with a number and a life of its own. Amendments have a tendency to change when no one is looking. Bills do not.

Our target list of potential cosponsors was growing. Key cosponsors could bring other supporters along with them. Boren allowed no grass to grow around him as he personally wrote hand-written, hand-delivered notes to senators, sending along information or editorials about his PAC legislation. Letters starting "Dear John," "Dear Jack," "Dear Ted," "Dear Jeff," "Dear Dennis," "Dear Warren," "Dear Lawton" were sent out to Stennis of Mississippi, Danforth of Missouri, Kennedy of Massachusetts, Bingaman of New Mexico, DeConcini of Arizona, Rudman of New Hampshire, and Chiles of Florida. This was a great investment of time for Boren, an effort uncommon to the U.S. Senate from anyone but serious legislators.

The first senator to sign on after the invitation to cosponsor was sent out was the senior democratic senator, John Stennis of Mississippi, a pillar in the Senate. The impact of his cosponsorship was important not only for its obvious support and vote but for the influence it had in lobbying Sen. Robert Byrd, the Democratic minority leader, to join as well. Stennis was greatly revered, almost like a father, by Byrd. I saw that—just as I would defer arguing with my grandfather over social or political issues as a boy—senators have a special reverence for the opinions of their political elders and mentors.

In his history in the Senate, Byrd referred to this personal rapport that epitomizes several relationships between lawmakers. He recalled the advice he received from Stennis on his first assignment to chair a subcommittee in the Senate and discussed his respect: "Senator Stennis was someone who would take time out of a busy day to give me a note of encouragement. He was one of my all-time favorite senators—a paradigm of fairness, rectitude, and integrity."

Stennis was added as a cosponsor to the amendment and the freestanding bill on October 30, the day after it was introduced. After six weeks of lobbying from Boren and Stennis, Byrd was added as well.

While developing our offensive strategy, we still had to focus on defense. The first line of "staff defense" had to be played with a hostile crowd. Perhaps the most insightful baptism by fire I have experienced in my relatively short academic and professional career came on November 22, 1985. I was invited to a special luncheon meeting of Democratic senators' aides to address questions on the intent, substance, and politics of the Boren-Goldwater PAC amendment. The group to whom I would speak was not the legislative assistants charged by their bosses to analyze, research, and advise on campaign reform bills but the administrative assistants. AAs, by the nature of their jobs, are the political contacts for a senator in the noncampaign season, which runs just under five and a half years. Even though I was the invited guest to the weekly Democratic AAs lunch/meeting, I felt more like the main course.

Boren's AA, Charlie Ward, had asked me a few days prior to the 22nd if I could join him at the lunch. As most lunches I attended with Ward were political fluff events, I did not think twice about agreeing. Yet Ward's slight hestiation when he invited me let me know it would not be an altogether friendly crowd.

I also remember discussing the luncheon opportunity with Common Cause lobbyist and the former Democratic policy staff director, Susan Manes. She seemed to be very concerned about my going in there alone, as I recall. Yet I assured her confidently that I had spoken to other groups about campaign reform and felt comfortable with the subject. I would just make a "populist appeal" to them. She still looked worried.

In the previous few weeks of telephone calls, meetings, and other encounters with Democratic staff, I knew there was opposition to the bill, as Democrats were prime recipients of PAC cash. But nothing could have prepared me to fully defend Boren's bill when faced with the opposition of these more experienced and seasoned staff members.

The luncheon was held in the Lyndon Baines Johnson Room, just off the Senate floor. Ward knew everyone there, and introduced me to a few of them as we entered and wandered over to the buffet table to construct a sandwich and grab a Diet Coke. After people had eaten and settled down a bit, attention turned to one AA who informally opened the meeting, introduced Ward and me, and let me do a five-minute rundown of the bill's provisions.

"Senator Boren's concerned about the increasingly large role PACs play in campaign financing. Challengers are at a great disadvantage and more and more—particularly House members—are getting over half of their money from PACs," I said.

After a few more naive comments and technical descriptions of the bill's intent, I opened the floor to questions.

"What makes you think this 'bundling' provision is going to work. Doesn't it mean that our fund raisers won't be able to collect money from donors?" asked one AA.

"Why the hell does Senator Boren care if somebody gets half their money from PACs? It's all disclosed, and at least you know which interest the money comes from." declared another. "And that's more than you can say about individuals," he continued, hinting at Boren's style of not accepting PAC money.

"Don't you know the Republicans will eat our lunch on getting big money contributors if you raise the contribution rate to $1,500?" asked another.

For fifteen minutes I defended the substance of the bill's bundling provision to a group of people who were charged by their senators to be conduits of campaign contributions themselves. Questions were fired at me from Nebraska Sen. Jim Exon's AA and from Roy Greenaway, AA to Sen. Alan Cranston of California. I somehow managed to end the encounter without losing my temper, breaking a sweat, or starting to cry. But I know my face must have shown tension with the technical and political nature of the questions and charges. This group would have no part of any populist appeal that I could make. These were the stinging wasps of campaign finance operations for their senators, and I was a stick stirring their nest.

Ward later likened my experience to "a Christian being thrown to the lions." In a computer message sent to the staff later that afternoon, Ward wrote, "Just call him Daniel. He went into the Lions Den (Democratic AAs' luncheon) today and tamed 'em just like Daniel did. He did a superb job. . . . This AA was mighty proud of him." Ward was generous.

It did not take long for other senators, sensing that national focus would soon come to campaign finance reform, to dust off their reform proposals. Further, the seniority-respectful Senate was about to show who was boss on the topic. I started to hear rumors that Sen. Charles McC. Mathias, Jr.'s Rules Committee was "coincidentally" about to have hearings on the issue of campaign reform. Knowing that Boren could quickly be blind-sided by such a development and left out of the process, on Halloween I drafted a letter to the chairman from Boren.

Dear Mac,

Early this week, I introduced the Campaign Finance Reform Act of 1985, S. 1806. Senators Goldwater, Kassebaum, Levin, Rudman, and Stennis have joined as cosponsors so far.

While I have stated my intent to bring up the proposal as a possible amendment to the pending Compact of Free Association, S.J.Res. 77, I understand there may be a chance that hearings will soon be held in the Rules Committee on campaign reform.

Should it be in your plans to have such an agenda, I would greatly appreciate your consideration of allowing time for hearings for S. 1806. With the growing bipartisan support being expressed in this legislation, I believe it could be the best chance for reform in our election process in several years.

Sincerely,
David L. Boren

After Boren signed the letter, I copied the ranking Democrat on the Rules Committee, Wendell Ford of Kentucky. A hearing was confirmed for the next week, November 5, at 9:30 A.M. No reply was ever received from the Republican chairman, but the real slight to Boren was yet to come.

Even though an off-year for most state and federal elections, that Tuesday was an election day for several citizens around the country. It was a perfect, symbolic day to begin the first formal Senate consideration of campaign reform in many years. In the chairman's opening sentence, I knew his views on the Boren-Goldwater PAC bill were less than cordial.

Despite the fact that Senator Boren warned on the Senate floor that he would force a vote on his PAC bill, followed up with a "Dear Colleague" letter, a separately introduced, bipartisan bill, and a letter requesting this very hearing on his and Senator Goldwater's legislation, Mathias stated that the committee "meets this morning to take testimony on Senate bill 1787, a bill that I introduced."

After statements by Senator Hart, also a cosponsor of the Mathias bill, and Senator Mitchell, Boren was finally invited to give his statement before the committee. After explaining his bill and his rationale for it and answering questions from senators who sat on the committee, Boren responded to a final question. Senator Simon brought the discussion back to his and Senator Mathias's bill.

"What is your reaction to the proposal [for public financing] by the senior senator from Maryland?" Simon asked.

Boren concluded a long answer by saying, "I just do not want to see the vision that some have of the perfect solution to a problem inhibit us from going forward with what might be a possible and very meaningful reform in the system. . . . I realize that those who are for public financing would view my proposal only as an interim step. Even if they want to view it in that way, I think it is an interim step that is well worth taking."

Mathias had the last word. "We will try to persuade you, but in deference to the next witnesses, I will not do it now." The persuading would come later.

Dole was the other Republican leader in the battle who would be the hardest to pin down on the issue of campaign reform. His reaction to Boren's declared war on PACs was one of evasion. Despite his seemingly strong statements in favor of doing something, the specifics never came. But the first chore after our bombshell approach on October 2 was to pin Dole down to a time agreement and give us a vote on the amendment.

CHAPTER FOUR

"Find Me a Vehicle"

When one man seeks to rule another, it is his own freedom he destroys. For then, he must do, not what he wants but what is expected of him.

—PAUL HARVEY

ON THE NIGHT of the 1988 New Hampshire Republican primary, Sen. Bob Dole was asked by NBC network anchorman Tom Brokaw, during a live, prime time interview, if he had anything he would like to say to the primary's winning candidate, George Bush. Frustrated by a surprising defeat after his big win in the Iowa caucuses, Dole glared into the camera and said, "Tell him to stop lying about my record!"

The result of this less than gracious congratulatory greeting from the Kansas senator to the vice president resulted in a field day for television political commentators. Talk of "mean-spiritedness" plagued Dole much the way the term "wimp" was at the time a millstone around the neck of the eventual nominee.

Such a reputation attached itself earlier to Senator Dole during his failed vice presidential campaign with the incumbent president, Gerald Ford, in 1976. In that race against the Carter-Mondale ticket, it was Dole who often played the role of "hatchet man" for the Republican ticket. But Dole broke from that form at a crucial juncture in the campaign finance reform debate of 1985.

The real breakthrough to getting a commitment for consideration of the Boren-Goldwater PAC limit bill was in attaining a time agreement from the Senate majority leader. Of course, Dole was under intense pressure from members of his party not to "give" to Boren under any circumstance that would allow this bill to come to a vote. However, Boren had the leader's back against the wall with his unwillingness to let his legislative vehicle be freed up. The only way for Dole to get the Compact of Free Association treaty passed before the end of 1985 was to negotiate with Boren.

Dole obviously wanted Boren to agree to a Dole-Mathias offer to have the Senate Rules and Administration Committee hold early hearings on the Boren-Goldwater bill. Boren saw this as nothing more than a convenient delay tactic. Further, while some Democrats thought Boren's bill was a good way to show up the Republicans, most were not at all anxious to vote against PACs at a time when they would be soliciting funds from those giving arms of special interest.

Boren held his ground on abandoning his amendment on this must-pass bill. The administration greatly wanted the compact passed before the Congress broke for its month-long August recess. At this point, all Boren really wanted was a vote—up or down—on his amendment.

"I'll declare a moral victory and go home if I can get 25 or 30 votes," Boren repeatedly told me.

Up to now, neither of us really believed we were in a position to see this thing pass. At a minimum, Boren wanted another "must-pass" bill to which he could file his amendment before the end of the year. That was the request.

But the savvy Boren, who saw the artful abilities of Dole on the Finance and Agriculture committees on which they both sat, knew he would have to go into any negotiating meeting with both barrels loaded. So he found a night session in which the Senate was working late and corraled his two most distinguished allies to join him when he approached Dole. He wanted not only his partner, Barry Goldwater, but another whose longevity in the Senate and high respectability would not be overlooked by a "quick-fix" Dole. No one could fill that role better than Stennis, the most senior member of the Senate.

Earlier that year, after his second inauguration, Ronald Reagan paid special praise to Stennis who had just recovered from cancer surgery, which cost him the amputation of his left leg. With the wintery winds howling outside the Capitol where the inauguration was to be held, the president, after the traditional, lengthy greetings, said, "This day has been made brighter with the presence . . . of Senator John Stennis." The crowded Rotunda audience gave thunderous applause to the esteemed but quiet Southern gentleman.

Ten months later, when Boren approached Dole in the Republican cloakroom just off the Senate floor, this was the scene. On one side of Boren was the godfather of Republican conservatism, Barry M. Goldwater, leaning on a cane to rest his artificial right hip. And on the other was the eighty-four-year-old southern patriarch of the Senate, sitting straight and attentive in his wheelchair holding the Senate Calendar resting against his one leg.

Boren began the relatively quick session by simply saying, "All we want is a vote on this amendment, Bob." Boren actually would have been willing to let the compact pass by withdrawing his PAC amendment, but he wanted more than just hearings. He wanted a specific date for the vote on the legislation. Both Goldwater and Stennis, in addition to their strong nonverbal communication, added their views on why this was an important issue that deserved a floor vote.

"Bob, we all need to do something about these damn PACs, and Dave and I just want a vote on it," Goldwater said.

Here were two men who meant no threat to Dole's leadership. Goldwater had already announced that he would not run again for the Senate after his term expired in 1986. Stennis would be expected to make the same decision when his term ended in 1988.

The conversation steered to Boren's bottom line position: let the Compact pass, find another must-pass bill to which Boren-Goldwater could be considered as an amendment, and develop a time agreement for a vote. A weakened Dole, faced by two revered men of the Senate, must have seen a vision of himself in twenty years if his dream of attaining the White House proved evasive. The mean-spiritedness was lost for a moment as Dole barked out to a Republican staff member, "Find me a vehicle!"

This time, it was the Low-Level Radioactive Waste Compact, S. 655. It would allow several central states to engage in interstate contracts on disposal of certain wastes, and it needed to be passed. But unlike the Compact, its deadline was not until the end of the year. Dole gave Boren a time agreement on November 14 to allow four hours of debate and "one" vote on the amendment in early December. We got what we wanted.

RETURN TO THE FLOOR FOR A VOTE

The opening day of debate of the Boren-Goldwater reform amendment was also the one hundred twenty-second anniversary of the Statue of Freedom's completed placement atop the Capitol's gilded dome. The five-sectioned bronze work stands 19 feet 6 inches high and weighs nearly seven and a half tons. Her headpiece encircled in stars cannot be seen from the ground far below by the thousands of native and international tourists who gaze at her lofty throne atop the Capitol. To the average American, those symbols might as well be dollar signs. But the desire to erase that increasingly evident symbol was not shared by all senators.

The debate on the amendment was limited to two days, December 2 and 3, for two hours each day. Boren, for the Democrats, would manage the bill and control the one hour each day. Sen. John Heinz, the late Pennsylvania Republican, would control the other hour. Heinz, managing floor time for opponents, opened his debate by raising a number of issues concerning the manner of the amendment's consideration. His continuous call to delay the bill's deliberation evoked Senator Boren's ire. After raising substance issues against the amendment, Heinz resorted to arguments on procedure.

These problems alone make the need for a more deliberative process obvious in my view. . . . Questions of this nature should compel a more thoughtful approach to this legislation. At the very least, it should be amendable, and certainly it should be the subject of committee hearings. . . . Why, then, if it does not affect 1985 and 1986, are we dealing with it in such a precipitous and preemptory fashion?

These comments raised Boren's temper to the boiling point. He turned to me, sitting next to him at the leader's desk, and asked for the chronology I had put together about the progress of reform bills since 1974. Boren rose and was recognized. He was ready.

> MR. BOREN: *Mr. President, how much time remains to those in support of the amendment?*
> PRESIDING OFFICER: *Thirty-five minutes.*
> MR. BOREN: *Mr. President, I yield myself four minutes.*
> *Mr. President, I am sorry that my colleague from Pennsylvania has been so alarmed by the precipitous way in which we have been dealing with the subject of campaign reform in the Senate. [With voice raising to a shrill and sarcastic tone.] It reminds me a little bit of Rip Van Winkle. [Heinz turns with stern face to watch Boren as he continues to speak.] I wonder if my good colleague from Pennsylvania has just awakened from a loooong nap and thought . . . . [Heinz now rising, red-faced, approaching Boren, who still is speaking in a slow and almost mocking tone] . . . that this was the first time that the Senate has ever discovered this matter.*

Heinz, now standing next to Boren, interrupted him in an urgent, firm voice shielded from the microphones.

"David, I'll call the rule! That's out of order! I'll call the rule on you!"

Heinz was referring to Rule 19 of the Standing Rules of the Senate which prohibits any senator during debate to "directly or indirectly, by any form of words, impute to another senator or other senators any conduct or motive unworthy or unbecoming a senator." The rules of Senate debate require that no personal references to senators be made and that all debate be directed to the presiding officer. While I did not realize what Heinz was talking about at the time, it was obvious he felt insulted.

Boren, stunned, stumbled in his speech, stopped, shielded his microphone, and mumbled an apology to Heinz, then said, "Let me continue." Heinz, red-faced, slowly turned to sit again, eyes still affixed to Boren. Boren spoke again.

You know, it has been pending here now for eleven years, since the FECA was passed and amended in 1974. We tried to deal with it in 1977, S. 926. After three cloture votes, we failed to break a filibuster. . . . Then, of course, we had the Obey-Railsback amendment, H.R. 4970, in 1979 . . . [which] passed the House because a threatened filibuster by opponents blocked its consideration by the Senate. In 1981, S. 9 was introduced by Senator Byrd, similar to the Obey bill. . . . In 1983, H.R. 2490 and H.R. 4428 were introduced on the House side, and I introduced the companion bill, S. 1443. Then earlier this year I introduced S. 297.

We have been struggling now for eleven years to bring this matter before the Senate and get a vote. We have had two filibusters that prevented it. On November 5, I appeared before the Rules Committee and testified for approximately one hour, answering questions from members of the committee and subjecting myself to cross-examination of this very proposal. . . .

Yet we are asked by the senator from Pennsylvania, why are we rushing pell-mell in the consideration of campaign reform? Well, I would say that if the Constitutional Convention had proceeded with . . . the same degree of speed that we are dealing with campaign reform here on the floor of the Senate, they would still be attempting to write the Constitution of the United States to this good day.

Boren later inserted the full chronology into the *Congressional Record* to show the unprecipitous nature of the cause. But other uncharacteristic flare-ups occurred that day as well.

Most Senate debates seem to follow a monotonous pattern — statement, quorum call, statement, quorum call — without an exchange of questions or real debate. By the time most issues are brought to the floor, the real compromise has been made in committee or the cloakrooms and positions of senators have been solidified. This is why, to the surprise and disillusionment of most visitors to the Senate gallery, very few senators are ever in the chamber at one time. Except during roll call votes, senators and staff monitor floor action in their offices through a "squawk box," closed audio coverage, or of course in recent years, by television. But this debate started out different. Boren wanted it to be a real debate. But Heinz did not.

MR. HEINZ: *Mr. President, I am not going to argue about why in one state a limitation of $100,000 will guarantee the purity of the electoral process in that state and how a limitation of $750,000 in another state will guarantee the electoral purity in that state. I do not know how that really is going to work, but those kind of issues, maybe we can get into some other occasion.*

MR. BOREN: *Mr. President, will the senator yield?*

MR. HEINZ: *Not at this time . . .*

(*After inviting a discussion, Heinz reneged and went on, but Boren would persist.*)

MR. HEINZ: *When the PAC contribution ceiling is reached [under the bill] every other PAC is frozen out. Who does that hurt? I suspect it is going to hurt small, less well-funded grass roots. Who else benefits?*

Mr. President, there is one other group that benefits more than anybody else. They are called incumbents. Believe me, I do not have anything against incumbents. Some of my best friends are incumbents. In fact, I can think of quite a few on both sides of the aisle that I would like to see return here for many years to come.

MR. BOREN: *Will the senator yield?*

MR. HEINZ: *Only very briefly.*

MR. BOREN: *Just a brief question: Of the PAC money that was contributed last year, does the senator know what percentage of it went to incumbents and what percentage of it went to challengers?*

MR. HEINZ: *I read the* Washington Post *the same as the senator from Oklahoma. I would be happy to put that in the* Record *later. I do not yield further.*

What Heinz meant, I did not know. Not known for his debate skills, he refused to engage Boren in a direct exchange. Boren used his opening speech to relate Goldwater's regretted absence from the Monday session. Goldwater was at the bedside of his wife, who was ill and hospitalized in Arizona. The Goldwater statement read by Boren was personal and strong.

Having served twice as chairman of the National Republican Senatorial Committee [NRSC], I full well understand the opposition that may come, not only from the Republican occupant of that chair at the present time but from his counterpart on the Democratic side. . . .

The answer is not greater spending by political parties or anyone else. The answer is less campaign spending by all sources, and PACs are the place to start.

It was a great statement. I wished that Goldwater had been there to read it.

The December 2 debate on the amendment ended with Rules Committee Chairman Mathias publicly appealing to Boren to allow his committee to be the "first step" at finding a solution for problems in campaign finance. Mathias was strongly opposed to writing a new law on the Senate floor, both out of jurisdictional pride as the chairman and out of defense for his party, which feared the effects of the amendment. But Boren respectfully declined to back off his commitment to see the amendment through to a vote by stating, "There are many of us who have watched this subject being around for a long time. Not the senator [Mathias] from Maryland but many others . . . say, 'Let us wait until after the next election.' "

He then turned to Heinz to vent his growing anger and criticism.

The Senator talked about preserving PAC financing because we need to be sure that we help the challengers. I do hope that those who are challengers for public office . . . will look at statistics before they call in to honor the senator from Pennsylvania, before they send out the invitations and ask everyone to come to honor him as a friend of . . . challengers. . . . Last year, political action committees contributed 4½ times as much to incumbents as they gave to challengers. It is certainly in the interest of any challenger for political office that all of us [in the Senate] have to go back to the grass roots, to the citizens, to ask for those contributions, a dollar at a time, a person at a time, just as we have to ask for those votes.

An hour and 58 minutes of the debate time had been used that first day. Heinz had two minutes left. He declined to use it.

The next day's debate and vote was much more spirited as senators in support of our amendment could not be scheduled for floor time fast enough. I had the difficult duty of calculating how much of the hour could be allocated to senators wishing to speak. I constructed a memo for Boren's and my use that morning. Many of the nine cosponsors wanted to speak. Three noncosponsors wanted to speak. But first, my list reserved almost twenty minutes for Boren. He would have to counter the charges by opponents and make the most comprehensive and coherent statements.

My telephone messages for those two days were continuous. Aside from the normal inquiries and press calls, aides were calling to ask for time to speak on the floor before the vote. But first, I would have to assemble the names of who would and could speak.

Cosponsors Bingaman and Kassebaum spoke the day before so would forgo another floor appearance. Cosponsors Chiles and Goldwater were absent. Finally, with some direction from Boren, I constructed the chart: Hart, 7 minutes; DeConcini, 5 minutes; Levin, 5 minutes; Stennis, 10 minutes. Those were the cosponsors. Byrd, as the minority leader, would be granted 3 minutes. Rudman, our lone speaking Republican cosponsor, would be allocated 5 minutes. And Thomas Eagleton of Missouri and Daniel Patrick Moynihan of New York, neither cosponsors but both supporters, could have 3 minutes each. That would leave Boren just 19 minutes.

But by the time we got to the floor, adjustments were to be made. Moynihan, in an arrogant tone, demanded 5 minutes; 3 would not do. The same courtesy would be given to Byrd who helped get us to this point. But we earned some of the time back when Rudman gave up his floor appearance — probably feeling pressure from his Republican caucus at joining the Democrats. So Boren still controlled his 20 needed minutes.

But something strange had developed that morning well before the vote was to occur. Word started to filter back to me that during an informal morning press visit with reporters in the well of the Senate chamber, Dole made comments about the upcoming vote as not being such a showdown after all. Everyone wants campaign reform, we just needed to find the right way to do it, was his message to the media.

No one knew what such comments really meant. Why was Dole so calm about what appeared to be a developing partisan embarrassment for the Republican Senate? Rebels of his caucus had joined with Boren to force this vote. It would be decided one way or another. Wouldn't it? Not necessarily.

Sitting with Boren on the floor, we soon heard that Dole wanted to delay the vote until after the caucus luncheons, the Tuesday ritual of Democrats and Republicans. When Boren told me, I responded like a kid robbed of candy.

"They can't do that? We've got unanimous consent. We have to have the vote at noon!" I argued.

"But Dole's got Byrd convinced that we should let the caucuses talk it over before the vote. We won't lose our vote. Nothing will change that, I assure you," Boren said.

During the closing arguments against the bill being made by Sen. Pete Domenici of New Mexico, Heinz, Dole, Byrd, and Boren caucused on the floor. Dole slipped to the back of the chamber and Heinz rose to speak. "Mr. President, I ask unanimous consent that the Senate now stand in recess until the hour of 2:00 P.M."

Boren looked at me and said I should go get a quick bite of lunch. He would go to the caucus and meet me back on the floor before 2:00.

I got back to the chamber after a hearty bowl of Senate Bean Soup and onion rings—a staple of life at the time—and awaited Boren. After the luncheons adjourned, Boren wandered in, saw me, and came back to the black leather couch where I sat. He had information from the Republican luncheon meeting as well.

"Well, they're all throwing the towel in," Boren said with a half-dejected sigh.

"What do you mean?" I asked.

"No one wants to vote against our bill, so they're going to move to table, vote against their own motion, and then Dole will bring the bill down," Boren replied.

My anticipation for a close vote and dramatic finish was washed up. Dole's done it again, I thought. I then realized what the Dole strategy was. He only promised Boren "a vote," translated in the Senate as "one vote." This meant that a motion to table could be defeated, and with the Senate precedence of recognition, Dole would immediately be recognized by the presiding officer. Rather than moving to an immediate vote or approval by voice vote, Dole could change the business of the Senate and call up the farm credit legislation that was waiting on the calendar.

I shuffled off to sit by Boren during the next few minutes before the vote. The Senate came to order. Dole was recognized and asked that each side be given three extra minutes each for debate "before a motion to table is made by the distinguished senator from Pennsylvania."

Boren interrupted Dole with an inquiry on the parliamentary maneuvers left undiscussed. "Will the distinguished majority leader make that request contingent upon there being no intervening motions, points of order, or anything but the debate to proceed going to a vote on the motion to table? Also, on the yeas and nays, the motion has not been lodged, but I assume it will be. May I have the opportunity to request the yeas and nays on the motion to table?"

Boren was worried that Dole or another opponent might "move to recommit" the amendment to the Rules Committee. He also wanted to make sure that Republicans had not rehearsed a quick exercise to create a "voice vote" on a tabling motion that would displace Boren's rights.

After the agreement for three minutes on each side, Mathias addressed the Senate as though the tabling motion already had passed. He rose to reiterate his intention to continue early hearings on Boren's and other reform proposals "as soon as practicable after the Senate reconvenes in January."

Boren then reminded the Senate that "if our amendment is not tabled today, it will remain alive, and it will remain attached to the pending bill that is on the calendar." This was a veiled declaration that despite the time they thought they bought by tabling it, Boren's bill would be back if Rules continued to drag its feet.

Then, with the rapt attention of the Senate, uncharacteristically listening in the chamber at their desks, it was time for Heinz.

Mr. President, I am going to make a motion to table in a minute. And I'm going to ask all my colleagues to vote against the motion to table in the sense that, and with the idea that, the vote is a vote for further consideration of the issue. The senator from Maryland [Mathias] has said that he will hold hearings. The majority leader has made his pledge that he takes this issue very seriously. So I am going to make a motion to table. I am going to ask my colleagues to vote against it. I am going to vote against it. I move to table the Boren amendment and ask for the yeas and nays.

With that, the vote was taken. Only seven senators voted to table it, among them Phil Gramm of Texas, Simpson of Wyoming, Helms of North Carolina, and the lone Democrat, Edward Zorinsky of Nebraska. Those voting with Boren and the disingenuous Heinz numbered eighty-four. (Nine Senators did not vote.) After the tally was announced, the Farm Credit System Restructuring and Regulatory Reform Act of 1985 was called up by the Republican presiding officer. With S. 1884 now the pending business, Boren was prevented from moving to accept the untabled amendment by voice vote or by a roll call.

But Boren wasted no time in confronting Dole on the floor.

Mr. President, if I might have the attention of the majority leader for just a moment. In light of the overwhelming vote that we just had against tabling this campaign reform proposal, . . . I wonder if the majority leader might give us some assurance that early next year, say, by the first of March, . . . we would have an opportunity to bring either the pending matter . . . or the recommendation of the committee . . . back to the full Senate for our consideration?

Dole hedged.

I am not certain I could give any commitment. . . . It may take longer than that to find a consensus approach. . . . I am certainly willing, if we can work out some bipartisan way to approach it, to bring a bill up.

After the vote, the news media reported the result. Correspondent Phil Jones correctly reported for the "CBS Evening News" that the "Republican leadership maneuvered to delay a vote on campaign reform until next year." Dole told the reporter that it "appeared to us that we should try to work out something next year. But we don't think the Boren approach is the right one." He would grow to regret that position.

Before the adjournment of the first session of the 99th Congress, the Senate had to pass a number of pressing bills. Boren again went to the floor to press Dole for an agreement to allow debate on his PAC amendment to S. 655. The only public skirmish in the otherwise cordial relationship between Dole and Boren erupted on December 19. Dole was trying to pass the low-level nuclear waste compact as well as a reconciliation bill and a continuing resolution to fund government services. His anger was apparent.

If we cannot get an agreement [on the compact], let's just forget it or pull out the Oklahoma-Arkansas compact and go ahead and pass the others. There is no need to punish the other states because the Senator from Oklahoma feels that the campaign finance reform is more important than dealing with low-level nuclear waste. That is a judgment he has made.

Boren responded by saying he was willing for the bill to be called up at a certain time. Thus, Boren said, "We could bring it up prior to the May recess . . . [around] the 15th of April."

Dole barked back that Boren "has moved from the next session, which he agreed to on December 3, to the first few weeks we are back. He has not moved the other way."

Boren defended himself. "The senator from Kansas knows that is not the fact."

Dole quickly retorted, "That is what the *Record* says."

Boren argued back, "The senator from Oklahoma is not willing to give away a vehicle on which the distinguished senator from Kansas said we could attach this." He further explained on the floor that he could not give up a live vehicle for no real commitment.

Senator Simpson of Wyoming tried to play peacemaker between Boren and Dole. Eventually an agreement was reached in those closing hours before the year's adjournment. A Boren press release bragged of the accomplishment.

Fighting off procedural tactics which would have effectively killed it, Senator Boren today won an agreement from the Senate for consideration early next year of his amendment limiting the amount of special interest money going into House and Senate campaigns. Efforts were made on the Senate floor to strip off all provisions, except Boren's, on S. 655, turning that bill into what Boren termed "a mere shell." Boren fought this action due to his fear that doing so, without a definite agreement to bring up his provision again in 1986, would sound a death knell to his efforts at campaign reform.

PRESSING, PLANNING, AND PAUSING

There was continued activity in 1986 but at a slower pace, with the legislation having been placed in committee for hearings. I secretly hoped for stalemate in the committee so we could force the amendment back on the floor. The individual positions of Rules Committee members ran the gamut. Senator Mathias wanted public financing and spending limits. Senator Helms wanted campaign reform as a way to pass a national "right to work" law by clamping down on labor union dues. Others were pro-PAC, anti-PAC, and all over the board.

Boren was assigned a large responsibility after the amendment was tabled in December. Minority Leader Byrd appointed him to head a study group of ten Democratic senators to figure out a strategy on the issue. On the one hand, it was a way for Byrd and frightened Democrats to get a hold on a rebel reformer like Boren. On the other, it was a chance to build some support for our legislation. But the group, appointed in late December, did not formally meet for quite some time.

We needed this forum to keep the troops happy, if not in line. Luckily for us, only one senator took the Campaign Finance Subgroup of the Conference's Strategy Group—as Byrd referred to it—as a serious activity. Senator Bingaman sent Boren a couple of ideas relating to PACs: to set the individual PAC limit to a lower limit ($100 or $250), and to restrict PAC administrative and solicitation costs. Others who showed up for that pro forma session discussed the issue of tax credits for small contributions, PAC bundling of contributions, and a "code of good broadcasting" for television stations as a device against independent expenditures. The subgroup never expected to devise a consensus bill, but Boren knew opening up the process would only delay the chances of his narrow legislation.

A strong undercurrent of distrust for Boren was running through the party faithful of Senate Democrats. They viewed him as a PAC-basher and populist. I began to consider that the real problem was not just where the money came from but how much it took to get elected.

That view was obviously held by Byrd as well. I was not at all sure what Byrd really thought because access to him was very limited. Staffers were not allowed to sit in on many of Byrd's meetings with their bosses. On one occasion, Boren asked that I join him in a strategy and substance meeting on campaign reform with the Democratic leader.

Waiting just inside the John F. Kennedy Room reception area of the second floor suite of the Capitol, Boren looked as nervous as I was. When Byrd's secretary told Boren to come back to the his personal office, Boren advised me to sit tight so that he could ask if I could join in the session. David Pratt, Byrd's leadership staffer charged with coordinating his efforts on campaign reform, was waiting as well. After a few minutes, Boren peered around the corner of the passage leading to Byrd's inner sanctum. In a hushed tone, he indicated it was okay to enter.

In my delicate steps back to the office, I felt the same

nervousness portrayed by the Cowardly Lion in *The Wizard of Oz*. As I entered the room, I saw Byrd enthroned in a chair at the head of his large wooden conference table. Much to my surprise, he was shrouded in billowing smoke from an enormous cigar (much like that of the Wizard's image in his electronic palace in Oz).

After a polite and perfunctory introduction, which Byrd failed to acknowledge, Boren continued in a conversation with Byrd. He asked Byrd for his advice and assistance in pressing Dole to give us a shot at considering the Boren-Goldwater amendment. All the while Byrd listened to Boren spell out the ways and whys of this reform bill, he worked with his cigar to keep it burning. Striking a huge kitchen match, Byrd's puffing on the cigar created a large flame and consuming clouds of smoke. Despite his seeming preoccupation with this burning wad of leaves, he was paying close attention. He interrupted Boren to pledge his commitment.

"David, I don't know how many more years I'll be able to serve the people of the great state of West Virginia, nor how long my colleagues will ask that I serve as their leader. But two things will occupy my energy as long as I serve out my time."

Byrd went on to explain that his goal was to see that congressional salaries were raised to an appropriate level and that campaign reform to stop the money chase would be enacted. He would make good on his first promise in a controversial plot years later. And he would demonstrate historical commitment to the second.

Before the meeting's end, Byrd made it clear that he supported spending limits and public financing personally. But he also shared his feelings that without the votes to pass it, a good start would be Boren's reform. He said he would help us in every way to press Dole to bring our bill up at the appropriate time. With this surprising show of Byrd's strong support, our meeting was a huge success.

A couple of months later, Boren went to the floor armed with a speech I drafted for him. Delivered on April 21, his forty-fifth birthday, Boren read it with youthful fire and determination. To most, it seemed like just another of those "vigil" speeches to get him to the floor for a quick press release. But the real purpose was to publicly remind Dole, the Democrats, and the press that he was indeed going to push the issue of campaign finance reform and that he would remain its leader.

This speech was built around simply inserting a *Wall Street Journal* article by Brooks Jackson into the *Congressional Record*, but it turned out to be a little bit more.

Mr. President, the cries for reform of our congressional campaign finance laws are loud and clear. The public is increasingly aware of the critical growth of special interest influence in our Congress. Because of this understanding of the problems, which at least indirectly contribute to the current legislative stalemate in Congress, we can hope to see substantial reform in this session of Congress.

In October of last year, when I announced I would attempt to bring my proposal to limit the influence of political action committees and modify our campaign finance laws, it was with the intention of putting this vital issue squarely on the national agenda for action. It is my hope that with the agreements made by the distinguished majority leader and the leadership of the chairman of the Rules and Administration Committee, we can address this issue on the floor very soon in the next couple of months.

My proposal, which is pending as an amendment to S. 655 on the Senate Calendar, has a broad base of support . . . [as] eleven members of this body have joined in putting forth this legislation as an attempt to put confidence back in our congressional elections.

Then, Boren inserted the *Wall Street Journal* article in the *Record* and reminded his fellow senators, "I will be anxiously awaiting a committee proposal on campaign finance reform. In the absence of such a proposal, I will work with the leadership to secure a time frame and agreement to have S. 1806 brought directly back to the floor."

Two months later, Dole asked for unanimous consent to limit the amendments in order to pass an unrelated bill. His June 6 efforts were focused at arriving at a time agreement and whittling away extraneous amendments. Boren seized the opportunity to press Dole publicly on getting a time agreement for his reform bill.

MR. BOREN: *Mr. President, reserving the right to object, and I will not object, I wonder if the majority leader will yield briefly. I have listed an amendment on campaign reform dealing with political action committees. The majority leader and I were discussing this in good faith, to try to determine a time to bring up S. 655. The majority leader will agree that we have had good faith negotiations on that, and we will try to bring it up at a reasonable time within the schedule.*

MR. DOLE: *The senator is correct. We are discussing different options.*

MR. BOREN: *I am not trying to pin down the majority leader, but we discussed bringing up S. 655 for consideration at least before the end of July.*

MR. DOLE: *That is correct.*

MR. BOREN: *I would like to start a process that I hope will be a helpful one and ask that my amendment be stricken from this list, in light of the majority leader working in good faith with us.*

MR. DOLE: *I appreciate the cooperation of the distinguished senator. That is one less.*

This colloquy between Dole and Boren demonstrated that Boren was gaining control over the issue. Dole was becoming trapped by his previous mistake of delaying a vote on the Boren amendment. As Paul Harvey has suggested, one loses one's own freedom when one "seeks to rule another."

The *Washington Post* finally helped our cause with a story on July 26, 1986, the same day the Dole-Boren colloquy appeared in the *Congressional Record*, with a headline that read, "PAC Funds to Senators Up 53% in Two Years." The Tom Edsall story was based on much of the research and work of Common Cause, which put out a study in the form of a press release. (This practice by groups like Common Cause is one of the most valuable resoures in Washington.)

In a page A4 article, the *Post* printed a paragraph that listed the top twenty-two Senate PAC recipients, who netted a minimum of $500,000 in PAC funds. Of them, fifteen were among the majority Republican party. All but three were incumbent senators (Henson Moore, Jim Jones, and Tom Daschle were House members).

While waiting for Rules Committee action, which was as productive as watching paint dry, we discovered a unique Republican activity thanks to an Oklahoma banker and PAC treasurer. Boschwitz had sent him a letter and survey requesting information on how they ran their PAC and how they would feel about Boren's legislation. The Boschwitz letter, dated July 14, asked for their participation in the survey to help the Senate "understand what the proposed changes will really do."

The survey asked a number of statistical questions, such as how many contributed to the PAC, the average contribution to the PAC, and the size of the contributions it made. The poll also asked some qualitative questions like, "Would the Boren proposals change the operation of your political action committee?" and "Do you believe PAC reform is needed?"

Boschwitz, who would become chairman of the National Republican Senatorial Committee the following year, was laying important groundwork with the same people he intended to write later to ask for contributions to Republican Senate candidates. He knew that it would be easier in the future to solicit those PACs for contributions to the national GOP if he had been their protector against the Boren PAC legislation. At least the survey was ethically executed, however. Even though responses were to be sent to the senator in his Hart Senate Building suite, the letter clearly stated that it was "not printed at government expense" (but obviously paid for by the NRSC).

AUGUST HEAT

A little before 11:00 A.M. on July 31, the two party leaders were struggling on the Senate floor to come closer to working out an agreeable schedule to finish two weeks of business before the August recess. Byrd was in an unusual negotiating position with respect to Dole in scheduling of the Boren-Goldwater legislation.

On that morning, after discussing a time agreement for a defense authorization bill, Byrd mentioned to Dole, "Also, there is the Boren PAC amendment, which has to be woven in between now and August 15. I understand that the distinguished majority leader has an agreement with the distinguished senator from Oklahoma."

Dole responded, "I hope to be able to begin the Boren issue on the 11th of August and complete it on the 12th. That is our present intention. That would be before the recess. I have indicated that to Senator Boren. He also understands that if some other matter delays it, it could be a little later."

We were finally moving. Dole had finally, publicly kept his promise. The next day, August 1, the Democratic leader took to the floor to formalize the deal.

MR. BYRD: *Mr. President, I take this time because I see the distinguished senator from Oklahoma [Boren] on the floor. The distinguished majority leader, yesterday, stated again his intention to bring up the Boren PAC legislation. That is the campaign financing reform legislation. I am a cosponsor of that legislation, and I am very interested in seeing it brought up. . . . May I ask the distinguished majority leader, is that still the intention of the majority leader?*

MR. DOLE: *Mr. President, I would say that it is still my intention, but I would also say that it depends on what happens to the debt ceiling, South Africa, aid to the freedom fighters, and a lot of other things that are piling up. I certainly intend to keep my word to the distinguished senator from Oklahoma. It may mean staying here all day today and all day tomorrow to do it, but I am prepared to do it. It seems to me if we make that commitment, we ought to do it before the recess.*

MR. BOREN: *I appreciate the statement that has just been made.*

MR. DOLE: *Let me just say to the Senator from Oklahoma, if we get something else jammed up in there that we cannot dispose of, it would pose some problems for the majority leader. I think we have to all understand if we are going to do all these things, and I certainly made this commitment and I will keep it, it is not going to be any bed of roses around this place the next couple of weeks. . . . [I] want to do what the distinguished senator from Oklahoma desires to do.*

MR. BOREN: *Mr. President, I appreciate those comments. I know there are problems for the majority leader and the minority leader in arranging schedules, trying to move the Senate along. I would point out that when we released the subject matter in S. 655, we did so with the knowledge that we would have a chance this year early enough in the year to have access so that we could complete action on campaign reform and the House could still act. I appreciate the majority leader's commitment to bring this up before the August 15 recess.*

On August 6, as an important colloquy occurred seeking agreement on a prerecess schedule of Senate business, the heat was turned up. After outlining timing procedures and consideration scenarios of a South Africa bill and a Contra aid bill, Senator Byrd brought up the Boren amendment again.

MR. BYRD: *We are discussing these two issues with the understanding that the commitment to the senator from Oklahoma would have to be kept. The distinguished majority leader, of course, would be within his prerogative, within the context of the commitment to the senator from Oklahoma, to schedule that measure for action.*
MR. DOLE: *I think we have outlined the general framework [for action prior to the recess]. . . . With reference to the senator from Oklahoma and his priority, we are going to try to do them all. I do not know if we will do them all, but if we do not get this agreement, there is no problem with doing his. If we do get the agreement, we may have to alter it some.*

The agreement was set. The Boren amendment and one "Republican alternative" would be considered with one vote each. On August 9, in a memo to the staff of cosponsors, I informed the fourteen Senate offices of the Monday and Tuesday schedule for our amendment's consideration.

A Boschwitz alternative was carefully designed to help his party gut the Boren amendment. His "Dear Colleague" letter of August 11 stated his approach.

First, my amendment requires the disclosure of all so-called soft money to the national party committees (given principally by corporations and labor unions). Second, it prohibits PAC contributions to political parties (an easy way to avoid the Boren restrictions). And third, it would remove (for first amendment reasons) rules requiring broadcasters to give air time to offset independent expenditures.

He went on to explain that other amendments—on which he wanted a Senate vote—were to double party contributions limits to candidates, reverse the Boren amendment change on the individual contribution (leaving it at $1,000), prohibit retiring congressmen from shifting campaign funds to personal use, and establish a bipartisan commission to study further campaign reforms.

On the day of the vote, Boren let his Republican partner make the opening statement. In it, Goldwater reminded the Senate of "what James Madison in the *Federalist Papers* said we should be, agents of the sovereign people and not the instruments of narrow factions." Goldwater concluded, "By curbing the influence of PACs, it would help to assure that the outcome of elections will be determined by the broad public consent of the voters and not by those who give the most money. I urge the Senate to adopt this proposal and help return the power over elections to the people, where it belongs. That is what this amendment is all about."

Boren, Boschwitz, and the other usual cast of characters spoke and argued on the merits of the two amendments. When the dust settled after the debate, the votes were taken. The Boschwitz tally was 58 to 42. The Boren ballot was 69 to 30. The Senate, wanting to appear strongly in favor of campaign finance reform, passed both amendments.

After the glow of a 69 to 30 victory, it was time to find a way to move to final passage of the legislation. It would take one-hundred senators unanimously agreeing to limit debate and a vote of final passage before the measure could be sent to the House of Representatives.

Boren met with his archrival, Senator Boschwitz, at 9:30 A.M. on August 14, one day before the scheduled month-long recess was to begin. If we did not move before the recess to secure a time agreement for final passage, there would be no chance of moving the legislation in 1986. The usually cordial Boschwitz and Boren always got along well, and the chemistry served them well for this meeting of the minds. They did agree on a way to move on the bill in September and give the go-ahead to Dole.

Time agreements in the Senate are just that—agreements on timing. The Senate operates on the standard of unanimous consent. They set the time to convene, the time to vote, the number of amendments to be considered, the hours of debate. In the absence of a unanimous consent agreement in the Senate, nothing can really happen, except disagreement, discussion, and filibuster.

The day after the Boren-Boschwitz summit, I was due in Oklahoma City at 8:00 A.M. for the wedding rehearsal of my best friend, Denis Rischard. I was in the wedding party and certainly expected to attend the rehearsal and dinner. However, as the time agreement had not been reached, I delayed my plans and tried to reschedule for Saturday morning, well in advance of the 7:00 P.M. service.

After some lengthy negotiations with Senator Dole, Boren saw no way but to allow a time agreement request to be made of the Senate. But first Boren checked with me to make sure Common Cause and some of the cosponsors were supportive of the agreement. Then he found out about my plans to cancel my flight.

"You have to go back to be there for your friend," Boren said. "We've got things pretty well nailed down on the time agreement. Either they [the Senate] will take it or they won't. There's really nothing else you can do."

"But I'd feel better being here to see what happens," I replied.

"Greg, you'll always regret missing this important day in Denis's life," Boren calmly said.

After thinking about it and realizing the senator was right, I said I would call the Combined Airline Ticket Office (CATO), Congress's travel agent, and see about later flights on Friday. I rescheduled for a 1:30 flight that would get me into Will Rogers World Airport in Oklahoma City at 5:06 P.M., barely in time for rehearsal.

I felt extremely nervous as the early hours of Friday, August 15, passed. I was packed to go straight to National Airport but had the whole morning to wait for Dole to propound the consent agreement to conclude consideration of the approved Boren and Boschwitz amendments. Time passed to no avail, so I bid the office and the senator good-bye, saying I would call in from Chicago.

At 2:30, while I was somewhere over Ohio in an American Airlines passenger jet, Senator Dole took the Senate floor.

> Mr. President, I am going to propound a unanimous consent request, and I hope there is no debate on it. I will propound it, and I hope we can get it agreed to.

I ask unanimous consent that following the conclusion of morning business on Monday, September 8, the Senate resume consideration of S. 655, with the Boren and Boschwitz amendments attached, and at that point it be considered under the following time agreement:

Six hours total for debate to be equally divided between the senator from Pennsylvania [Mr. Heinz] and the senator from Oklahoma [Mr. Boren] or their designees:

That all amendments be limited to 40 minutes each, to be equally divided and germane or relevant to the Boren and Boschwitz amendments and in the first degree only;

That in the event a substitute amendment is adopted, it be treated as original text for the purpose of further amendments;

Ten minutes on any debatable motions, appeals, or points of order if so submitted to the Senate;

That no motions to recommit with instructions be in order and that the agreement be in the usual form, with the exception of a Simon amendment dealing with public financing.

I further ask unanimous consent that during the Senate's consideration of S. 655 there be alternate recognition for the offering of amendments and no amendment dealing with a commission on campaign financing be in order.

Further, I ask unanimous consent that following the conclusion or yielding back of time, the Senate proceed immediately, without any intervening action, motion, debate, or quorum call, to third reading and final passage of S. 655, as amended.

Now, I would ask unanimous consent that following the disposition of S. 655, the Senate turn to the consideration of Calendar No. 834, S. 528, a bill to establish a bipartisan commission on campaign financing, and it be considered under the following time agreement:

One hour total debate, to be equally divided in the usual form;

That no amendments be in order except the committee reported substitute;

Two minutes on any debatable motions, appeals, or points of order, if so submitted to the Senate;

That no motions to recommit with instructions be in order;

And that the agreement be in the usual form.

Finally, I ask unanimous consent that following the conclusion or yielding back of time, the Senate proceed immediately, without intervening action, motion, debate, or quorum call, to third reading and final passage of S. 528, as amended.

This tediously constructed agreement was hammered out over

hours and days. It resembled more of a parliamentary contract than a schedule of the Senate doing its business.

After its full reading, this took place:

PRESIDING OFFICER: Is there objection?
MR. HELMS: On behalf of a number of senators, I do object.

Our 1986 efforts were quashed by three simple words: "I do object." Helms was honest, though; he did represent a number of other senators. But we will never know who they were. It is possible that Senator Dole could have gone to Helms and asked him to object for their side. Boschwitz could have been in on it as well, merely going through negotiating motions to keep Boren off-guard.

Despite the death blow to our plans to move forward to a vote before the 1986 elections, my anger and frustration were calmed by hope for the future. The inaction of the Republican Senate majority to grapple with campaign finance reform might play to an angry electorate. A rule of politics kept running through my mind: "What goes around, comes around."

PLANNING FOR NEXT YEAR

On the high school football team my junior year, I remember all too well that after losing the last game of the season, Coach Lykes would tell everyone that we should now start thinking about next year. And now, nine years after that losing game, Senator Boren gave the same pep talk. Instead of discussing returning starters or his quarterback's throwing arm, the senator spoke of improvement and expansion of legislation to address the deterioration of the electoral process.

In an October 8 speech on the Senate floor, Boren summed up his work on campaign finance reform.

Mr. President, as the 99th Congress comes to a close, I wish to discuss for apparently the final time in this session, the volatile issue of campaign finance reform. . . . For the first time in nine years, the

U.S. Senate took a vote on a major change in our campaign finance laws. Not since 1977—when S. 926 was debated and has three cloture votes taken—have the major changes to the Federal Election Campaign Act been on the agenda of the Senate.

The actions on S. 1806, as an amendment to S. 655, show a tremendous move of support for sweeping changes to bring back our system of financing campaigns to the directly accountable, grass-roots level.

Before the litany of "thanks" were doled out by Boren, he summed up his commitment:

While action cannot be expected in the dark of the 99th Congress, it is hoped a renewed spirit of urgency, compromise, and resolve can set the stage for passage of a comprehensive bill in the 100th Congress. And if not then, let me make very clear that so long as I serve in this body, I will do all I can to see that reform is made in the area of campaign finance.

I want my colleagues to know of my interest to expand and modify my legislation. . . . Many—who see and experience the depth of this "crisis of liberty," as Senator Goldwater refers to it—rightfully believe that we must go much further in overhauling the system. . . .

I am optimistic about the ultimate success for campaign finance reform. We must not tire in our efforts until the task is completed. We have an obligation to our fellow Americans and the future generation to preserve and protect the integrity of the election process.

Ten days after the election, which gave the Democrats a majority and all of us plenty of time for the results to soak in and the celebratory drunk to wear off, I drafted a letter from Boren to the thirteen new senators elected. Each of that group, the "Class of '86," was sent a letter of congratulations on their victory seeking their support for campaign reform.

My letter stated that "if there is one common result coming out of the congressional elections of 1986, it was that the huge amount of money in the various races and the negative tone of the campaigns have deteriorated our election process." After boasting of the Senate vote of 69 to 30 and the 17 Senate and 115 House cosponsors of the measure, the letter from Boren stated his plans to reintroduce the bill "on the first day of our convening in January."

Two of the recipients received a special P.S. on their letter. Both House members Wyche Fowler and Timothy Wirth got the added missive, "As a previous cosponsor of Rep. Synar's H.R. 3799, I hope you'll be interested in helping again." Both eventually would. The day before that letter went out, I worked up drafts of letters to some of our cosponsors of the Campaign Finance Reform Act of 1985 asking that they too join in the continuing effort.

I warned Boren of some internal politics. First, the changing control of the Senate would result in Senator Ford of Kentucky taking over as the new chairman of the Rules Committee, replacing the retiring Republican chairman, Mathias. In a November 14 memo, I suggested that he "might be well served to make sure we haven't created a turf battle" with Ford since Boren was named the chairman of the Democratic Task Force on Campaign Finance Reform. I also suggested that Boren try to arrange a call from Senator Byrd to soften up Ford, at that time a seemingly brutal opponent to PAC limits.

Further, I informed Boren that as a member of the Steering Committee for the Democrats, he should consider who could fill what would surely be a new slot for his party on the Rules Committee. My memo read, "THIS IS VERY IMPORTANT, as that vote could be a determining factor on whether or not we get a bill out of committee next year."

CHAPTER FIVE

New Senate, New Bill

Doesn't it seem that step-by-step, we're being moved away from
pure democracy? You know, in ancient Athens, all the citizens
gathered in the agora and decided the issues. And when we got
too many people, we had to go to [a] representative form of
government, where elected representatives made those
decisions. And now, with the influence represented by things
like political action committees, doesn't it seem that the citizen
is being shut out of the democratic process?
　　　　　　　—HUGH DOWNS, "ABC News," March 20, 1986,
　　　　　　　after the "20/20" story, "Who Own$ Capitol Hill?"

　　Politics has got so expensive that it takes
　　　a lot of money even to get beat.
　　　　　　　　　　　　　　—WILL ROGERS

WHILE MOST OKLAHOMA FOOTBALL FANS were watch-
ing the 1987 Orange Bowl game pitting the Sooners against the
Arkansas Razorbacks in a classic revenge match, I could only
hear the game from a distant office television set. Instead of
participating in the Miami stadium on a balmy South Florida
night or watching it on television in the comfort and warm
company of fellow OU fans in Washington, I was hunched over
my computer terminal in my poorly lighted office in the Russell
Senate Office Building.

On the first day of the new year, I was piecing together the
beginnings of legislation to be introduced in just a few days by

my boss and the new majority leader of the Senate. In a battle against the clock, I feared that time was running out, just as it did for the Razorbacks. For twelve hours, with extra light provided by a fluorescent desk lamp, I retyped passages of old bills into the text of the old Boren-Goldwater bill. Any current of air in the office might have upset the delicate stacks of papers for the "new Title 5," the "Aggregate PAC limit" section, or section 3 on candidate reporting requirements. Reams of legislative language had to be melded together to make thirty-one pages of a new bill for the new Senate.

THE HARD SELL

Of course, I knew well before the elections or the Orange Bowl that our bill would change. But I feared the talk of spending limits and public financing would put Boren in the awkward position of either accepting the controversial idea as his own and risking criticism back home or rejecting the scheme and losing his leadership of the issue for the new majority party.

But the hard sell for public financing and spending limits came in a late 1986 meeting with Common Cause President Fred Wertheimer accompanied by Susan Manes. They came first to see me just ten days after the November elections. I knew—and feared—what they had in mind. While meetings with Manes were almost as regular an occurrence as my meetings with the senator, when Wertheimer came in also, I was prepared for a strong pitch for a new approach in a new bill.

Indeed, they made the case that with the 55 to 45 composition of the newly Democratic Senate, chances for a broader, comprehensive bill had substantially increased. They explained Common Cause had always been philosophically in support of public financing to better protect the Congress against special interest influence. They also made the point that Boren should remain the leader of such a reform because of the credibility he had earned among Democrats and Republicans on the subject of campaign finance reform.

I wasted no time in reminding them that he had publicly made arguments questioning the concept of a public financing system in the first Rules Committee hearing a year ago and that—perhaps more important to him—he would likely be strongly criticized by the state newspaper for support of a "liberal" program. In fact, Boren had gone to the Public Affairs Committee of the U.S. Chamber of Commerce just two months earlier, well after the August votes on Boren-Goldwater, and indicated his displeasure with public financing plans. A September 30 letter from the Chamber's political action manager thanked Boren for his remarks to the group the previous week and reiterated their opposition to "further restrictions on political action committees." In addition, they applauded his comments indicating his "desire to avoid taxpayer financing of congressional elections."

I did not expect Wertheimer and Manes to care what the Chamber position was, but I wanted them to understand that I could not expect Boren to support the concept so quickly. It would look too awkward, I thought.

What I did not tell them was that the day before, I sent out letters from Boren to the seventeen cosponsors of S. 1806 as well as the eleven new Democratic senators-elect. In it, I had Boren ask for their support for that same bill, to be reintroduced "on the convening of the 100th Congress." (This would prove to be a confusing and conflicting message. But Boren signed the letters and agreed to stake out the leadership position.) After a typically lively, frank, and respectful conversation, I suggested that Wertheimer and Manes talk with Boren directly. They jumped at the chance. But it would take a few weeks to arrange the meeting.

Within a week of our meeting, *Roll Call*, Capitol Hill's newspaper, ran a story headlined, "Hill Anticipates Campaign Finance Reform." The story reported that "Boren plans to resurrect his proposed PAC-contribution limits on the first day of the 100th Congress, increasing pressure on lawmakers to rein in the campaign finance system." It also noted that incoming Majority Leader "Byrd favors public financing of congressional elections and has already indicated that overhauling the system will be one of his top priorities" in the new Democratic Senate.

After returning from a brief skiing vacation at Crested Butte, Colorado, with friends from the office in early December, I met with Wertheimer and Manes again. In that encounter, on my twenty-sixty birthday, I agreed to help arrange a meeting for them with Boren that next week.

To my surprise, Boren cleared his calendar and was ready to meet on the afternoon of the next workday, the 15th. While the Senate was adjourned until the new Congress could be sworn in, Boren was still very busy getting ready to undertake his new leadership role as chairman of the Senate Select Committee on Intelligence. With the switch in Senate control and more senior Democrats on Intelligence preparing to head other panels, Boren would soon take the helm.

I briefed Boren before that afternoon meeting. "You know, they're going to make a pitch that you should author a bill on public financing," I warned him.

Boren, assuming as much, only asked, "Well, what do you think?"

"I can see where that's probably where we need to go, but it'll sure be hard to convince the *Daily Oklahoman* of that. Plus, we really don't have much time before the first day of the new Congress. Working out the right bill could be tough over the holidays. And our Boren-Goldwater cosponsors think we're putting that bill back in. It may be better to just reintroduce it and say we're working on a broader bill to address spending limits, for now."

Boren expressed his concern that Byrd was growing impatient as well. "Byrd keeps asking me about it, too. I wouldn't want to lose my position of being out front on this issue, with where the Democrats are. Why don't we just talk to them [Common Cause] about it."

With that response, I went back out front and escorted Wertheimer and Manes into Boren's office.

In his typical, friendly fashion, Boren showed his allies in and told them to get comfortable on the couches grouped around the fireplace. The Common Cause duo sat and chatted politics first, catching up on the latest revelations surrounding the Iran-Contra affair, which was just making news. They also questioned him about his new role as the chairman of Intelligence, a subject growing nearer to Boren's heart with each passing hour. After other niceties, the real issue was broached. Wertheimer gave the same hard sell to Boren—why it was time to push for a broad bill—that he gave to me weeks earlier. Unlike the reluctance I voiced on his behalf, Boren surprised us all.

"Well, it seems like the only right thing to do."

Before I could adjust my expression of amazement or check my pulse, Boren had already launched into a series of questions on how a public financing bill could be constructed.

"An important thing is to make sure that the bill would have a high enough threshold to qualify for the funds, so that fringe candidates couldn't get public money. We should leave our PAC limits alone, even though some Democrats would want them to go up: with public funds, they won't need as much PAC money. If anything, they should go down. And the spending limits need to show real reductions in what's being spent in elections."

Wertheimer jumped in. "We think we've got some good [legislative] language ideas we'd like to show you that would address all that. We just have to be careful that you treat minor party candidates similar to how the presidential system handles them. The Court has upheld that."

The meeting concluded with the understanding that Boren would talk to Byrd to finalize a process and strategy. Several issues needed resolution for the new bill. Would it be a "Byrd-Boren" or "Boren-Byrd" bill? Would they seek to get numerous cosponsors before introduction? When would it be introduced? Who would draft it?

The answers came just two days later. Boren had a private, 10:00 A.M. meeting with Byrd on December 17. First, Byrd and Boren agreed to push a spending limit/public financing bill with Boren continuing as the reform issue leader. Byrd would be his "primary cosponsor." Second, no other cosponsors would be sought prior to introduction. Third, the bill should be ready to be introduced on the first day of the session, January 6. And finally, Boren, as the bill's author, would be responsible for its drafting (that meant me).

The news of these decisions reached me as I was preparing to pack my car for a Christmas trip to Oklahoma. After Boren gave me his and Senator Byrd's answers to the questions of "who, what, and when," he left the "how" to me.

In desperate need of a break with family and friends for the holidays, I left that night to drive straight through to Oklahoma. After the grueling 1,300-mile drive, I made it to my parents' home in time for a nap before going to the annual Christmas party in Norman sponsored by my friends, David and Carol Burr. Despite my fatigue and the rush of holiday parties and plans, my mind was still clogged with the burden of what lay ahead for me in Washington on my return.

I packed my Chevrolet for the return trip to D.C. on Saturday, the 27th. I would leave before 5:00 A.M. the next morning, after one more holiday party at my aunt's home in Edmond. I arrived in Washington that Monday, with my first office appointment set for the next day: "2:30 P.M.—Scott Bunton—DPC."

Bunton was Byrd's staff director of the Democratic Policy Committee. That office serves as the Democratic Senate's staff for floor support, policy analysis, and parliamentary assistance. That Byrd would have this top "leadership" staff person handle the negotiations of campaign reform was a bit intimidating. As a free-lancing "personal" staffer for Boren, I was used to dealing with other staff LAs more than leadership office professionals.

But on meeting Bunton, my fears were allayed. He was cordial, respectful, and helpful. He knew I must have been frightened by the task before us. His manner was assuring. He only wanted to help. We went over some material on what the bill should look like, and I assured him that I could put it together in time for introduction. I merely needed to settle some issues individually with my boss on provisions in the bill and strategy.

Before leaving that first meeting, Bunton asked—in the voice of a wine steward anxious to fill the champagne flute of a prized patron of a five-star restaurant—what seemed to him a most important question. "Have you thought about a particular bill number you'd like reserved for this legislation when it gets introduced?"

Not realizing before then that the majority and minority leaders could reserve status-clad, low bill numbers with the Senate bill clerk at the beginning of a new Congress, I only replied, "Well, no. Not yet. But I'll let you know." I could not think of a lucky number, so I left to start the task of drafting.

After working with draft language given to me by Common Cause and old provisions from last year's Mathias-Simon public financing bill, I needed to bring the senator up to date on our progress. I did so in a New Year's Eve memo and specification sheet that I faxed to him in Oklahoma:

> [Here's] a 3-pg. spec sheet on the bill, which should help you get more familiar with it. The only undecided issue to date is the amount on the aggregate PAC limit to parties, which I will get on Friday, the 2nd.
>
> I met with Scott Tuesday and will again at 2:00 P.M. Friday. I should have the final or near-final draft to him for Sen. Byrd at our mtg. then. He indicated Tuesday that *S. 42* is the lowest # the [bill] clerk can get us. I hope that's alright.
>
> I'm coordinating with Brett [Wesner, Boren's new press secretary] on Press stuff. Byrd should be able to do press with you—he'll do statement right after you do on Tuesday [January 6]. I'll give you final run-down on timing later after I talk to Scott again.

Now the only thing to do was finish splicing together the provisions of legislative language that Bunton and I had from old bills, hopefully, before we met again on Friday, January 2. Normally, the Senate Legislative Counsel's office, another of the many support staff offices in Congress, would draft the actual legislative language that I was constructing on my office computer. As I was not a lawyer, I had to quickly learn how to put the words together. But I feared that with many last-minute changes, it would best be held on my own computer.

Which leads me back to typing out pirated provisions of public financing schemes, forming it into what Boren and Byrd would introduce in a matter of days, while hearing the sounds of the Orange Bowl emanating from a nearby office. There I felt the lonely pressure to have the bill ready for final approval from the Senate majority leader, the staff director of the Senate Democratic Policy Committee, and the reform leader and my boss, Senator Boren.

JANUARY 6

The hours leading up to the first day of the 100th Congress were a hectic mesh of telephone calls, late nights at the office, and meetings to go over the final language. In between drafting the bill, planning for press attention, and responding to questions about the unveiling of our measure, I had to construct an introductory statement, draft a "Dear Colleague" letter, contact Senate offices about cosponsoring, and keep my senator informed.

In that December 31 memo to Boren, I had also raised the issue of what to do about senators who had already indicated they wanted to cosponsor a "reintroduced" version of the aggregate PAC limit bill. Seven of his colleagues had already informed Boren of their desire to do so. This late shift in strategy would have to be delicately handled as the plans and egos of senators were involved. The January 5 letter to the seven read, in part,

I greatly apreciate your willingness to again cosponsor our campaign finance reform bill to limit the financial influence of political action committees. However, my plans to introduce the exact language as S. 1806 from the 99th Congress have recently changed.

Tomorrow, I will introduce S. 42—the Senatorial Election Campaign Act of 1987. It is much broader in its scope than the previous legislation. It includes a provision to establish spending limits through a system of voluntary, partial public financing of Senate general elections, in addition to the aggregate PAC limit and other provisions.

I apologize for having not discussed this with you earlier and hope to do so soon. I greatly appreciate your help on this issue in the past and hope to visit with you soon about this legislation.

In an effort not to offend those senators wanting to be on "the" campaign reform bill, it was important to send this communication. Four Democrats did join Byrd in time to be considered "original" cosponsors: Chiles, Kennedy, Stennis, and newly elected Terry Sanford of North Carolina. Senator Bingaman was upset at being notified of the change so late and not being included as an original cosponsor. But he, John Melcher of Montana, DeConcini of Arizona, and our first Republican, Robert Stafford of Vermont, were added to the list within days.

I tried to prevent any other breakdowns from occurring before we went to the floor to introduce the bill. I spent most of the day before the 6th and that morning on the telephone with last-minute details and explanations. In addition to calls to the Senate Legislative Counsel's office for technical corrections to the bill, which I finally consented to let them see, I was on the telephone to the Congressional Research Service (CRS) for figures to be used in Boren's speech. CRS is a research arm of Congress, under the Library of Congress. Their specialist, Joe Cantor, had become a helpful telephone companion who had answers to almost any campaign money question I had.

I took calls from a number of other congressional offices to answer questions about our planned legislative initiative. In that short time, I talked to staffers with Congressman Synar, Senators Stennis, Chiles, Kennedy, Mitchell, Kassebaum, DeConcini, Sanford, Daniel Evans (R-Wash.), Jim Sasser (D-Tenn.), and Don Riegle (D-Mich.) as well as Rules Committee staff and the press. But the hours were growing short; it was time to go to the floor.

The first day of the first session of the 100th Congress, like the beginning of any new session of Congress, saw many bills brought to the floor for introduction. Every pet project or position of a congressman is enhanced with his or her ability to tell constituents, "On the first day of this Congress, I introduced legislation to . . ."

Senator Boren had a few special bills to introduce as well. But none was as important to his colleagues as the Senatorial Election Campaign Act of 1987. His first effort on the legislation would be a 4:00 P.M. press conference with state press in his office with Congressman Mike Synar. Our state colleague had been the House sponsor of the aggregate PAC limit bill and was a willing leader to push the new and improved bill on the other side of the Capitol.

Boren asked me to sit in on the casual press briefing, mainly to see that he correctly answered any technical questions about the bill. This was a nervous moment for me, because I feared that with the short amount of time we had to discuss fine points of this bill, Boren might get tripped up on details. Of course, in my three and a half years with Boren, I had never seen him get tripped up by any reporter, constituent, or senator. But I still had an anxious feeling. Maybe I was nervous because I did not understand the bill that well either.

The *Tulsa Tribune*, the *Tulsa World*, and the Gannett reporters, as well as Al Cromley of the *Daily Oklahoman*, were among those present for the unveiling of this public financing bill. I could hear my heart pounding during one tense moment, when Cromley, the dean of the press delegation, pressed Synar about the need for a "public financing scheme." Synar, known as a quick wit and short-tempered maverick, started his response with an insensitive, "Now look, Al . . . ." Cromley really was not surprised by Synar's support for the idea. It was Boren's support that would make his story.

But as I feared, the next day's *Daily Oklahoman* ran Cromley's story under the headline, "Boren Adds New Wrinkle to Limit Election Spending." The lead paragraph left no mystery as it read, "U.S. Senator David Boren renewed his campaign finance reform drive Tuesday, but this time with a new wrinkle—public financing." With such a focus on taxpayer financing, I knew the next step would be an editorial against the bill.

Rushing back into his office in the late afternoon with his press secretary, I handed Boren a cleaned-up, revised copy of the

introductory statement he had looked over previously. Attached
was the summary of the bill, an "English version" of the
legalistic language, and finally and most important, a clean,
final copy of the bill that I had printed out from our office
computers.

I asked Boren to put his signatures in the upper right-hand
corner of the three documents. This was a required procedure for
the Senate's "official reporters of debates," those stenographers
who walked the Senate floor recording any debates that took
place. Their transcripts would have to be incorporated with those
documents that senators would "insert for the record," like
lawyers submitting evidence in trials. The debates and inserted
material were all to be printed in the *Congressional Record*, the
official record of congressional proceedings and debates.

After settling a few issues with the press secretary, it was time
to go to the floor. The only thing remaining to do at this point as
the first day's session was winding down was physically introduce S. 42.

Boren and I walked over to the Capitol, via the tunnel under
the Russell Senate Office Building. We were accompanied by
Tripp Hall, a state field representative who was visiting Washington that week and wanted to see a bill introduced. We entered the
"Senators Only" elevator, one in a bank of six elevators marked
just for the lawmakers, which took us from the basement to the
second floor. A hard right and we were thirty feet from the door
to the Senate chamber. Boren went straight in, telling me to meet
him inside. I went to the back lobby entrance, where all staff have
to check in and be issued a "floor credential" in order to gain
access to the hallowed ground. With Boren's speech, summary,
and bill in hand, I gingerly walked to the Democratic side of the
lobby and entered the chamber.

Boren, as he had on my first time on the floor, motioned for a
chair from a page to be placed next to his, as well as a lectern
stand for his speech. The Senate was in a "quorum call," the
deliberately slow reading of the roll to ascertain a quorum,
typically used as a procedure to kill time during off-the-floor

negotiations or to wait for a senator on his way to the floor to speak.

It had been a typical first day of the Congress with 282 bills and 76 resolutions introduced. Besides the usual housekeeping procedures in starting up a new session, like the formal election of the president pro tempore and notifying the House that the Senate had assembled, the Senate had its first roll call vote on establishing the Select Committee on Secret Military Assistance to Iran and the Nicaraguan Opposition, which passed 88 to 4.

But now the chamber was quiet. Sen. Thad Cochran (R-Miss.) had just completed a speech honoring Senator Stennis, the fourth Mississippian to serve as president pro tempore of the Senate. Sen. "Spark" Matsunaga (D-Hawaii) was presiding in the chair. Only one more bill would be publicly introduced with traditional floor speeches before this first day would adjourn.

Byrd, the only other senator on the floor, approached Boren with a proud and confident smile. The few visitors in the gallery, the floor staff, pages, and television cameras were focused on Boren, awaiting his request to address the Senate. But first he must talk to the majority leader and his primary cosponsor.

"David, I've reserved a special number for your bill. I'm making it 'S. 2,'" Byrd whispered.

Boren smiled and whispered back with a humble and graceful tone, "Why, thank you, Mr. Leader."

Boren turned to me and showed his pleasure with a gleaming smile and upturned eyebrows. Words were not needed to express his satisfaction with the majority leader's symbolic gesture.

I could tell that one form of legislative priority in a new Congress was the assignment of low bill numbers. Earlier that day, S. 1 was given to the Water Quality Act of 1987, better known as the Clean Water Bill. In a consistent clean sweep, the majority party leader gave the next top billing to a bill for clean campaigns. Byrd had returned to his Senate desk at the foot of the chamber's well, where he sat to listen to Boren introduce their bill.

Boren then sought and gained recognition to address the Senate.

Mr. President, last year, through a lengthy process and after much deliberation about the need for reform, the Senate had an initial vote to make major changes in our system of campaign finance. I was pleased to be joined by many concerned and sympathetic colleagues who had firsthand knowledge and experience with the alarming trend toward runaway spending in elections funneled by an unhealthy amount of special interest money.

Now in the 100th Congress, on the heels of the last election cycle, [we] must bring a renewed focus on the problems caused by money in politics and the divisiveness it promotes.

The senator next listed those who had already joined him in the fight. But he did not read the names as they were listed on the bill. "I am proud to join with [the majority leader] in this effort. Others have already joined us: Senator Terry Sanford of North Carolina, the past president of Duke University, . . . Senator John Stennis of Mississippi, the president pro tempore, . . . Senator Lawton Chiles, chairman of the Budget Committee, . . . and the senior senator from Massachusetts."

In a slight apparently not recognized by anyone but me at the time, Boren could not bring himself to publicly name his "liberal" colleague, Ted Kennedy, as an original cosponsor. Perhaps he feared how the state press would label this bill.

Boren explained the bill and inserted the "summary of S. 42," which I had not gotten around to changing to reflect the newly assigned bill number. He then concluded his remarks.

This is an American problem about which we are talking. We are talking about the integrity of this institution. We are talking about the integrity of the election process. How long will we wait, Mr. President? How many millions and millions of dollars will it take the average candidate spending in order to get elected before we realize that something has gone badly wrong with the present way in which we finance campaign in ths country? Mr. President, my hope is we will not wait another year. The 100th Congress must face up to its responsibility to the American people.

By this time, Chiles and Kennedy had come to the floor to add their supportive statements to the chorus. Again, the floor held no senators besides Byrd and Boren. In fact, Byrd had to take over the duties of presiding while Kennedy concluded his speech. Byrd was ready to make the final statement for the reform legislation. So during another quorum call, with no other senator in sight, he motioned to Boren to preside while he took his place on the floor to speak.

That no other senators were on the floor during this discussion symbolized more than the typical pro forma nature of the exercise. I would later learn that absence from the chamber during serious discussions of changing the system of campaign finance was deliberate, just as Dole's evasiveness the year before showed. Most interest centered around making speeches. But Byrd's words illuminated his intense sincerity.

It is my strong belief that the great majority of senators—of both parties—know that the current system of campaign financing is damaging the Senate, hurts their ability to be the best senator for this nation and for citizens of their respective States that they could be, strains their family life by consuming even more time than their official responsibilities demand, and destroys the democracy we all cerish by eroding public confidence in its integrity. If we do not face a problem of this magnitude and fix it, we have no one but ourselves to blame for the tragic results.

BOREN LEADER

Senator Boren's development as the acknowledged leader of campaign reform did not come easily. The change merits some additional discussion.

The formal effort to shift gears in our drive for campaign reform toward public financing began three days after the November elections. Those elections gave the Democrats control of the Senate, Robert Byrd the title of majority leader, and David Boren the driver's seat on the main vehicle for campaign reform.

In a November 7 letter to Boren, Byrd confirmed his instructions to "continue to work diligently during this intersession period" on a "carefully constructed and realistic campaign finance reform bill" that would be placed "prominently and early on the Senate agenda." Byrd directly instructed Boren to reassemble the Democratic Working Group on Campaign Finance Reform, which Byrd appointed nearly a year earlier to look at "some form of public financing arrangement."

Byrd had originally appointed Boren to head the group of ten Democratic senators after the amendment was tabled by the Senate in 1985. That December 11 letter was a landmark document and a landmark day for Boren in his work on campaign finance reform. It marked a transition for Boren from radical "bombshell" thrower to responsible leader for Senate Democrats. The letter was drafted on the same day that Byrd joined as a cosponsor on the Boren-Goldwater bill. Such a move by the leader was a strong indication of his commitment to the issue and his desire to work through Boren as the means to an end. The letter also indicated Byrd's desire that Boren move his thoughts beyond the current PAC debate.

The entire array of campaign finance problems encountered in seeking elective office, and the public perceptions of impropriety and catering to special interests that often result from the current means of financing campaigns, are more than sufficient justification for the Congress to take broader remedial action. I hope you can propose some ideas that look beyond PAC limitations—whether to be offered along with or instead of your earlier amendment or to serve as a longer-term objective.

The political objective was also stated. Byrd asked Boren to help "provide leadership to the senators I have asked to join you in devising recommendations to our 1986 strategy group concerning what Senate Democrats should do with respect to campaign finance reform." The appointed senators were Bingaman, Albert Gore of Tennessee, Kennedy, J. Bennett Johnston of Louisiana, Mitchell, Riegle, Sasser, and Simon. The committee's makeup was a politically shrewd maneuver by Byrd at the time. He was likely to be challenged as he sought another term as Democratic leader by one of the appointees, Johnston. Another,

Mitchell, had future leadership plans as well. Further, Byrd knew of the undercurrent of opposition within the Democratic ranks and must have felt it could be diffused by putting Boren in charge of hearing out disgruntled Democrats. This would be the purpose of such a leadership post for Boren through not only the Boren-Goldwater debate but through the 1987 Boren-Byrd legislation as well.

FAMILY FEUD

I have described the early efforts of 1985 and the intrafamily disputes and ill-will of Democrats. But this does not measure the in-fighting, jealousy, and mistrust shown among the Democrats in reworking the legislation behind the scenes in the 100th Congress.

Several days after we introduced the bill, I received word that Senator Cranston was working on his own campaign finance bill and was seeking Democratic input and support. His free-lancing would not have been so important to me except that he was trying to keep Mitchell from cosponsoring S. 2. Boren and I saw Mitchell as a very important and respected catch. We wanted his support.

Cranston was also reportedly telling others that *he* was really the "leadership's point man on the issue." I had information that such a claim was made to Anne Wexler, a former Carter administration official and current lobbyist for the AMA, Chamber, and other big PACs."

In a January 22 memo to Boren, I warned him of these developments. With Cranston serving as the Democratic whip and knowing of Mitchell's hope of becoming the next majority leader, I told Boren that "due to the future 'leadership' implications of this [Mitchell/Cranston] alliance, I think (as does Common Cause and others) that we must work to get Mitchell on board."

The problem persisted for another month. I received more confirmation that Cranston was working with Mitchell to construct a bill with much higher aggregate PAC limits, a much lower qualifying threshold to get public funds, no change in the individual PAC limit, and some unspecified language on soft money. Such a bill would be seen as a sham—not worthy of the name "reform" and a retreat from an already established pro-reform position of the Democrats.

As Byrd was working particularly hard to get numerical Democratic support, several names were missing from our list of cosponsors. Besides Cranston and Mitchell, the senators waiting to see Cranston's bill before cosponsoring S. 2 were Bill Bradley of New Jersey, Moynihan, Johnston, Tim Wirth of Colorado, John Kerry of Massachusetts, Daschle, and Max Baucus of Montana (in that order of importance to us).

By February 19, four weeks after we discovered Cranston's plan and six weeks after we introduced our bill, S. 2 had thirty cosponsors, including two all-important Republicans. While I would have rather seen Boren spend his precious time convincing the other party to support his measure, he and Byrd would have a "prayer meeting" with the defiant senators.

At Boren's request, Byrd called together Senators Cranston, Mitchell, Ford, Kerry, and Kennedy for a 3:00 P.M. meeting in S-221, off the Senate chamber. Byrd opened the meeting by reporting the progress of cosponsors and followed with a strong pitch for unity. No mention was made by Boren or Byrd that either was at all aware of the covert effort by Cranston.

Kerry, then chairman of the Democratic Senatorial Campaign Committee, had two of the committee's political staffers in this policy meeting. After some 15 or 20 minutes of rambling conversation on strategy and substance of changes needed in S. 2 to make it more acceptable for Democrats, Byrd got to the real point of the meeting.

"Now, will each of you cosponsor this bill? Ted, I know you're already on it."

Boren and I looked at the shameless faces of the plotting band of staff and senators. An uncomfortable silence was broken quickly enough by Kerry, who said, "Of course, Mr. Leader, we'd just like to have a chance to work on details that need fixing in the bill." Little more was said, and detailed discussions were cut off as Byrd had to leave. The meeting adjourned. The point was made. After another month of conversation and co-opting, Cranston, Mitchell, and Kerry threw in the towel on March 24 and decided to cosponsor S. 2.

Despite these strategic barriers that had to be overcome, the singular, Democratic obstruction for our new bill was the opposition of the new Rules Committee chairman, Wendell Ford. The only observation I could make about Ford's views on reform during Boren's initial assault on the issue was that the Kentucky senator was a friend of PACs. He was unenthusiastic about Boren's effort to put a clamp on them. An exchange from the November 1985 Rules Committee hearing helps to illustrate.

MR. FORD: *Mr. Chairman, I might just say to my distinguished friend, I am up for reelection next year. I already have over 2,000 individual contributors. . . . Of course, in Oklahoma, with all those rich oil people, it does not take very long for you to get enough from individual contributions and you don't have to worry about raising the PACs. But we have a little different situation in some other states. . . . PACs represent a real interest of local people and employees. . . . Those people are part of the system . . . [with] an interest in their PAC's activities, and [they] feel like their money means more when contributed though their PAC.*

MR. BOREN: *Fine. I think, Senator Ford, those are exceptions. I think there are situations like that, and that is the reason my proposal does not ban PACs altogether. . . . The usual situation is not [like] that. It is usually the group of lobbyists here in Washington making the decision. I just say in the footnote that the way my wheat farmers and my oil men are doing lately, I may have to come to Kentucky to tap your tobacco farmers in my next election, but . . .*

MR. FORD: *You just continue to support the tobacco legislation . . . [Laughter]*

MR. BOREN: *If I see any other individuals out here that want to support good government, I am going to encourage them to help my colleague from Kentucky. I think that would be a wise investment in good government, as well as an investment in this legislation.*

MR. FORD: *You have always been an astute politician. [Laughter]*

Despite this humorous banter, Ford's concerns were not just keeping a tap on PAC money, which abundantly came his way for that 1986 election. His concern seemed to be that the cost of getting elected kept going up so quickly that PAC money was the only way to keep pace. This view was reflected by an earlier statement in that same hearing: "Campaigning is almost like the medical profession. All of us want to use or have access to every new discovery or technique. . . . This desire to take advantage of the newest developments becomes a very personal thing in a political campaign, and I am no different from anyone else."

He further discussed the costs of the "new phenomenon called tracking polls," computers, and direct mail. Ford had come to the realization that "how much" money it took to run for office was (if not more) important as "from whom" the money came. But that realization was slow in developing.

After Boren and Byrd introduced S. 2, it was first referred to the Senate Rules and Administration Committee, where its new chairman would help decide its fate. But a news story about Ford started a long family feud on the issue. "Ford May Block Campaign Reforms" was the *National Journal*'s headline on a January 31 article. Described as "a potentially formidable roadblock" to the top priority bill, S. 2, Ford was portrayed as our first hurdle before we could focus on Republican support for the bill.

Ford had said after the vote on Boren-Goldwater that "everyone knew that proposal was going nowhere. . . . We ought not restrict PACs." In this interview, he went on to raise his objection to public financing, saying, "Campaign finance is a serious question, but it is not in the league with economic issues, trade and agriculture."

Bringing this stray back into the fold would be a difficult task for Boren and Byrd. Ford was a cagey, old-school politician. His devotion to tobacco, horses, and bourbon earned him the respect and reelections from Kentuckians since his service as governor. He was most comfortable chairing his Rules Committee, shrouded by a delicate cloud of cigarette smoke broken only by the air current from his gravelly voice as he badgered a witness. Any meeting with the man served as a reminder of his state's large cash crop. That gruff voice could cut as easily as it could charm. He would often open a negotiating session with, "Now I'm no lawyer, but I got good horse sense."

But this caricature of a tobacco state senator would be incomplete without the understanding of his real first love. His devotion to the three primary industries of his homeland were only challenged by his affection for politics. Like few others, Kentucky became known as a state where politics was a contact sport. With a developing dynasty of his own, other campaigns would become important ventures for Ford. The biggest was the 1984 Senate race that he helped coach for incumbent Dee Huddleston. In that campaign, Ford sought to help his Democratic friend and colleague fight off a challenge from a slick, media-conscious Republican, Mitch McConnell.

Huddleston was defeated by the negative campaign television ads of the challenger. McConnell's upset victory was characterized by "hound dog ads" depicting a search for the absent incumbent. They accused Huddleston of speaking for honoraria to lobby and interest groups instead of voting in the Capitol. The ad was honored with placement in the classical archives by negative campaign strategists.

The defeat of his friend would leave a sore spot that Ford would never forget. That was lucky for us.

A MIGHTY FORTRESS?

Support for S. 2 was built gradually. Before the end of that January, we had added eleven Democratic cosponsors to the bill, joining the five originals from January 6. Byrd was the master of twisting the arms of his colleagues, allowing Boren to focus on meeting with Republicans. The tally continued with thirteen more cosponsors in February, ten in March, and four in April. It would have the appearance of a mighty fortress.

Boren kept up his end of the deal, too. In unusually aggressive fashion for a bill sponsor, Boren made personal, individual appointments with his colleagues to lobby for S. 2: Senators Arlen Specter (R-Penn.) and Rudman on January 21; Rhode Island Senators John Chafee (R) and Claiborne Pell (D), a Rules Committee member, on February 2; another committee member, Christopher Dodd (D-Conn.), and Kassebaum on February 3; Senator Simon on February 5.

I recall that part of the motivation for Boren to continue his meetings was to show Byrd he could produce. Byrd obviously had the same competitive spirit. However, the difficulty of getting one Republican to support us in that tense partisan time was equivalent to about ten Democrats that Byrd could produce. Calls coming in from Senate staffers to sign on was a heady experiene. The routine was that an LA would call me and ask that their boss be added. I would then type up a "unanimous consent" request to be submitted to the floor which looked like this: "Mr. President, I ask unanimous consent that my distinguished colleague from Arkansas, Senator BUMPERS, be added as a co-sponsor of S. 2, the Senatorial Election Campaign Act of 1987."

After getting Boren's signature, I would then walk to the Capitol and visit the Democratic Policy Committee office on the first floor, where the staff would see that the "U.C." sheet made it to the floor staff. There, it would be added to the *Congressional Record* via the recorders of debate after a routine perusal by the cloak room staff for the Democrats and Republicans.

After a while, with more than forty names coming in over three months, it became a chore to get the names added by the necessary procedure. I first had to let Boren know that a senator was added to the bill. I would inform Bunton (for Byrd) and Manes (for Common Cause), so that they would call off the dogs on those offices and thank them instead. I would then add the name to my ongoing list of cosponsors and my chronology. And finally, I would have to double check the *Congressional Record* the next day to be sure the name actually made it into the "Additional Cosponsors" section.

Byrd and Boren both took a time-out from their meetings and arm-twisting long enough to testify before Ford's Rules Committee on March 5. A second hearing was held on March 18 to allow the rest of the senators wishing to testify an opportunity to do so, again, an unusual circumstance. Then two more days in April were allowed for testimony from outside interest groups, academics, and PACs.

One of the strategies we undertook was to get as much outside support as soon as we could. In addition to the coalition of outside groups (see chap. 6) that any serious legislative effort works to amass, we sought out individuals to give support as well. I thought that it would be worth a shot for Boren to write to his partner from the year before, Barry Goldwater, now retired, to inform him of the change to the bill and explain the reasons. The letter would have to be delicate, because I knew the conservative Republican could blow a gasket at the notion of public financing.

The letter I wrote for Boren to sign was as follows:

As we discussed late last year before you left the Senate, the fight to clean up the congressional election process could greatly benefit from our continued interest and commitment.

I wanted to send to you some material on a bill I introduced the first day back in the 100th Congress. I hope that you can take a close look at . . . an expanded version of the bill we pushed together last year.

Like you, I have felt the real solution to problems in campaign finance is to have overall spending limits. However, the only practical way to do so, without appearing to go against the *Buckley v. Valeo* Supreme Court decision, is to tie the limits to a system of voluntary, partial public financing. An attempt to amend the Constitution could take years.

Unlike some bills in the past, S. 2 has a provision to require several, small, in-state contributions as an eligibility requirement to receive the public money. As well, it specifies that if a nonparticipating opponent twice exceeds that state's spending limit, the limit is taken off for the participating candidate. This helps ensure that there is a budgetary ceiling on what the program ultimately costs.

I am sure you share with me the strong feeling that with the tone of, and money pumped into, the 1986 elections, moving to this system is a small price to pay to preserve and secure the integrity of the election process and to restore public faith in the Congress. . . .

I greatly valued our partnership on this issue in the 99th Congress. Knowing your sincere concern for this institution, I look forward to having your help again.

Sincerely,
David L. Boren

When I typed "public money" and "public financing" on that February 23 letter, I felt real fear that not only would Goldwater oppose such a scheme but that it would become public and the Republicans would use it to argue against the bill. But good news came in a March 7 response from Goldwater.

I have had a good opportunity to read your proposed legislation, and frankly, Dave, I like it a little better than what we put in last year.

The important thing is to eliminate the growing, dreadful use of money, money to get elected. It is a costly procedure, and I think any kind of a law that would prohibit, or limit, expenditures on certain items, such as television and other advertising, would be a boon to everyone running for politics.

As I sit on the outside now and look back at my time of campaigning, I almost get sick at the amount of money I had to spend to achieve what I did.

My best wishes are with you for your success in this. I think you are doing a great thing for our country.

With all good wishes,
Barry Goldwater

Boren immediately agreed with my suggestion to circulate the letter to Specter, Rudman, William Cohen (R-Me.), and Kassebaum to get their cosponsorship of the bill. The problems and strategies were coming a mile a minute, however. Just as we thought that the Rules Committee hearings would focus reform attention on S. 2, another proposal took hold, a constitutional amendment. On March 10, I warned the senator about my "grave concern that should the constitutional amendment idea be pushed too hard, it would take the place of S. 2."

The amendment would essentially overturn the 1976 Supreme Court's *Buckley v. Valeo* decision, which disallowed Congress's right to set spending limits on the grounds that it was a First

Amendment violation. They did uphold the public financing/ spending limit program in the presidential system as a way to enforce "voluntary" limits.

My memo warned, "Senator Simon—after you left the [Rules] Committee hearing [on March 5]—indicated to Sen. [Ted] Stevens [R-Alaska] that he would hold 'early hearings' on this proposal. This would have the effect of being a 'study commission' roadblock that caused us problems last year. It can be used as a way for our opponents to say they're for campaign finance reform." I told Boren that he should talk to Byrd to short-circuit the Simon promise of hearings. Yet the press picked up on the new avenue for reform.

Still another twist was found by a House member. A *National Journal* article on March 21 talked of a proposal to amend the rules of the House to limit what a member spent on elections. The article said that the proposal by Rep. Jim Bates (D-Calif.) "could be enforced by public scrutiny and House disciplinary action." Such an idea might have been advanced in the Senate as well to diffuse our bill. I told the *National Journal* reporter that the "proposal could raise constitutional problems" since it would apply to incumbents but not challengers. Luckily, that idea went nowhere. We could not say the same for the constitutional amendment. It would be an idea that was well received by the likes of Stevens, Ernest Hollings (D-S.C.), and others we needed on our bill.

By April 29, our bill was reported out of committee by a favorable but party-line 8 to 3 vote. A few weeks later, the committee staff, with our input, filed Committee Report 100-58. (Committee and conference reports describe the contents of bills in laymen's terms, without "legalese.") After a committee report is filed, it is placed on the Senate Calendar, where it technically sits until called up for consideration by unanimous consent. When that happens, it becomes the pending business of the Senate, ready for debate, a potential time agreement, and passage.

By May, the heavy-handedness of Byrd was starting to cost us goodwill among Republicans. Byrd had been getting Democratic cosponsors in proportions that would suggest that our party was anxious for the bill to pass as a vehicle for partisan advantage. Further, Byrd was the real force behind Ford's brisk action in getting a markup completed with unanimous Democratic support.

I warned Boren in early May that Senator Chafee's staff person told me his boss—even though a cosponsor—was having problems with the bill. Chafee's unsettled attitude was confirmed to me by a friend who was told at a fund raiser for the Rhode Island senator that "Byrd's running the show now" and that his view was that it was being "politicized." The same report came from our other Republican cosponsor, Senator Stafford of Vermont. In talking to his aide the morning of May 6, he said the 8 to 3 committee vote out of Rules was a "Byrd-rigged, partisan event."

I warned Boren of this as well, so he could smooth the ruffled feathers of Republicans. However, it was obvious that they were merely reflecting the pressure they were getting from staunch opponents in the GOP camp, instead of their own views.

There was also information that came to me about a Republican bill that was being constructed. It was Stevens's substitute amendment that was defeated on party lines in the Rules Committee. The amendment would have raised the individual contribution limit from $1,000 to $2,500, lowered the PAC limit from $5,000 to $2,500, doubled party contribution limits, and provided for a 100 percent tax credit for political contributions. I also received word that McConnell and Packwood were working on a bill as well, one that would eliminate PAC contributions. This idea was perceived as heresy by PAC-dependent Democrats, despite their reformist colors.

Boren's response to the situation from the May 6 memo was to "talk to Common Cause and target a meeting with a group of Republicans. We need about 10 or 12 of them to get cloture. This means we must fashion a compromise and need to think about that compromise."

The next day was filled with more meetings. I had a speech before the Banking Law Institute, followed by a late afternoon

Democratic Task Force meeting of staffers. It was more an airing of partisan disgust that Democratic senators were feeling about how the current bill would cut their boss's PAC receipts than a strategy of how to get a bipartisan bill. The next morning, I accompanied Boren to a C-SPAN televised breakfast speech before the National Conference of State Legislators. From there I went to the Common Cause offices to pump up the coalition of interest groups that endorsed our bill.

Then there were the telephones. Calls came in from the staffs of Senators Hollings, Sanford, McConnell, Bumpers, Gore, and Levin—all with questions about how our bill was changing and how it would really affect them or to ask when the bill was coming to the floor. I talked to staffers at the Democratic Policy Committee and a curious PAC manager from American Express. Plus, I talked to the editorial page writers from the *Washington Post* and the *New York Times*. Those were the most productive conversations of the day. At least I could see their editorials in the newspaper eventually. Finally, I had to meet with Common Cause's Wertheimer and Manes and with Bunton from Byrd's staff. We had to get a grip on this monster of a process that was turning far too partisan. And not by our hands.

So with all this time needed to hand-hold Democrats, when would there be an opportunity to get a meeting of those "10 or 12 Republicans"? It would never happen.

The pressure to fortify the walls of the "mighty fortress" was too great. The "leadership group staff" representing Boren, Byrd, Ford, Kerry, Kennedy, Mitchell, and Cranston continued to meet throughout the busy spring. Our job was to secretly come up with a revised version that would placate the uneasy Democrats before S. 2 would make it to the floor. The meeting that earned us the cosponsorship and support of Cranston, Mitchell, Ford, and Kerry cost Boren an opportunity to bring his bill to the floor without any major changes.

No fewer than eighteen meetings of this covert, core group of staff persons took place between that February 19 Democratic summit and the end of May. The meetings were run by Bunton on behalf of Byrd and by me on behalf of Boren. While he and I explained the rationale for various aspects of the bill, each of the other staffers—two from some offices—had the opportunity to shoot us down. The dance of each meeting was the same. A problem was discussed. Options were identified. Debate ensued. A new topic arose. Time ran out. The next meeting time and place was set.

One of the first issues to be brought up was the aggregate PAC limits of S. 2. Our bill allowed for a PAC limit that ranged from a low of $175,000 for a state like Montana to a maximum of $750,000 for California. The problem for Roy Greenaway of Cranston's staff was that $750,000 was an arbitrary ceiling as opposed to the natural cutoff point from the formula. Even though we all knew Greenaway wanted his boss to be able to raise a million or more from PACs, he tried to sell us on changing it for fairness sake.

Despite my arguments that such a boost would be an obvious signal to our opponents that we were catering to PACs, the group wanted to placate Cranston and other senators with a larger PAC limit. Thus, there and after, the PAC limit would be raised to $825,000 for a state like California and nearly $200,000 for the smaller states.

One of the improvements made in the bill rewritten by this staff group was coverage of primary elections. While the Boren-Byrd bill did not deal with any kind of spending limit in the primary, we knew it was a weakness. Time pressures did not allow us to figure out how to fix it. But the process of the meetings allowed us the chance to work out a system in which a candidate would have to agree to limit up front what he or she spent in the primary election to be eligible for the public financing benefits in the general election.

Other issues were examined, and changes were made in a draft recommendation to the senators involved. The spending limits would be raised while the "threshold requirement" on in-state fund raising to be eligible for public funds would go down. The rewards for a complying candidate who was victimized by a high-spending candidate would rise as well. The number of changes we recommended went on and on.

The tedious, exhaustive meetings, usually held in a Capitol conference room or at the Democratic Policy Committee in the Hart building, at times took their toll on our patience. The aides from each of the five other personal staffs, as well as from the Democratic Senatorial Campaign Committee (DSCC) and the Rules Committee, did, however, develop a rapport and a trust out of the long process.

But still, trust was not a quality that always ran high in the process. After getting slight indications of approval from Boren, one covert strategy I engaged in was to have amendments to S. 2 drafted unbeknown to the negotiating Democratic staff. Since there was disagreement on some issues, if the Senate were ever in a position to really amend a live piece of legislation, I wanted to be prepared.

The three amendments dealt with lowering the PAC contribution, restricting the "franking" privilege for congressional newsletters, and disallowing the tax exemption of Senate campaign committees that did not abide by the spending limits. Nearly all of these would have been privately opposed by the staff group. Another favorite axiom of this game was "Trust everyone, but always cut the cards."

BATTLE BEGINS

On June 2, Boren was to have a private meeting with Senator Byrd at 11:00 A.M. I was to have a lunch meeting with a lobbyist from the American Israel Public Affairs Committee, or AIPAC. There had been talk and speculation among several of those involved that the bill would be coming up soon. We just did not know when Byrd wanted to try to schedule it. I remember asking Bunton, who politely and diplomatically explained, "Senator Byrd, I'm sure, is developing a strategy in his mind and will discuss it with Senator Boren." But I did not expect what happened that day.

While lunching at La Colline, with a view of the Capitol dome, I explained to the AIPAC lobbyist that the reform bill could come up in a week, maybe two. Little did I know at the time that Byrd was on the floor, clearing the calendar to make S. 2 the pending business for the next day.

Byrd's action was quiet, deliberate, and secret. A Senate Calendar with no pending business listed under "Unanimous Consent Agreements" is the only circumstance under which a senator may call up an item listed on the calendar without debate. Typically, in the middle of a session, as we were that June, the calendar has at least one or two items listed. Only with it cleared can an item be brought up as the pending business without "unanimous consent." For several days, without drawing any attention, Byrd worked to see that the calendar was clear of any unfinished business so that he could call up S. 2.

In the quiet late morning, Byrd did just that. He announced it would be the first item of debate the next day, June 3. On returning from my "lobbyist lunch," Boren was the first to let me know that we were getting ready to go to the floor. But reaction from others was quick to follow.

My friend and confidante, Laurie Sedlmayr of Senator De-Concini's office, was the first to call me to inquire about "the plan." Somewhat embarrassed and angry at my ignorance of Byrd's strategy for my boss's bill, I said, "I don't know what the hell he's doing!" I assured her that even though the commander-in-chief, Byrd, was calling a surprise attack, Boren, the field general, was ready for battle tomorrow.

Dave Smith, the aide to Senator Kennedy, was the next to call. He was extremely upset and felt such a strategy was unwise. How could we be sure we were ready for the opposition?

His perspective reminded me of the work I had ahead of me to ready opening statements and material for the floor. It also reminded me that Democrats do not like being told where and when to go to battle. I tried to assure him that we needed to stay calm and prepare for the floor together. I reminded him that Kennedy was an important spokesman for our cause, and we needed his leadership on the floor tomorrow.

Back on the floor the next day, we found out what Byrd intended.

As I look at campaign finance reform . . . I do not now see 60 votes to invoke cloture on the bill. I am not sure we would ever get 60 votes to invoke cloture on S. 2. But if we can get the bill up and debate it, see where the problems are, hopefully, we can deal with the legislation and whatever amendments the Senate feels would be appropriate, whatever changes have to be made, make them, and in that way, perhaps arrive at a bipartisan consensus that will support passage of meaningful and effective and needed legislation. But we can only do that if we get the measure up. I do not think we would ever reach a consensus on this bill unless we get it up and start debating.

Dole responded:

I think there is a great deal of interest in reaching some consensus. I think the biggest problem on this side would be the public financing portion. . . . One way to find out is to debate the motion to proceed or the bill itself, to have the people who have an interest *on* the floor.

A NEW FOE

Senator Ford, as Rules Committee chairman, first acted as a manager of the bill, a big change in procedure from our previous assault on the floor. However, unlike the unconventional trial, this effort was going by the book: (1) bill introduction; (2) committee hearings; (3) committee approval; (4) full consideration on the floor.

During his opening remarks about the report of S. 2 from his committee, Ford explained that Rules approved a "committee amendment in the nature of a substitute." This was the work of our much more limited group of Democratic leaders. As he was explaining, Senator McConnell, his junior colleague from Kentucky, interrupted him to "yield on a point" to which Ford curtly replied, "If my colleague will wait until I finish."

As mentioned previously, the animosity between Ford and McConnell was perhaps the greatest blessing for our gaining the

Rules chairman's support. The undisguised and mutual loathing between the two would keep the speeches spirited during debate.

After another couple of minutes, Ford ignored the Republican and turned to "yield the floor now to the distinguished senator from Oklahoma." And I, at Boren's side, watched the senator give yet another speech explaining his remedies for the ills of campaign finance as the tiffed McConnell waited.

Stevens and Packwood were the next to speak on their side of the aisle, to be followed by McConnell. In his opening salvo in this fight, he staked out his ideological disagreement "that somehow campaign spending is bad." McConnell said, and would repeat for years into the future, that "we spend more on advertising pet food in this country than we do on campaigns." So, he would ask, what's the problem?

By default and persistent attendance on the floor, McConnell became the Republican point man on campaign reform. Dole would have difficulty excluding him from any negotiation arrangement because the Kentucky senator interjected himself so boldly into the S. 2 debate. In 1985, Senator Heinz led the opposition to the Boren PAC legislation. In 1986, the role was passed to Senator Boschwitz. From 1987 forward, McConnell would grasp the baton in the race.

A *New York Times* editorial years later best described the ascent of our new foe, Mitch McConnell.

The system is broke and Congress . . . can finally fix it. But it won't if Senator Mitch McConnell, Republican of Kentucky, has his way. To him, reforming the odious way of financing Congressional campaigns is not an ethical question at all, just partisanship. He helped torpedo reform legislation . . . and appears ready to do it again. . . . [His] intransigence is hard to understand, even on partisan grounds. The proposed spending limits would reduce the huge fundraising advantage now enjoyed by Congressional incumbents, most of whom are Democrats.

But the piece clearly indicted the GOP leadership: "There's ample room for negotiating a bi-partisan agreement—if Senator

Dole will mobilize reasonable Republicans behind it. . . . Senator Dole's silence now creates a vacuum into which Mr. McConnell gladly rushes."

The vacuum that McConnell sought to fill, along with Senators Packwood, Helms, and Gramm, was indeed strong. Other Republican members would not publicly buck the tide for reform. After the opening debate on S. 2, the Republicans took a hard-line position, influenced by these four senators. In a June 11 letter to Byrd, Dole wrote that his Republican caucus met the day before and "had the opportunity to discuss in some detail the issue of campaign financing reform." He went on, "In considering changes in the bill, I thought it would be helpful for you to know that our caucus was able to reach near unanimous support on three basic issues: 1. Opposition to any public financing; 2. Opposition to any expenditure limitations; 3. Support for applying any campaign financing changes to both the House and Senate." This, from the Republican leader who nine days earlier characterized the problem as being "public financing" alone.

Another Dole letter was being circulated among Democratic staffers around that time. The letter went from Dole to the FEC chairman certifying and agreeing to spending limits and accepting public funding as a candidate for the presidential nomination. Dole sent the legalistic letter on May 15 stating he and his committee would "not incure qualified campaign expenses in excess of the expenditure limitations prescribed" in the law, in exchange for "matching public funds." But no senator or staffer was bold enough to take the document public. Not yet, anyway.

The chronology of S. 2's life in 1987 reads like a tragic medical history. Like a terminal cancer, from the first failed operation, the supporters kept going in to repair partisan damage, only to show no improvement and with complications developing from repeated surgery.

After the opening debate June 3 and a week's worth of speeches, the first cloture vote to limit debate and force a vote occurred on June 9. That vote failed by a 52 to 47 margin. Had Senator Gore been present, we would have been 7 votes short of the necessary 60 votes to stop the filibuster.

Two days later, yielding to Republican opposition, Byrd laid down an amendment to cut in half the public funds going to candidates complying with limits. This was done after we all agreed that if public funds were the GOP sticking point, we would lessen the pot and see if we picked up votes.

We did not. No votes changed in the second cloture vote on June 16; the tally was 49 to 46. For next three consecutive days, Byrd hammered in cloture votes to make the nation focus on campaign financing and make the Republicans stew in their opposition. But it did not work:

June 17 — 3rd cloture motion failed, 51–47;

June 18 — 4th cloture motion failed, 50–47;

June 19 — 5th cloture motion failed, 45–43.

By July 1, we decided to call the opposition's bluff. Despite Democratic unease, Boren filed "Amendment 429 in the nature of a substitute," which would remove all direct public financing. We further hoped it would remove Republican opposition to S. 2. Instead of a grant that candidates would receive for agreeing to limit campaign spending, our new legislation would provide funds if, and only if, noncomplying opponents started to out-spend them.

As the plan germinated in the press and on the Hill, the Republicans became more creative in their opposition. McConnell and Packwood were publicly promoting their bill to prohibit contributions from PACs to candidates, leaving open a loophole to parties. Other notions and ideas were tossed out to divert attention from the Democrats who proved they were willing to deal.

Before the August recess, Byrd allowed S. 2 to come back to the floor, from which it had taken back seat to other pressing Senate business. It was our strategy that the bill could be left as the pending business so that members visiting their states over the summer break could hear from constituent supporters of S. 2. On the September 9 reconvening of the Senate, debate continued. Before another cloture vote was taken, we tried to explain the arguments as best we could. There were two major fallacies in the opponents' arguments against S. 2. They believed the bill would not curtail PAC money and that it would keep challengers from being able to spend money against incumbents.

The PAC argument for Republicans went like this. Since S. 2 does not lower the $5,000 PAC limit and since Democrats get most PAC money, S. 2 is good for Democrats and bad for Republicans. Supporters of S. 2 would try a different tack: S. 2 sets aggregate limits on all candidates getting PAC money, and since more incumbents are Democrats, S. 2 is bad for Democrats and good for Republicans.

The facts were borne out from a look at the 1986 Senate elections had S. 2 been in effect. In that election, all Senate general election candidates received $45.7 million in PAC contributions. Had S. 2 been law, only $20.7 million could have been received. The effect was felt by incumbents, not Republicans or Democrats.

The spending limit argument went the same way. Opponents argued that the stifling of "free speech" campaign spending would harm challengers trying to unseat the Democratically controlled Senate. Supporters of S. 2 argued that these "ceilings" were a mere outer limit that would do more harm to incumbents who outspend challengers. And since most challengers were Republicans, they should like limiting the Democratic incumbents.

Again, a look at the 1986 aggregate election cycle spending showed that $182.3 million was spent by Senate candidates. That figure is deceiving since a challenger would rarely bump up against the limit, while incumbents would be the ones limited. S. 2 would have effectively limited that to $175.1 million and leveled the playing field. Still, such a small difference was a problem for Boren, who wanted to show overall spending would be racheted down more dramatically. In fact, the U.S. Chamber of Commerce, in their opposition to S. 2, made that argument. They noted that the bill would have cut election cycle spending in 1986 "a mere 4 percent. . . . If the goal of S. 2 is to limit substantially the cost of campaigns, it certainly fails on that count."

But the opponents, Republican senators and groups like the Chamber, were not interested in limiting campaign costs or spending. They both would argue their bottom line goals included broad-based citizen participation. What they never understood was that citizens were turned off by big money politics and slick election campaigns. But in the process, individual senators did not want to be limited by the S. 2 numbers.

On September 10, the sixth cloture vote was taken. No movement from the summer was made except for one Democrat, Hollings of South Carolina. He stated he would give us his vote on cloture but still would not support final passage if we ever got that far. (The only way his vote was secured was through a promise to hold hearings on his favorite reform idea, a Constitutional Amendment to authorize congressional power to set spending limits.) The final tally that day was 53 to 42.

In the five days until September 15, we had gained Senators Exon, Dodd, John Glenn (Ohio), and John Breaux (La.) as cosponsors. While these four Democrats put our total number of cosponsors at fifty-two, we will needed the magic sixty to break the filibuster.

Boren's final appeal to the Senate reminded them that cloture was a procedural hurdle to limit debate.

If we invoke cloture at 11 o'clock this morning, the amendments of the senator from Kentucky [McConnell] and others will be in order. All we are asking is that the Senate be allowed to proceed by the invoking of cloture on this bill . . . before this year's work of Congress is completed. We would have a full airing of the entire matter. Agreements could be reached. Amendments could be offered. Undoubtedly some changes in the pending legislation would be made. But we should have a chance, Mrs. President.

Within minutes of his appeal, the seventh vote on Boren's bill was taken, falling short 51 to 44.

In the end, it was a gross and selfish miscalculation by the

Republican Senate. The minority party could have been concerned with getting strength in their numbers instead of worrying about how the bill would effect them personally.

The first session of the 100th Congress began with Boren's introduction of S. 2. There was a Republican response to the subject that day from Dole. He agreed with Boren and Byrd that

it is a matter that I feel should be addressed. There are a number of concerns that many American have, and there are a number of concerns that contributors have. There are a number of concerns that candidates have. There is a perception of special interest influence in political campaigns, regardless of party and regardless of candidate. I do no believe there will be any effort to stall any such legislation.

Dole was wrong. His caucus, led by fringe extremists, did in fact stall the will of the majority with their use of the Senate rules. We would have to wait until the next year to see if S. 2 was stalled for good.

The Boren for Senate campaign in 1984 held an open house at its Oklahoma City headquarters while I was still a field representative for the senator in the state. Posing with me are Senator Boren's son and daughter, Dan and Carrie Boren (front); my father, Curt Kubiak (center); and Sen. David Boren (right). Photo credit: Office of Senator Boren, photo by Barbara Webb.

Boren and I walking through the basement of the Russell Senate Office Building to the Capitol in a common routine of briefing on the run. An antique senate subway car is displayed in the background. Photo by Michael Geissinger.

The issue of campaign finance reform was a topic of several weekly Democratic caucus luncheons in the Mansfield Room of the Capitol. After one such meeting, I am making a point to Sen. Tim Wirth (Colo.) and Senator Boren at right. Other staffers are Bob Rozen, legislative aide to Majority Leader Mitchell (back to camera) and Jack Sousa, chief counsel for the Senate Rules and Administration Committee. Photo by Michael Geissinger.

Finding a moment off the Senate floor, I take some instructions from Senator Boren during the 1990 debate on campaign finance reform. Photo by Michael Geissinger.

The core Democratic strategy group on campaign reform shares a light moment before a meeting in the majority leader's private conference room. Left to right: Jim King, staff director of the Senate Rules and Administration Committee; Diane Dewhirst, communications director for the majority leader; Sen. Wendell Ford (Ky.); Sen. George Mitchell (Me.), majority leader; Senator Boren; John Deeken, Boren staffer; and me. Photo by Michael Geissinger.

After a Democratic caucus luncheon in April 1990, Sen. Alan Cranston of California (left) pressed Boren and me on an issue relating to the reform bill being considered by the Senate. Seven months later, the Senate Ethics Committee opened public hearings on Cranston's conduct relating to the Keating Five affair. Photo by Michael Geissinger.

On the way to one of many votes on the Boren bill, fellow staffer John Deeken summons an elevator in the Russell Senate Office Building as I discuss strategy with Senator Boren. Photo by Michael Geissinger.

A familiar occurrence in the halls of the Capitol—an impromptu press conference. After a discouraging breakdown in negotiations with Republican leaders
in 1990, Senator Boren was surrounded by reporters off the Senate floor, while I
waited to the side (left). Photo by Michael Geissinger.

CHAPTER SIX

The Allied Forces

Law of Legislative Action: The length of time it takes a bill to pass through the legislature is in inverse proportion to the number of lobbying groups favoring it.

JUST ABOUT ANY LEGISLATIVE BATTLE on Capitol Hill will involve alliances between a lawmaker and at least one national lobbying group. Seldom does a lawmaker initiate a bill that is not preceded or followed by the support of a lobbying interest. Many of the hundred and hundreds of Washington-based groups have talents, constituencies, and resources to tap into a legislative effort. But few can bring the right combination of talent and respect that we had with our primary partner.

COMMON CAUSE

From that first meeting with lobbyists for Common Cause, an important partnership was forged between Boren and the group. Boren would not have been a natural ally of the traditionally liberal citizens' lobby. The organization's roots were founded on the principle of working "to improve the way federal and state governments operate"—primarily through a clean and open government agenda. Such an agenda was made up of reforms in open meetings, laws, lobby disclosure, campaign finance, conflict of interest standards, and the federal budget process. Yet their interests grew to include the issues of arms control, civil rights, Contra aid, and judicial nominations.

Typically, their views on these additional issues were not consistent with those of a moderate to conservative southern senator like David Boren, who supported strong military spending, aid to the Nicaraguan "freedom fighters," and the nomination of Robert Bork to the Supreme Court. But the intersection of commonality for the lobby group and the senator came from their more distant backgrounds. Common Cause and Boren's political career bloomed at about the same time, both against the backdrop of the Watergate scandal. Common Cause was founded in 1970, three years before the unfolding of that national scandal. Boren started his run for governor in 1973 against an incumbent rumored to have legal and ethical skeletons, misdeeds that would later send him to federal prison. The tenets of open government, clean campaigns, full disclosure, and the power of people over money were the pillars that built their common altar.

Boren brought a commitment to write and lead campaign finance reform legislation. That vow was firm and understood. Common Cause brought something to the alliance as well. They had four capabilities of varying value that were necessary: advice, both technical and strategic; media access, especially editorial page writers; research capabilities; and a grass-roots network.

Besides myself, no individuals spoke with or advised Boren more on campaign reform than Fred Wertheimer and Susan Manes. Their presence in the office became so common during times when our bill was up for debate that one staffer joked that our reception area was a satellite office for them. Aside from the actual technical assistance with legislative language, Wertheimer and Manes were consummate strategists. Any knowledge Wertheimer may have lacked in inner-Senate mores, Susan possessed from her years of experience on the Hill. National press writers whom Boren had not met, Wertheimer knew on a first-name basis. When the two would ask for Boren to commit to something I felt was too much, I spoke up to spare the senator from having to do it.

The professional relationship was an efficient and effective combination of knowledge, savvy, and trust. When strategy differences occurred, meetings or telephone calls would straighten them out. Only once was there a flare of tempers between Wertheimer and Boren that interrupted an otherwise smooth relationship.

Between the heated debates over the Boren-Goldwater PAC legislation in 1986, Wertheimer felt that the senator was not making enough time to meet with him and Manes and wanted to discuss it with Boren. I felt insulted that Wertheimer did not trust me to be a proper intermediary for the busy senator. I let Boren know.

A meeting was held in which the four of us caught up on strategies and plans to push the legislation forward. As the meeting broke up, Boren asked Wertheimer to stay just a minute more. After Manes and I left Boren's personal office, the two titans conversed. Ever the defender of hardworking staff, Boren told Wertheimer, "When you talk to Greg, it's as good as talking to me. I am committed to this bill, but I can't spend as much time meeting with you as you'd like."

Just as upset as Boren, Wertheimer apparently thanked Boren for his commitment but reminded him that only he could lead this charge. His leadership would require his time and that it all would be worth it. Both principals, feeling the stress of long hours and frustrating setbacks, agreed that they needed each other for the fight to go on.

The cause was aided immensely by the media that reported on Common Cause studies and the editorials written supporting Common Cause reforms. In the week of a vote on our bill, Common Cause delivered huge reams of packaged editorials from all over the country. Their news and clipping service scanned newspapers to find how successful the Common Cause editorial advisories had been. As is pointed out later, hundreds and hundreds of these would make their way into our debates.

Common Cause was also very helpful in the purposeful timing of their released studies. Since newspaper investigation and research teams usually consisted of a reporter reading someone else's study, a research effort for Common Cause was always worth a story in the *Post*. After the first cloture vote on S. 2, they released a study entitled "S. 2 Would Have Cut PAC Contributions to Senators Elected in 1986 by Two-thirds." The four-and-a-half-page press release came with four charts that ripped apart the Republican argument that the bill would not have reduced PAC receipts because it did not lower the individual PAC limit from its $5,000 level. The detailed report came out five days before the second cloture vote, a great device for coverage from the media.

Common Cause had effective, grass-roots state organizations that helped put political pressure on senators back in their home states. One effort that was a direct hit on Dole occurred in the midst of the 1987 cloture votes on S. 2. That June, twenty-six state organizations, led by Common Cause Iowa, issued a statement and press release calling on the minority leader and presidential candidate to "help end the filibuster" on the bill. The diverse group included the Police Executive Forum, the Association of School Administrators, Church Women United in Iowa, and Farm Aid Agricultural Services. Their statement called for three essential ingredients to comprehensive reform: campaign spending limits, public financing, and an aggregate limit on what a congressional candidate can receive from all PACs.

Some of the efforts backfired, however. Through the summer recess of 1987, Common Cause spent large sums of money to place ads in state newspapers of senators who voted against cloture. Several senators felt unfairly stung by the charges made in the ads. In hindsight, they might have indeed been counter-productive to befriending lost Republicans. But Wertheimer and Common Cause were not afraid of taking off their gloves.

THE CENTER AGAINST SOFT MONEY

The Center for Responsive Politics represented a different kind of outside influence on the campaign finance reform debate. But as with most legislative issues of substance, there is likely to be as least one think tank that has an opinion or research available on the issue.

Most people recognize the name of the Brookings Institution, or maybe the Heritage Foundation or the American Enterprise Institute. These are just a few of the organizations typically called "think tanks" which are a cross between a lobbying organization and a research university. Such organizations are given a different kind of respect in the legislative process. They give an appearance of "nonbiased advocacy," which in itself describes a struggle against academic research and politically jaded punditry.

Joe Queenan described think tanks in a September 20, 1992, *Post* opinion piece as "most usefully thought of as a form of workfare for policy wonks whose labor never has been and never will be rewarded by the marketplace." Still, some do provide useful views for public perusal.

The Center for Responsive Politics, founded in 1983 "as a public interest research organization to help rebuild public confidence in Congress," had former Senators Dick Clark and Hugh Scott on its board of directors. Its biggest contribution to the public debate over campaign reform was its research into "Soft Money: A Loophole for the '80's," the title of its booklet released in November 1985.

"Soft money," defined most simply, is money intended to affect federal elections that is not subjected to federal rules and limits. For instance, if I live in Oklahoma and want to help get David Boren elected to the U.S. Senate, federal law limits my direct contribution to his reelection campaign to $1,000 for each of two elections (primary and general) he could face in his six-year election cycle. However, federal law would not prohibit my giving a $5,000 donation to the State Democratic Party and telling them to use it for his election. While there are federal ceilings on what the state party can spend on Boren's election directly, there are no, or loose, limits on how they collect and spend funds on his elections indirectly.

Abuses of this loophole started to become noticed in the 1980 presidential election when the national Republican party helped collect and pass along between $10 million and $15 million to state parties. Since the spending limits on presidential elections were effective with the Carter-Ford race in 1976, party activists and fund raisers had been eager to find new ways to influence the electorate under new money restrictions. The money changers got some unanticipated help from Congress, which made a seemingly minor change to the law. As the center's publication noted, "After the 1979 amendments took effect on January 8, 1980, Democratic and Republican lawyers quickly found that they could help state and local committees take full advantage of their unlimited spending authority without disturbing the FEC's [Federal Elections Commission's] regulatory ban on national party funds."

Once soft money distribution systems were created, national parties were able to collect and transfer unlimited amounts of money to their state and local affiliates. And in return, these affiliates could spend whatever other money they raised on election activity—especially those activities benefiting federal candidates.

An ominous warning came from the *Post* editorial of August 31, 1984, which said, "Through even the smallest loophole in the federal campaign spending laws, once it is discovered, vast sums of money will soon flow." It noted that "both the Republican and Democratic national committees have announced drives to raise some $20 million of soft money (the Democrats say the Republicans will raise $50 million to $70 million) on top of the $40.4 million of public funds and $6.9 million in national party spending allowed during the general election period."

The center's greatest contribution to the campaign finance reform debate was bringing the issue to our attention. The growing influence of soft money would surely lure other senators to it as an issue to be wrestled with, yet its complexity made it right only for the most serious of reformers.

PAC UPON PAC

Throughout this book, I refer to PACs in a distant manner. They seem to either have an identity like that of a villain in a Batman or

Superman comic book or take on a personality associated with the manager who runs them. But all in all, they represent the great diversity of views in this country, whether their desire for influence is ideological or economic. Political action committees are in many ways a mirror of this country, reflecting the multiplicity of our character. For a mere glimpse of that reflection, consider the following registered PACs as part of the landscape of American political influence:

National Coalition for a Free Cuba
Fireman's Fund Employees' Committee for Responsible Government
Christian Voter's Victory Fund
Puget Sound Bancorp PAC
Wal-Mart Stores, Inc., PAC for Responsible Government
National Pro-Life PAC
Texas Citrus and Vegetable Association PAC
Chocolate PAC
American Institute of Certified Public Accountants Effective Legislation Committee
Bakery, Confectionery & Tobacco Workers International Union Local 6 PAC
Gun Owners of America Campaign Committee
U.S. Committee Against Nuclear War
Ambulatory Operations, Inc., PAC

All of these PACs appear in a March 1988 listing from the Federal Election Commission.

PACs have their defenders. Highest on that list during the early fight for reform was the U.S. Chamber of Commerce. In a letter to senators before the August vote on Boren-Goldwater in 1986, the Chamber pointed out all the facts supporting PACs:

1. 70 percent of PACs contributed less than $20,000 in 1984.
2. PACs are limited to $5,000 contributions.
3. Chamber survey respondents of corporate employee PACs showed an average $295 contribution to House candidates and $1,103 to Senate candidates ($960 and $1,508 from association PACs).
4. Four and one-half million individuals contributed to PACs.
5. Their average annual contribution is approximately $114.

In the Rules Committee hearing earlier that year, a Chamber spokesman was asked by Senator Simon of Illinois if he had "even one scintilla of concern about the impact that money is having on elections in this country." The PAC manager and Chamber member responded that any negative impact of big money in politics "outweighs what [he sees] have been some real advantages to political action committees." He closed his testimony by claiming the 1974 reforms were a "cause for celebration . . . [for the] positive impact on the American public and on the electorate vis-à-vis the fact that we have a better informed citizenry out here now."

During the Chamber's talk show called "It's Your Business" from early 1986, the Chamber president, Dr. Richard Lesher, made his claim: "I don't think we have a major problem" with PACs or campaign financing. He then got into an argument on the influence of money and public financing with two senators also on the show.

DR. LESHER: *People in office are worried about constituency services. All that would dry up if you didn't have to go back to those same people and ask not only for their vote but for their money.*

SENATOR DECONCINI: *President Reagan is accountable, Dick. And he was public financed into office. There is an accountable President, and I think that's . . .*

SENATOR MATHIAS: *Dick, that's a shocking argument, that a constituent who doesn't contribute money to his senator doesn't have the same expectation of accountability as one who does because—and that's exactly the principle—you say that . . .*

DR. LESHER: *I'm telling you, the organizations we have today lay their concerns right at the feet of Congress and say worry about these things. Solve these problems.*

SENATOR MATHIAS: *And we won't contribute if you don't do it the way we say. That the thing we're trying to get away from.*

DR. LESHER: *We would have a regal Senate that can thumb their noses at their constituents and be reelected.*

SENATOR MATHIAS: *You never thumb your nose at people who vote.*

SENATOR DECONCINI: *Try running, Dick. You don't thumb your nose and get elected.*

DR. LESHER: I'm telling you that raising money makes you more accountable and makes you much more conscious of what the people want.

Clearly, what Lesher's constituents at the corporate-funded Chamber of Commerce wanted was the status quo system of PACs making Congress accountable to them.

Another tough guardian of PACs was the Public Affairs Council, a coalition of corporate interests. Boren spoke during the heat of the Boren-Goldwater PAC amendment at their 10th Annual Political Action Committee Conference in Washington. Boren shared his sincere concern that it was unhealthy to the democratic process for elected representatives to depend on so much money from the interests in Washington instead of the citizens of their home states.

Soon after his closing point, he fielded a question from corporate PAC manager who quoted a member of Congress telling him, "I really appreciate having the ability to raise money from groups like yours in Washington. That way, I don't have to bother the people of my district for contributions." The PAC manager, probably seeing the red face and disdainful eyes of the Oklahoma senator growing more intense, finally asked Boren a question about the congressman's view.

"What's wrong with raising money through PACs, which people, voters, give to, so congressmen can concentrate on issues instead of raising money door to door?"

With an indignant tone, Boren solemnly and sternly barked out, "Well, thank God the Constitution still says we have to *inconvenience* the people back home to vote for us, or else we could just settle the whole thing right here in Washington!"

The conference went on for another full day, during which the PAC people heard from then Wyoming Rep. Richard Cheney (and later secretary of defense) who spoke on "The Case for PACs in the Public Interest Is Salable Politically" and from Roger Ailes, president of Ailes Communications, who advised participants about "putting 'sell' into PAC communications."

But I was fascinated by the conference and went back to hear a

vice president of the American Medical Association, the doctors'
lobby and PAC, discuss independent expenditures. The session's
theme piqued my interest.

"What are the campaign funding alternatives should PAC
restrictions become a reality? Many say that independent expenditures will increasingly substitute and to some degree replace
contributions to candidates' committees." The AMA public
affairs official began his speech by boasting of the $400,000 it
spent in independent expenditures in 1984 and the million dollars
it would spend in 1986. His only direct charge against the current
law or proposed changes was that the current $5,000 limit on
PAC contributions was "out of date." The AMA PAC made
$1,839,000 in direct contributions to congressional candidates in
1984 (up 36% from 1980). As the PAC's funds would continue to
grow, the official was telling us that limits would keep it from
helping candidates directly. But independent expenditures could
help achieve the same goals of the PAC—defeating congressmen
or helping elect a congressman or challenger—without any
limits.

It was a warning to me that this loophole in campaign law,
carved by the First Amendment and protected by the *Buckley v.
Valeo* decision, would be a continual challenge in our legislative
battle. No senator would be willing to cut off a fund-raising
spigot if no barrier were placed in front of independent ads by
their enemies, First Amendment or not.

There is a "pyramid effect" of PAC contributions that deserves mention as well. Despite the seemingly democratic mosaic that PACs do represent in their numbers, their funds and
influence can be aggregated in much stronger ways than the
Chamber's "$295 average House contribution" figure might
suggest. Senator Hart described the exponential influence of
PAC contributions in an ABC interview in March 1986:

We're not talking about $5,000 [PAC contributions]. We're talking
about, as I said, $50,000, $100,000, $250,000, or more from the
insurance industry or the banking industry, or the airline industry or,

you name it, it's not any specific industry. It's every industry. They pyramid them. It's not one PAC. It's dozens of PACs.

But despite the growing influence of PACs, I had to remind myself during the struggles to reform them that they were only acting out of self-interest and survival. After all, this was the system we created for them in the reforms after Watergate.

LOBBYISTS—"THE ONES THAT COME TO THE PARTY"

If PACs "represent" people with money and a cause, then a lobbyist is usually the one who "carries" the money and the cause. PACs so far have been faceless interests. But lobbyists put a face on the interest.

Out of fairness, it is not a proper equation to put PACs and lobbyists on the same plane at the same time. There are PACs that technically hire no lobbyists and lobbyists who run no PACs. But no PAC manager talks to candidates in need of funds without lobbying for the PAC's interests. And few lobbyists are given access to lawmakers who do not have something to offer him or her. Like PACs, most lobbyists find that money, in the form of campaign contributions, is the "flowers and candy" most lawmakers like to courted with.

According to Senator Byrd's history of the Senate published in 1991, a newspaper correspondent in 1869 wrote a "vivid description of a monster in the Capitol building":

Winding in and out through the long, devious basement passage, crawling through the corridors, trailing its slimy length from gallery to committee room, at last it lies stretched at full length on the floor of Congress—this dazzling reptile, this huge scaly serpent of the lobby.

That description of the lobbyist and PAC managers who roam the halls of Congress today may be a bit dramatic. Margaret Thompson better defines lobbying as "the process by which the interests of discrete clienteles are represented within the policy-making system."

The term "lobbyist" comes from the practice of representatives of business or petitioners of Congress who would congregate in the side and rear lobbies of the old Senate and House chambers. From this vantage, they could engage a particular member to discuss special legislation or efforts to help the represented interest. Today, lobbyists come in many forms. They can be representatives of trade associations, member associations, law firms, corporations, labor unions, universities, financial institutions, consulting firms, public relations offices, coalitions of associations, states, cities, foreign countries, ideological/interest groups, and religious organizations, to name a few. But often employed in their duties to influence is money, the seed of political power.

ABC's news correspondent John Stossal got a good indication in a 1986 interview with Sen. Steve Symms (R-Idaho) about what lobbyists and PAC managers want from members of Congress. Symms, who was facing reelection that year, submitted to an interview with "20/20." The story related that despite Symms's service for such a small state, he had received over $500,000 in PAC money just through 1985. The descriptive interview was straightforward but grew tense.

MR. STOSSAL: *Why do the people [PAC managers and lobbyists] give you the money?*
MR. SYMMS: *They want to see Steve Symms reelected to the Senate. It's just that simple.*
MR. STOSSAL: *These people are giving money to you just because you're a good senator, not because they want something?*
MR. SYMMS: *Well, maybe it's what they don't want.*
MR. STOSSAL: *What don't they want?*
MR. SYMMS: *They don't want bigger government. They don't want higher taxes. . . .*
MR. STOSSAL: *Money is going to the tax committees. Why, if it's just for good government?*
MR. SYMMS: *Power!*

Then the reporter turned to the subject of a $1,000 per person (per lobbyist) fund raiser Symms held that week, concurrent with

Finance Committee consideration of the Tax Reform Act of 1986. The exchange grew heated and sharp.

MR. STOSSAL: *At your party there were people from the banking industry, loan companies, General Electric, the American Insurance Association . . .*

MR. SYMMS: *Well, these people are patriots too, you see!*

MR. STOSSAL: *I'm sure they are, but don't they . . .*

MR. SYMMS: *I mean, there's nothing evil. What' evil about it?*

MR. STOSSAL: *Nothing necessarily, but they all have specific agendas about taxes, that . . .*

MR. SYMMS: *Well, if you're representing, ah, say, an insurance industry and Congress is in a position to tax an insurance that would completely wipe out the way you've been selling policies, don't you think it's only natural that they would be concerned about it?*

MR. STOSSAL: *I'd be very . . .*

MR. SYMMS: *. . . And that they would want to talk to people on the Senate Finance Committee to try to explain this. It's the right to free speech.*

MR. STOSSAL: *But so only the people who contribute $1,000 get to speak?*

MR. SYMMS: *No, that's not what I said. They're the ones that come to the party. . . . There's absolutely nothing evil about contributing money to elect somebody to the United States Senate, unless you don't believe in the Constitution.*

And what a party it is in Washington! One of the best I attended was not a fund raiser but the "annual award-winning outdoor cookout" sponsored by the U.S. League of Savings Institutions, the lobbying arm of the savings and loan industry. The league rented out the Washington Sailing Marina, just south of Washington's National Airport on the Virginia side of the Potomac River. According to the invitation, they were to serve "beer, wine, and 'strong' drinks at 6:00 P.M. with a complete rib/chicken barbecue from 6:30 to 9:00 P.M." The casual affair was for all the friends of the industry, banking aides, committee staffers, or anyone else who would be able to help the industry lobby to keep regulations soft during the boom year of the mid-1980s.

I will discuss later the influence of the savings and loan industry with Congress. But suffice it to say, the league, like all major financial lobbies, was able to earn the ear of policymakers with more than strategically placed PAC contributions.

Barbecue and beer constituted the hospitality and attention that staff and members could understand and enjoy. After all, there was no "Citizens United Against Real Estate Growth" PAC that lobbied Congress against lax savings and loan regulations. There was no "National Association of Tougher Lending Laws" that sponsored a crab feast or cocktail reception, as a device to balance what savings and loan lobbyists were telling Congress.

Some lobbying was more personal and steeped in luxury. I was quickly ostracized in good fun by my office mates at the time when I accepted a trip on Boren's behalf to Palm Springs. A lobbyist with the insurance industry had invited Boren to come to the Rancho Las Palmas Resort and Country Club in the California desert in February 1986. It was to be a preliminary fund raiser with industry representatives and a breakfast speech for an honoraria, probably $2,000. Yet, for whatever reason, Boren had to cancel. He suggested to the lobbyist that I be able to go in his place. Boren asked that I speak at the breakfast and in return have a couple days to see the beauty of the desert and maybe play some golf.

I did attend the conference and spoke at the one official meeting. I recall there was a great deal of sophistication in questions about the upcoming tax reform act being debated at the time. But still, I thought that had Boren been here, they would have paid his transportation, lodging, and meals and still paid him $2,000 to tell them what I did. Of course, he's a senator and I'm a staffer. The two-day affair was more about desert sun, golf, food, and drink than capital gains tax relief and corporate rates. Thankfully, such honoraria practices have since been reformed out of existence.

It was my first of several junkets while on the Washington staff. I do feel that to a degree, they are an appropriate mode of communication for lawmakers and lobbyists. Speaking at conventions that happen to be in places most people dream of going to is not in itself an evil. But golfing vacations in resort communities in exchange for one thirty-minute speech are more about leisure and lobbying than about tax policy and insurance.

Several examples of how monied lobbyists try to help senators and curry their favor come to mind. At the 1988 Democratic National Convention in Atlanta, I coordinated the senator's activities as he chaired the Oklahoma delegation. Prior to my departure, Cody sent me a computer message from a railroad lobbyist. The message was "Joe La Sala — of Union Pacific — 662-0160 — has a ritzy RR dining car available and wants to do an event with DLB — pls. call." After consulting with Cody and Cox, the AA, I decided Boren did not have the time in his schedule for such largess.

But, of course, we did have time for a "breakfast reception" sponsored by our state's Kerr-McGee Corporation honoring the senator and his wife on the first morning of the convention. We accepted the favor of friends over that of strangers any day.

Another Oklahoma institution having a party that week was lawyer/lobbyist J. D. Williams of the Washington firm of Williams and Jensen. An invitation from him offered "the convenience of the Atlanta Suite on the 15th floor of the Omni Hotel" on Wednesday evening, July 18. The free flow of booze and political punditry would create a festive atmosphere indeed.

J.D. was the embodiment of a power lobbyist. I was fortunate to often be on the same side of issues with him. I helped his firm on a banking issue in 1987, not knowing at the time that what J.D. wanted was the bill to be obstructed more than his amendment to be attached. But the central credo of a good lobbyist is "to get you to do what *he* wants you to do, while making you think it's what *you* want to do."

We did not always agree on issues, however. As a staunch gun owner, he — like the National Rifle Association — saw my advice to Boren to support a 5- to 7-day waiting period on gun purchases as "gun control." And I never saw him at an Oklahoma State Society function that he would not rib me about how Boren's "turned liberal" by supporting spending limits and public financing to reform campaign finance.

A token that I took from the Hill was a book given to me by Williams. *Standing Ovation* was written by a friend of J.D.'s who dedicated it to him. The book, on how to be an effective speaker often quotes Churchill. On the inside of the book, Williams inscribed it, "Greg: Would Churchill support public financing? J. D. Williams"

CANDIDATES WITH A CAUSE

An anti-PAC, proreform movement among actual candidates also helped focus attention on the call for change. The effort blossomed when Republican challengers from twenty states wrote an open letter to President Bush in 1992 urging him to sign the reform bill Congress sent to his desk. But the modern seed for reform was planted by a Democratic candidate for Congress in Charlotte, North Carolina, in 1986.

On June 18, I received an unexpected call from the campaign of D. G. Martin, Democratic candidate in the 9th District of North Carolina, urban Charlotte. The campaign aide I talked to asked many questions about the Boren-Goldwater PAC amendment and boasted that "D.G. doesn't accept PAC money and wants to make a campaign issue out of it." He asked whether or not Boren would be willing to come to Charlotte to get exposure on his PAC issue and help D.G. at the same time.

I let Boren know in a memo the next day that this candidate, Martin, was going to do a thirty-minute cable television show on the issue and invited him to be the guest. He responded that he could not do it because he planned a family vacation at that time but that it would be okay for me to do it. His only request was to "just stick to PACs and not mention the election." As I had never been to Charlotte or appeared on a cable television show, I decided to do it. Two days later, I called the campaign to regret for Boren and accept for myself.

On June 30, I caught a 10:15 A.M. Piedmont Airlines flight into Charlotte. A campaign aide met me at the airport, from which we drove into the city. Passing by Heritage USA, the soon-to-collapse empire of Jim and Tammy Faye Baker, I was reminded of the influence and power of money in more than just politics. It made its way into religion as well.

Before we started taping, I had a chance to meet Brooks Jackson, the *Wall Street Journal* reporter who was tracking D. G. for a book he was working on. D. G. impressed me as a sincere patriot who believed in his rhetoric against the evils of special interest money. The taping for the cable show went well. Afterward, D. G. took us to one of the fine barbecue joints in that state. After the feast of "pulled pig," brisket, and slaw, the next stop was a meeting with the editorial board of the *Charlotte Observer*. Unaware of this stop on *my* itinerary and unaccustomed to being questioned by such a board, I nonetheless backed up what D. G. had told them earlier about the need for reform legislation like Boren's. I caught a 5:25 P.M. flight home, having promised D.G.'s campaign manager that I would give some technical help to their campaign.

It was soon after I was back in Washington that the request for a "draft" bill came from their campaign. It seemed D.G. wanted to expose a copy of H.R. 1, the first bill he would introduce if elected to Congress. I was busy with S. 1806 but was glad to help.

In a July 2 press conference, D.G. revealed his plan to eliminate PAC money in congressional elections, lower the individual contribution rate to $500, limit candidates to $10,000 of their own money, and set spending limits on campaigns. I later received the "D.G. Martin anti-PAC proposal" from his campaign manager touting H.R. 1 as "a bill to return Congress to the People." His material warned that the "pre-Watergate days of influence-peddling and back-room manipulation" were closing in on us and that "we'll be heading toward scandals that will sicken us all" unless we change policies and laws now. D.G. would not get his chance to introduce that bill. He was defeated by the well-financed incumbent, Alex McMillan.

A united effort by House challengers was organized after the 1988 elections. A group calling themselves the Coalition to End the Permanent Congress started in February 1989 to form "a nationwide coalition of 1988 challengers, plus other recent challengers from both parties, [who] could call attention to the negatives of a 'Permanent Congress.' "

The letter from two Democratic challengers—one from Kansas and one from Missouri—complained of "running against a well entrenched and financed incumbent." They proposed a meeting in Kansas City to bring attention to the "Permanent Congress [which] passes budget busting legislation that favors the special interests that provide their campaign funds."

Seeing that such a group could bring bipartisan support and attention to our effort, I encouraged Boren to accept their invitation to speak at their meeting. Again he had to decline. I would have gone in his place except for the lure of a National Guard junket starting that weekend to Maryland, Alabama, Louisiana, Florida, and the Virgin Islands. Somehow, in my now fatigued and cynical state of mind, I felt I deserved a leisurely week viewing environmental projects of the military more than I needed to hear a choir of challengers preach to the altarboy of reform.

I did, however, draft a letter for Boren to send to their conference. The May 20 letter read,

> I wish to recognize and applaud your concern about the growing barriers in our free and fair electoral process. By being in Kansas City today to meet and discuss the serious challenges facing our system of democratic elections, you are starting what I hope will be an effective campaign for change.

After discussing the cost of winning a campaign and the 8 to 1 ratio of PAC money going to incumbents, the letter continued,

> Aside from the obvious advantage these millions of dollars give to sitting incumbents, it is naive to believe that it hasn't some impact on legislative business or behavior. With more and more campaign funds coming from narrow interest groups or out-of-state sources, who can we say is truly represented in Congress?

The meeting of a dozen or so that May afternoon also spurred them to make an agenda of issues in need of repair that included limits on the franking privilege, reductions in excessive staff, and lids on the financial influence of PACs and special interest money. The challengers got some of the press attention they wanted. The *Washington Post*, *Wall Street Journal*, and *National Journal* all covered the meeting with similar headlines declaring, "Defeated Hopefuls to House Protest Incumbents' Edge"; "Also-Rans Decry 'Permanent' Congress"; "Unfair Fights for Challengers?" And while other local and video press covered the meeting, it was a hollow cry in the lonely woods of reform.

A similar effort took place three years later when Republican challengers from twenty states wrote to President Bush asking him to sign the campaign reform legislation in 1992. Further, fifteen former members did the same thing, led by John H. Buchanan, Jr., a Republican from Alabama who served from 1965 to 1981.

In an op-ed piece, Buchanan wrote that "the current system has muted the competition as well as discourse on issues. A growing number of incumbents run unopposed or face challengers with negligible resources to mount effective campaigns." On his and those Republicans' behalf, he urged the president's support of spending limits and partial public financing by signing a bill that would allow challengers "to compete on a level playing field against well-funded [mostly Democratic] incumbents."

Off-the-Hill Republicans were more united in the call for reform than Bush and the incumbents. Yet their united voice was ignored by the president. One candidate for the Senate stopped his race mostly because of the constant demands of fund-raising. Former Florida Gov. Reubin Askew abruptly withdrew from a U.S. Senate race in 1988, bringing new national focus to the issue.

It was bad news for Florida Democrats who hoped to keep control of the seat being vacated by Lawton Chiles. The *National Journal* reported the "unexpected development" of Askew's withdrawal, despite his "big lead in the public opinion polls over candidates of both parties." Such a decision in the heat of the political season in the big southern state was reached with great difficulty and soul-searching, said Askew.

I found myself increasingly concerned about the extraordinary cost of running a statewide campaign in Florida today. Of course, I knew that before I announced my candidacy in December. But frankly, I underestimated the time and effort it would take—and how [the system would hamper] my ability to have more direct contact with the voters.

As I've said during this campaign, something is seriously wrong with our system when many candidates for the Senate need to spend 75 percent of their time raising money. It's just not right.

Fifteen months later, after canceling out of a "booze cruise" on Chesapeake Bay compliments of the J. D. Williams and Jensen lobby/law firm, I received a telephone call from Governor Askew. He called on a Friday in August from his Orlando law office to first tell me he had accepted a fellowship at the Institute of Politics at the Kennedy School of Government in Cambridge, Massachusetts. He wanted to introduce himself to me, inform me of his new duties at Harvard University, and ask some questions about campaign finance reform. He accepted the fall fellowship to lecture a class entitled "Political Campaign Giving and Spending: A System in Need of Fundamental Repair."

Despite his service as governor in the Sunshine State, Askew was born in Oklahoma. So we got well acquainted during a conversation about our Sooner State roots before discussing the reason for his call. Despite his having read the book by Jackson, he needed plenty of information and background on the recent reform efforts in Congress and knew that I could help. But the more important thing he wanted came in a later telephone conversation—my participation in the first discussion class on October 11. After getting routine permission from Boren and the office AA, I agreed.

My trip to Boston was perhaps the most memorable "speech" I made on campaign reform. The event was quickly put on my permanent résumé and biography. The class syllabus read that Congressman Mike Synar, House sponsor of reform legislation, was to join "Greg Kubiak, campaign election law specialist and chief legislative assistant to . . . Boren," but late votes in the House prevented Synar from attending. Thus, the stage was mine to make my case, answer questions, and probe issues. The class of twenty or so intellectually curious students had a willingness to engage in direct debate that made the Senate's embrace of the issue look like a farce.

In a letter to Askew the next day, thanking him for the opportunity to appear before his study group, I related that "I came away from the evening gaining a great deal from the probing questions and interchange," unlike the unconnected and missed dialogue I had grown accustomed to with partisans in Washington. For me, it was an insight into the honorable call of education, thanks to an honorable man from Florida.

The last candidate who deserves mention as someone who falls somewhere between a concerned candidate and a cynical crusader is Jerry Brown. As a presidential candidate, the attention he received was automatic — much greater than any Senate or congressional candidate could receive for national purposes. Brown tried to make his 1992 presidential candidacy a referendum on what he called the "unholy alliance of private greed and corrupt politics." His charge was that "our democratic system has been the object of a hostile takeover [and] . . . money has been the lubricant greasing the deal." (A different view of Brown's background with political money comes in chap. 8.)

One newspaper columnist labeled the former California governor "a certified eccentric," a kinder, gentler label than those given him by his opponents. But the same pundit drew a conclusion about Brown that I shared while watching his 1991–92 candidacy discussion of big money politics: "Brown is the only serious presidential candidate who has limited his own contributions to a maximum of $100 and the only one in either party with the courage and the integrity to spread the ugly truth about the money corruption of our politics."

OTHER ARMIES

One of the often used devices in lobbying for a legislative cause is the coalition. The bringing together of diverse groups who would not ordinarily be united on an issue can give great impetus to legislative efforts.

When Byrd and Boren were pushing the Senatorial Election Campaign Act of 1987, we took the time to develop a strategy with outside interest groups. A fairly strong coalition of groups had already been assembled by Common Cause. But Byrd wanted more of the assembly's allegiance paid to him and S. 2 than to Common Cause. He assigned the coordination of the effort to a Democratic Policy Committee staff person, Sally Mernissi. She constructed a joint letter for Byrd and Boren to sign. The letter said,

> The decision to seek office is as much a financial decision for the potential candidate as it is anything else, and campaigns as a rule become "money chases"—with candidates risking the appearance of becoming beholden to the moneyed interests who finance the campaigns.
>
> It is our firm belief that we must this year make the changes in our campaign finance system . . . [and place] enactment of this bill at the top of our personal priority lists for the 100th Congress.
>
> We hope you will join us in making 1987 a year when we see enactment of legislation that will allow candidates for office to take their cases to the people rather than to moneyed special interests, halt the staggering growth in election costs, and enable senators to spend their time representing their constituents instead of raising money for their next campaigns.
>
> Sincerely yours,   Robert C. Byrd   David Boren

The between-the-lines interpretation of this letter was pointed. It could have read like this:

> You have benefited from Democrats in the Senate who have paid attention to your agenda and given you access to promote it, despite the fact that you don't have a PAC and don't give us campaign contributions. You have fared well by your friends in the Senate who have helped you with legislation you like.
>
> Now, we are coming to you for *your* endorsement of *our* bill. If you expect to continue your good relationship with us, you should get on board. Otherwise, you may not have the kind of "open door" you've come to expect from the new majority leader.

This letter went to approximately sixty groups ranging from the National Council of Senior Citizens, the United Methodist Church, and the National Audubon Society to the Fraternal Order of Police, the American Agricultural Movement, and the National Federation of Business and Professional Women's Clubs.

There was great power in the roster we were able to distribute to Senate offices in May 1987 in preparing for the S. 2 debates. That roster listed sixty-five groups, including the American Association of Retired Persons (AARP), a feared and respected senior citizens lobby.

One group that was almost too late to join the fight for reform was the League of Women Voters (LWV). I drafted an October 8, 1985, memo to Boren, who wanted me to get them and Common Cause briefed and on board with our effort. In it I informed the senator that LWV lobbyist Mary Brooks "is discussing it with their other people and will get back to me later." Boren was confident, as was I, that an endorsement would come from the LWV in short order. Little did I know it would be over two years before the league would support our legislation.

There were other minor players in the allied forces whose agenda was to clean up Congress. One group calling themselves the National Citizens Campaign to Clean Up Congress was well organized but for selfish reasons. In fall 1989, they held a rally and declared October 30 "National Clean Up Congress Day." However, while they claimed that their efforts were to direct attention to "the methods by which congressmen rig the campaign rules to ensure their own reelection," they spent time talking about congressional junkets, votes on pay raises, pensions for convicted congressmen, and campaign funds used for personal expenses. Even though they mentioned "huge campaign war chests from special interests," no specifics were mentioned on how Congress, or the people, should clean up the institution.

Probably the main reason for this was that the people listed on the national steering committee of this makeshift coalition were also vocal opponents of congressional efforts at campaign reform. Several of the persons also had affiliations with either

direct mail/consulting firms or PACs that engaged in independent expenditures themselves. These efforts from leaders of the
Conservative Victory Committee, the Conservative Alliance,
and United Conservatives of America were undertaken more to
elect conservative Republicans to Congress than to clean up the
people's forum of representation. For them, this was yet another
attempt to push their activist agenda under another name.

An unlikely army of allies was a loose coalition called Lobbyists and Lawyers for Campaign Finance Reform. The group
formed in 1987 without outside leadership. I first heard from
them in a telephone call on March 24, 1987, from Bill Baer, an
attorney from the firm of Arnold and Porter in downtown D.C.
He informed me of his willingness to form a group to broadly
support the notion of reform that would fit in nicely with the
Boren-Byrd strategy. We discussed his efforts at trying to get
approximately sixty people to sign on to a "Dear Senator" letter
in favor of strong, comprehensive reform. He asked whether
Boren would be interested in speaking to a breakfast meeting of
30 to 45 members of the group in a few weeks to spur the effort on
and create a press event. I quickly agreed.

I arranged a date, Friday, April 3, with Boren and his sched-
uler/secretary, Carolyn Quinn. I assured the senator of Baer's
promise for "press" at the event, which could mean anything from a
photographer from an "inside-the-beltway" lobbyist magazine to
network coverage. But we decided to take the chance.

The day before the breakfast, before breaking away from the
office long enough to pick up my visiting parents at the airport, I
received a faxed copy of their "Dear Senator" letter staking out
their position. It read, in part:

More has become the sour milk of American politics. That is why we
are today announcing the formation of Lobbyists and Lawyers for
Campaign Finance Reform, a bipartisan group of veteran Washington
lobbyists and lawyers willing to fight for fundamental campaign
financing reform. . . .
In short, our current system . . . diverts scarce time from the
issues; it elevates money above merits; it promotes cynicism in the

electorate. This is not good for you or your staff. It is not good for us or the clients we represent. Most important, it is not good for our democracy.

We do not offer up our own blueprint for reform. We know that the leadership of both Houses is pledged to such reform and that serious efforts are now under way to present comprehensive reform legislation to the Congress. We pledge, individually, and as a group, to support these efforts.

It was a masked endorsement of S. 2.

The next morning, I drove Boren to the law offices of Arnold and Porter, where we were met by a camera crew from CBS News—a victory in the fight for press. The evening news that night played the speech by Boren in a prominent way to show that even the perceived villain lobbyists were feeling victimized by the process.

In addition to national coalitions, a minor influence was felt from movements around the country. Arizona, a state born in the Progressive Era of political movement, was the first to show initiative on PAC reform during our battles.

Proposition 200 was a state referendum that would limit PACs to $2,500 for candidates, while individuals and small PACs could give up to $500—both half of the equivalent limits on the federal level. Any candidate who used $100,000 of his own money in a campaign would lift the limits for his opponent. The initiative also had strong penalties for public officials and candidates who violated the provisions.

One state representative, who helped coordinate the coalition for the "Clean Government Initiative," called me a year after we threw the aggregate PAC limit bombshell. His request was that Boren come to Arizona to help campaign for the state initiative as a national leader for reform. I convinced Boren to do so ten days before the ballot vote, November 4, 1986.

Our national press release, boasting Boren's role "as the national leader of efforts to limit . . . special interest money," said he had "accepted an invitation to speak in Arizona this weekend on behalf of an initiative, patterned after Boren's federal legislation." It noted that the measure, which secured 106,000 signatures, was also supported by Senators Goldwater and DeConcini, both of whom were cosponsors of Boren's bill.

On October 25, Boren and I flew from Tulsa to Tucson for a 10:15 A.M. press conference and then to a rally with coalition supporters at Phoenix's Glendale Community College. With speeches, press interviews and conferences, and the final rally with supporters, Boren helped to enhance the referendum in that State. It won with 64 percent of the vote and gave Arizona the toughest laws among twenty-four states with campaign finance limits.

Minnesota was one of the more important state legislatures to give serious deliberation to passing congressional campaign reform through state statutes. The Elections and Ethics Reform Act of 1990 was a Minnesota State Senate initiative whose findings related that "the need to raise campaign contributions has caused Minnesota congressional candidates to aggressively solicit contributions, diverting them from meeting Minnesota voters and debating pressing issues." Citing the U.S. Congress's inability to pass necessary reforms, the bill set a $3.4 million Senate and a $425,000 House campaign spending limit, under voluntary conditions similar to the current presidential system and Boren's bill.

Hubert H. Humphrey III, Minnesota's attorney general, wrote Senate Majority Leader George Mitchell on February 2, 1990, anticipating a Republican National Committee challenge of the bill once it was enacted. He said that while it was his "legal opinion that the Minnesota proposal would not be preempted by federal law," he wanted Mitchell's support to change the FECA "to explicitly allow states to establish voluntary limits on campaign spending" and avoid a lengthy legal battle. On April 25, the state legislature did indeed pass the first law to create spending limits and partial public financing of congressional campaigns.

While further court cases, state initiatives, and interest group activities would keep the issue of campaign finance reform in front of the electorate, only Congress could bring it about.

CHAPTER SEVEN

"Compel the Attendance"

Each House . . . may be authorized to compel the Attendance of absent Members, in such Manner, and under such Penalties as each House may provide."
—Article I, Section 5, U.S. Constitution

A majority of the Senators present may direct the Sergeant at Arms to request, and, when necessary, to compel the attendance of the absent Senators.
—Rule VI, Standing Rules of the Senate

AFTER THE SEVEN CLOTURE VOTES in the first session of the 100th Congress, 1988 began with no real expectation that the deadlock on campaign finance reform legislation would be reversed. However, a final attempt would be made to force the issue before a reluctant minority of filibustering senators after increasing the pressure for action.

PRESSURE MOUNTS

The presidential primaries were heating up in early 1988, and Bob Dole was under a great deal of public scrutiny about his opposition to S. 2. As the Republican leader, he was seen by many as responsible for the stalemate. With Byrd's assurances that the bill could come up again, the pressure began to mount.

I discussed with Boren the building campaign in the media to hold Republicans accountable as we counted down going to the floor again. In the January 12 Des Moines debate going into the Iowa caucuses, Dole was asked, "Why wouldn't you let this come to a vote? Why did you lead the filibuster? And as president of the United States would you continue to have the same opinion about campaign finance reform?"

Dole responded,

No, I feel strongly about campaign finance reform. I've said so and introduced legislation to do it. But I think we're getting a lot of these liberal Democratic questions thrown at us. And I think we have to address them. It's not campaign reform. In 1986, the Democrats talked about campaign reform, limiting the amount political action committees could give to candidates. But in 1987, they took back the Senate, they didn't change the PAC contributions. Still $5,000 for each election. . . . It doesn't even cut PAC spending. Second, it's public financing, which I think's wrong for 535 Senate and House races. And third, I'm a Republican, and I want the Republican party to grow. And this bill puts a cap on how much you could spend for Senate races. It's an incumbents' protection act. In the South, the Republicans are outnumbered 8 to 1, 4 to 1, 10 to 1. You put a limit on how much a Republican candidate can spend, and the South's going to be Democratic forever. So it's a Democratic incumbent in perpetuity bill. And we're not going to pass it.

Sensing that some of the partisan pressure could be eased on Dole and his colleagues, I drafted a letter for Boren to send out on January 29 to eleven GOP senators seen as crucial to developing any breakthrough compromise. It stated, in part:

As you know, Senate Majority Leader Robert Byrd had indicated last year our intention to recall S. 2 from the Senate calendar to continue consideration of campaign finance reform.

It is my sincere hope that when it does return to the floor for debate, issues which became far too clouded by partisan accusations and false rhetoric can be clarified. I think we all agree that major reform is needed, . . . [and] this measure, which is cosponsored by 52 of our colleagues, . . . [should] be considered. . . .

Negotiations and debate on this issue will occur, perhaps as early as next week.

Boren refused to sign off on the proposed letter, stating that Byrd wanted it to be a "complete surprise" when the bill came before the Senate. I felt then that the tactic used the year before would only be salt on the wounds of crucial Republicans. Just when we should have been more appeasing, Byrd was ready to play hardball. Negotiations would not occur without the threat of the bill coming back up for a vote, but a surprise attack would only make a united Republican Senate fight harder.

Tension continued to build with Senator Simpson being questioned about the filibuster posture of Republicans while on "Meet the Press." Dole was asked about it again at a Harvard debate televised on PBS. And editorials kept coming, too.

The *Los Angeles Times* chimed in on February 7: "Everyone seems to agree that there is a lot wrong with Congress. The institutional gridlock infecting the national legislative body has been reported on in depth. . . . Reform is offered as the cure, but few agree on just what course reform is to take, or how it would be implemented. But there is one obvious place to start, and that is with the money."

A week later, the *New York Times* dubbed S. 2 the "Political Clean Air Act of 1988," stating that "the smell of pervasive privilege and manipulation rises over Washington as one influence-peddling conviction follows another. In the next day or two, there will be a chance to do something about it—if Senate Republicans will finally abandon their adamant opposition."

A Sunday *Post* news story on St. Valentine's Day helped put Dole's role in the proper perspective. That article, headlined "Dole Called Key to Spending Limit Bill," quoted me as an (angry) "Democratic strategist." The story began, "Democrats are preparing to take . . . Dole at his word now that he is telling presidential campaign audiences that he wants to overhaul the rules for financing senatorial campaigns."

I gave the reporter her tone-setting quote for the story when I said of Dole, "He says he wants to negotiate a bill. Okay, we'll negotiate a bill. If he wants to get this thing off his neck, if he wants people to stop following him around with placards asking him where he stands, he can do it now."

Helen Dewar, the reporter on the story, noted our frustration that "Dole claims to be working hard on a solution, playing down his role in the filibuster . . . [by saying], 'It takes forty people to carry our a filibuster, and I'm only one.'" Still angry and willing to share my venom as an unnamed source, Dewar concluded the Sunday piece, "The key, said a Democratic aide involved in the maneuvering, 'is getting some movement from Bob Dole.' This is what Democrats have in mind for next week when the Senate returns from a week-long recess and Dole winds up his New Hampshire primary campaign. 'He knows he's going to get called on it. . . . He's going to get asked to put up or shut up,' said a Democrat. An aide said Dole has a speech prepared in response."

I tried to help Boren keep press interest alive. In midmonth, I developed a letter and information packet for twenty-five key press contacts ranging from network anchors and syndicated columnists to editorial writers and news correspondents. We wanted network, editorial, news story, and opinion piece coverage of S. 2 to put as much light and heat on the issue as possible. The personalized February 19 letter gave an update on negotiations between the four Republicans and four Democrats but mostly warned them that regardless of any breakthrough, Byrd was committed to bring the bill back.

Finally, as hope for negotiations broke down on February 22, a *Post* editorial that same day summed up the issue and set the coming scene for the U.S. Senate.

The sensible bill to limit congressional campaign spending and take the tin cup out of Congress' hands is back on the Senate floor. The Democrats tried for three months last summer to bring it up, but weren't able to; the Republicans filibustered. It was all very decorously done. . . .

Now Majority Leader Robert Byrd is saying no more Mr. Nice Guy. He is threatening to keep the Senate in session around the clock and make the resisting Republicans filibuster in earnest, old style. . . . The talks, which began last week, let [Dole] and the [Republicans] appear to be accommodative on the bill even if they are not.

Because the Republicans oppose public financing of campaigns, the Democrats have also backed the public money about as far out of the bill as they can. A candidate would be eligible for public financing only if he agreed to abide by the limit for his state, his opponent did not, and his opponent then exceeded the limit. The public money would be an insurance policy.

The uneasy Republicans parry this by saying they are also opposed to spending limits and public financing on principle. . . . The Democrats must ask them, and must ask themselves, which do they think is worse: A small federal presence in congressional campaigns or a large For Sale sign on the Senate?

LAST-DITCH EFFORT

The final formal effort to negotiate a bill took the form of a "group of 8" who were appointed by Byrd and Dole to work out a compromise. The Democratic team consisted of Boren, Mitchell, Levin, and Exon. The Republicans, announced by Simpson the morning of February 17, were McConnell, Boschwitz, Packwood, and Stevens. Byrd, who had committed to bring the bill back to the floor, wanted to force compromise by the Republicans. Dole, who was out campaigning for the presidential nomination, just wished it all away.

The next morning's *Post* had a bold, page A4 story reading, "Senate Leaders Seek Compromise on Campaign-Finance Legislation." It might not have been such a story had Simpson not made conciliatory comments that suggested "if they [the Democrats] will get serious with us on soft money, in-kind contributions, we will get serious with them on taxpayer financing and limiting PACs." Despite the staunch opposition to limits by McConnell and Boschwitz, the Simpson comment was a sign of openness that gave me hope.

After Simpson announced the Republican members to the Group of 8, we called members to the first, high-level meeting to occur the next day at 10:00 A.M. I advised Boren beforehand of the points that needed to be raised in this session: to discuss ground rules and a schedule of when the bipartisan group would report to their leaders, to subtly remind the senators that Democrats were committed to bring S. 2 back to the floor for a vote, and to distribute a paper entitled "Principles of Agreement" for their discussion.

Boren concurred with my guidelines, but like me, he knew that this exercise did not look very promising for ending the impasse, Simpson's comments notwithstanding. But that Thursday morning would begin our last-ditch effort. Boren, in true optimistic fashion, brought up his first item of business.

"Now before we get started, when can we meet again? How are your schedules?" Boren asked. "Does Monday work?"

After a few seconds of exchange, the first agreement was reached. The next meeting would be at 1:30 P.M. the following Monday. Quickly growing impatient at Boren's optimism that there would actually be anything worthwhile to discuss, McConnell jumped into the substance of the meeting by expressing that "a lot of people on our side" like the idea of going back to the aggregate limit on PACs legislation that Boren and Goldwater pushed in 1985. A free-for-all discussion ensued.

Mitchell pulled McConnell back to the argument for overall spending limits by telling him he "could make an argument for limits" as a way to help challenging Republicans. McConnell responded that the Republican minority in the House of Representatives was not a result of PAC money or too much spending but of gerrymandering by Democratic state legislatures.

Boschwitz, chairman of the National Republican Senatorial Committee (NRSC), praised Packwood and McConnell as "his leaders" in this group. He then argued that any agreement should include limits on state party GOTV (get-out-the-vote) efforts. As someone apparently stung by labor union help to the Democratic party in his Democratic state, Boschwitz was obviously unaware that members of his party nationally were the real professionals at funneling money for federal elections through state party structures.

Levin, a force in any bipartisan meeting, was quick to take up Boschwitz's offer to limit state party "soft money," as a look of consternation came over McConnell's face.

Exon tried to bring the group back to the issue of spending limits. He questioned his Republican colleagues. How could it be healthy that in a small state like South Dakota, $7 million was spent in the 1986 Senate race, when Boschwitz spent $6 million in the larger state next door?

As he had so many times during floor debate, McConnell responded that it was healthy for voting because in such states, "participation is up."

Exon merely replied, "So what?"

McConnell repeated another charge against limits, that they favor incumbents.

Boren finally jumped in to pull the discussion together by saying they must find some agreement on principles and reminding McConnell that "S. 2 is on the table," not the old Boren-Goldwater bill. At that point, he issued the "Principles of Agreement" I had constructed for him the day before. It listed the four Democratic senators followed by five points in outline form. The five points, with explanation and their rationale, were (1) overall spending limits, (2) enforcement/inducement of the limits, (3) aggregate PAC limits, (4) protections against "independent expenditures," and (5) disclosure of soft money.

By this time, however, no senator wanted to follow a program. But the discussion did come to a climax. Senator Levin asked a direct question of McConnell. "Four years ago, [when the Republicans still controlled the Senate,] would you say that spending limits would still favor Democrats?"

In his reply to Levin, McConnell showed himself to be more an immovable ideologue than a worthy partisan opponent: "Carl, I don't care, because I'm philosophically opposed" to spending limits.

While other GOP negotiators were there to see that Democrats created no partisan advantage with campaign finance law changes, McConnell was there as a detached loner. He showed himself not only opposed to a Democratic reform but closed to any rewrite of the law that was not of his handiwork. This attitude was clearly why he made few political alliances, even among Republicans. His later defeat for a Republican leadership position might have been due to what one colleague said of him: "Mitch has no friends among Democrats *or* Republicans."

Mitchell closed out the questioning of McConnell and the morning's meeting by asking him why he was so "philosophically against overall limits and not the millionaire's loophole," which allowed wealthy individuals to spend unlimited sums of their own money for their campaigns. McConnell endorsed the notion of widespread *financial* involvement of citizens in the political process by responding that the campaign funds could come "from a lot of people." He never did see the point that the *personal* involvement of people in the process was being threatened by the campaigns of slick media consultants and negative campaign ads, paid for by PACs and wealthy donors.

The second and last meeting of the group occurred Monday as planned. Packwood could not attend because of a speech he was giving at the University of Virginia. In a note to Boren on Friday, the 19th, he apologized for not being able to attend and warned Boren, "Don't take any precipitous steps without me."

Nothing "precipitous" happened. Nothing constructive happened either. The Republicans, who promised to present a detailed proposal to the Democrats, had a two-page outline of a bill entitled The Campaign Spending and Reform Act of 1988. While it discussed PACs, nonparty soft money, bundling, and broadcast rates, its mention of spending limits was heavily disguised. Listed under the provision to "establish a bipartisan commission," such a body could "examine and report on the effectiveness of taxpayer financing and limits on both candidate and noncandidate spending."

The Republican "good faith" effort in discussing real limits was to kick it to a blue ribbon commission, a way to ensure further delay. With such a response, there was an obvious impasse and no room for negotiation.

This was the last straw for the patient Democrats. After the 1:30 meeting, which was polite but shrouded with angry disappointment, Boren informed Byrd of the GOP position. Byrd called a 4:30 meeting with Boren and his three helpers, along with Senators Ford as Rules chairman and Kerry as Democratic Senatorial Campaign Committee chairman. I patiently waited outside of this meeting of the chieftains. When it was over, in a short time, the decision about what to do next was made: bring the bill to the floor, and call off the "gentlemen's filibuster."

TO COMPEL OR NOT TO COMPEL

On Tuesday, February 23, a great photo opportunity occurred for the benefit—and to the dismay—of both supporting and opposing members. Majority Leader Byrd directed Capitol workers to set up cots in the Mansfield Room of the Capitol to dramatize what an old-fashioned filibuster was supposed to be like. It was an old tradition to have sleeping pallets for tired senators to nap on in the wee hours between votes during all-night sessions. Around-the-clock sessions in modern days were reserved for budget deadlines so that omnibus spending bills could be passed to keep the government's doors open. But rarely would the majority leader of the Senate keep the day's session going on an issue that was not of imminent or landmark significance.

Senator Cochran, a Mississippi Republican, took a dim view of the tactic, claiming, "They [the Democrats] are just trying to attract some attention." But Byrd was unmovable. "There's no point in having an easy gentlemen's filibuster back in the cloakrooms. Let's have it right here on the Senate floor where the American people can see it. Let's let the American people ponder this: Do they want their U.S. Senate seats up for sale?"

Behind the scenes, however, in the weekly Tuesday caucus luncheons, Democrats were not looking forward to the theatrics of an all-night session in what many thought was a fruitless fight. Some were grumbling that such a move would only deepen the divisions between Democrats and Republicans. They feared that

Republicans could turn the issue around on the stubborn Democrats to show that they were using hardball tactics to get their way.

There had been a long drought and cynical chasm since the seventh cloture vote on S. 2 on September 15. But Republicans most assuredly got the message that another attempt would be made when on February 1 of the new year, a clear Senate calendar allowed Majority Leader Byrd to place S. 2 back on the calendar without the necessity of requesting unanimous consent.

To be clear, it should be pointed out that the "pending business" was not merely the bill, S. 2. To protect the majority proponents against the parliamentary devices available to the minority opponents, we devised a way to shield S. 2 from further amendments, motions, or intervening actions. The technical process is referred to in the Senate as "filling the amendment tree."

A bill can be changed by amendment (in the first degree), and that amendment can further be amended (in the second degree). Therefore, if S. 2 had been brought to the floor alone, the opponents could, for example, try to amend it by stripping out spending limits and public financing, in return for a congressional pay cut and a ban on PACs. Such a move is referred to as "loving a bill to death" — amending it with items that sound good on the surface but together make passage of the package unlikely. So, Byrd filed an extraneous amendment to S. 2, followed by a Boren second-degree amendment, that was the unaltered Boren-Byrd bill language. (This maneuver is referred to as "filling the amendment tree.") This would ensure that the first vote on S. 2 would be on the substance of the bill. Republican amendments on PAC bans or pay cuts could follow afterward.

There is also the possibility of a "motion to recommit." Such a motion is nondebatable and would be a likely way to diffuse criticism for voting against S. 2. Thus, Boren and Byrd made pending "motion to recommit the bill, with instructions" to Rules committee "to report back forthwith" that same Boren-Byrd language.

I realize that to the layman, such maneuvers look like lawyerly theatrics at best and political gamesmanship at worst. But as a nonlawyer who worked in the Senate for seven years, I can fully see that the founding fathers and subsequent Senate leaders sought to respect and protect the rights of minority opinion. That has always been a feature of the six-year-term, deliberative body, the U.S. Senate.

Three weeks and two days after Byrd placed the bill on the Senate calendar, the frontal attack began. With the cots set up, Byrd dared the filibuster to begin. It started quietly enough on February 23, 1988, when the Senate convened at 10:00 A.M. to consider and debate S. 2.

A guest chaplain from Byrd's West Virginia opened the Senate that day. He implored the Almighty to "let fear dissipate and the challenge of this day succumb to Your influence ministered through these vessels in the Chamber of law." While the fear did dissipate, the challenge would last longer than a typical day for most Americans. That "day" in the Senate would drag on for fifty-seven hours.

After a routine number of varied speeches on "morning business," Byrd addressed the subject and the bill, S. 2, on its being called up as the pending business of the Senate. There was no need for a final warning of what was in store, so he set the tone by saying only, "I know of no matter that is more important to the integrity of this institution or the integrity of our political process than the matter of campaign financing reform." A hush, as though the quiet before the storm, descended on the chamber as the Senate recessed at 12:47 P.M.

As the 23rd was a Tuesday, the Senate took its weekly break to allow both parties to have their caucus luncheons. Boren was present in the Democratic luncheon off the floor to appease the fears of skeptical Democrats who thought the threat of a real old-fashioned filibuster was ill-conceived. After addressing the caucus in support of Byrd's strategy, he passed around a piece of paper to get senators to sign up then and there for duty on the floor. With the likelihood of a late, or all-night, session, Boren needed warm bodies to make hot speeches.

The sheet came back to me with the names and times scribbled by the senators themselves: Harry Reid, Ted Kennedy, Jim Exon, George Mitchell, Jeff Bingaman, W. Ford, and so on. The luncheon, closed to staff members, adjourned around 2:00 P.M. I was waiting for Boren on the floor. Then the moment came for the session to reconvene and for a parliamentary battle. Weighted down with two armloads of binders and folders, tabbed and organized with facts, figures, and arguments, we were prepared.

Boren and I debated parliamentary tactics that could be used by the opponents to thwart our efforts at a "real" filibuster. Senate Rule XIX technically disallows any senator from making more than two speeches on one matter before the body without an intervening session. Boren and Byrd would obviously need to be on the floor most of the time of debate to guard the rights of the majority. However, as is usual, there are rarely more than three or four senators on the floor at a given time. The opponents of S. 2 could simply wait for Boren to make his "two speeches" and for no other Democrat to be on the floor, and they could control the debate. Likewise, if no senator was present to object, any senator could technically seek unanimous consent for the Senate to adjourn, thus killing our desire to force Republicans to filibuster.

Boren addressed the chair to seek recognition. Fearful of the possible use of the little-used two speech rule, he said, "Mr. President, I ask unanimous consent that I might make some introductory comments about the pending matter, S. 2, without it counting against the number of speeches that I may give on this subject."

McConnell—having assumed the floor manager's position, in this case Bob Dole's minority leader desk—did not object or was not paying attention. Boren began a long off-the-cuff speech that reviewed the bidding, reported on the Democratic caucus discussion, and explained the essential elements of a "real reform" bill. McConnell made a similar report only after getting assurances that he too would be spared from the rarely enforced rules of the Senate.

The Question is on the Amendment

Later in the afternoon, Stevens spoke of his disappointment at the breakdown of the Group of 8 negotiations:

Mr. President, I am saddened by the continued difference in the Senate over this bill because I think we could agree, now, on a campaign reform proposal that could actually apply this fall. I am certain we could devise one that would be in effect by 1990 and work and improve this system. But if we are to continue to battle over the question of whether expenditure limitations are the sine qua non, the essence of a bill without which the majority will not support the concept, then I think it is going to be a long, long debate.

At this point, Senator Burdick, a close friend of Senator Byrd's and one of the inspirations for Boren's convictions about the "PAC game," was the presiding officer. There being no other senator seeking recognition, Burdick announced, "The question is on the amendment." Such a call was the Senate's warning that without any further debate or previously consented time agreement, the Senate was prepared to vote.

Stevens quickly jumped to his feet and said, "Mr. President, I suggest the absence of a quorum."

Byrd, tiring of the delay and ready to force the filibuster, rose thereafter to address the chair as well. "Mr. President, I ask unanimous consent that the order for the quorum call be rescinded."

The presiding officer, Burdick, renewed his statement. "Without objection, it is so ordered. The question is on the amendment."

Stevens, growing angry at what was about to happen, repeated his request to the presiding officer, "Again, I suggest the absence of a quorum."

This time, after Burdick instructed the clerk to "call the roll," unlike the typical slow approach to the traditional delaying device, the clerk read the roll at a regular pace to "ascertain the presence of a quorum."

On that count, only seven senators were recorded as present: Boren, Byrd, Stevens, Burdick, Exon, Packwood, and Bill Armstrong of Colorado. Knowing that the Senate could technically be recessed without having a quorum of fifty-one senators present, Byrd stood again to address the chair.

MR. BYRD: *Mr. President, I move that the sergeant at arms be instructed—*
MR. PACKWOOD (interrupting): *Mr. President, I was going to move that the order for the quorum called be rescinded.*
MR. BYRD: *Mr. President, I move that the sergeant at arms be instructed to request the attendance of absent senators, and I ask for the yeas and nays.*
PRESIDING OFFICER: *Is there a sufficient second? There is a sufficient second. The yeas and nays were ordered. . . . The clerk will call the roll.*

Byrd's motion was another step in getting attendance of senators to assure that the Republicans could not force the Democrats out of session. Packwood's interruption may have been his attempt to gain the floor to request an immediate adjournment of the Senate as it lacked a quorum. But Byrd went the next step in getting the live quorum through the "motion to request."

Such a motion is merely a roll call vote, the absence from which a senator's roll call attendance percentage would decrease. No senator wants to purposefully miss a roll call vote. Incumbents seeking reelection have lost their seats after being charged as "absentee" senators. Therefore, the first vote was called.

The procedural vote began at 4:37 P.M. when a "motion to instruct" the sergeant at arms to request the attendance of absent senators was agreed to 71 to 18. Two more of these redundant and fruitless votes were called—one at 8:30 and another at 9:51 P.M. However, approximately fifteen senators missed those 57 to 17 and 57 to 21 tallies. It looked as though a Republican strategy was being developed.

Sen. Pete Wilson (R-Calif.) made a floor speech after that third vote. Simpson, still the Republican manager, thanked his

Republican colleague for his remarks and said, "We apparently have a large agenda of those speakers tonight and on into the morning. That is regrettable, but that is the test I guess that confronts us. But awaiting some members, I suggest the absence of a quorum."

Byrd, worried that some of his own members might have left to go home, asked to rescind the quorum call. Simpson, feeling confident in the evolving GOP strategy, objected to Byrd's request, and the clerk called the roll yet again.

Present at that time were twelve Democratic senators and Simpson. Seeing no quorum, Byrd jumped in again with a motion to instruct. That fourth roll call vote, called at 10:43 P.M., not only resulted in a 47 to 1 tally but confirmed for Byrd and Boren the Republican strategy. Republicans wanted to "boycott" the session. All the Republicans would have to do is ensure that one Republican senator was on the floor to guard their concerns, while all the rest avoided the floor. If enough Democrats were absent, without a required quorum of a majority of the Senate, Simpson could force the Senate to adjourn. With only forty-eight senators having answered that late-night roll call, the proponents faced the embarrassing prospect of having to adjourn the session. The required quorum of fifty-one senators was three short.

The Arrest

The only thing for Byrd, our parliamentary manager, to do was fight fire with fire. If playing by the rules is what Republicans wanted, Byrd was determined to give them a fight. Thus, he dusted off an obscure tool from the rule books which declared that in order for the Senate to properly function, a majority could "compel" the attendance of absent senators. Tradition had developed over time and precedent that "compel" could mean "arrest." So, at 11:00 P.M., Senator Byrd made the motion to counter the strategy of absent senators. They were purposefully trying to block the majority of the Senate who wanted to be in session to debate campaign finance reform.

I clearly recall Byrd on the floor as he stared directly at the presiding officer, Sen. Barbara Mikulski of Maryland. With a determined look, he said, "Madam President, I move that the sergeant at arms be instructed to *arrest* the absent senators and bring them to the chamber, and I ask for the yeas and nays on the motion." The word "arrest" was spoken with resolute authority. Boren's face had a nervous, cautious grin.

While the arrest motion passed by a vote of 45 to 3, it did not represent the needed quorum of fifty-one. Later, two lost Democrats would be found, but at least one more would still be needed to thwart the Republican strategy to force adjournment.

The three Democrats voting against the arcane motion, DeConcini and Alabamians Howell Heflin and Richard Shelby, represented more than just minority Democratic displeasure. Not only did the late hour, 11:00 P.M., not sit well but the strategy of forcing a compromise did not seem to be working.

Republican senators had been meeting in the cloakroom off the Senate floor to develop strategy. Seeing the impending manhunt for one more senator, they scattered. Once the motion passed, the sergeant at arms, Henry Giugni, and his assistants, scoured the history books to see how to "arrest" senators. This was the first time in over forty-five years that an arrest motion was to be carried out, and no one knew with certainty how to do it. The first thing to do was issue "warrants."

In 1942, the Senate was debating a bill to abolish poll taxes when opposing southern senators refused to attend the session. Warrants were issued, and public accounts indicate that three were arrested or escorted back to the chamber. Senate historians later reported that only twice since that arrest—in 1950 and 1976—was an arrest motion made and passed. However, in both those instances, the arrests did not have to be carried out as the threat alone brought senators to the floor.

As Senator Levin took the floor to make remarks about the bill, we knew that at our last count, only one senator was needed to make quorum. The sergeant at arms and a contingent of five

Capitol policemen, armed with "warrants," began their search for one lone, hiding Republican.

U.S. Senate—Washington, D.C., February 23, 1988
TO: Henry K. Giugni: Sergeant at Arms, United States Senate
The undersigned, presiding officer of the Senate, by virtue of the power vested in me, hereby commands you in pursuance of the order of the Senate, this day made, to forthwith arrest and take into custody and bring to the bar of the Senate *(name of absent senator)*, who is absent without leave, to wit:
Hereof fail not and made due return of this warrant.
In testimony whereof I have hereunto set my hand and caused to be affixed the seal of the United States Senate, this 23 day of February 1988.
BROCK ADAMS, Presiding Officer

Sen. Lowell Weicker (R-Conn.) was spotted in the Capitol and approached by the band. However, his large frame, raging temper, and obstinate condition suggested that they look for a less violent subject. Senator Symms was seen in the Capitol but outran his pursuers.

Resorting to the Russell Senate Office Building, the posse had a lead from a cleaning lady that Packwood was hiding out in his personal office. Giugni had a master key that he used to enter the office and ambush the Oregon senator. With one door bolted and another blocked with a large chair, Packwood would later say, "I thought I was safe." Hearing the door opening, Packwood went to hold it shut, but the force was too great. The fifty-first senator was caught.

Packwood agreed to be escorted to the Capitol but stopped short of the Senate chamber doors. Packwood told Giugni and the officers that that would be as far as he would go. They would have to carry him the rest of the way. With no animosity at the late-night theatrics, two officers lifted the senator and carried him feetfirst onto the floor.

At 1:17 A.M., with the quorum roll call still pending, Packwood, on regaining his feet, announced, "Here." The session could go on.

Byrd thought of one way to keep the senators' feet to the fire in session. He temporarily went to the "executive calendar" at 2:30 A.M. to allow a vote on one of the president's nominations. This vote would be of interest to Republicans who wanted to support President Reagan and not miss another roll call vote. With Byrd threatening to call up nominations, Republicans would no longer stray far from the floor.

After the wee-hour arrest and the maintenance of quorum, the late debate on reform continued. Weicker, out of hiding and ready to debate, took to the floor at around 3:00 A.M. on February 24. He was armed with the Senate Watergate committee reports from years earlier to use in his defense against public financing of elections.

I nearly started to doze off on the comfortable staff couches in the rear of the Senate chamber during Weicker's discombobulated speech. But two more "bed check" votes called at 3:02 and 5:47 kept me awake. I went back to the office after the vote. I took off my tie and shoes and laid on the couch in our AA's office for an hour-and-a-half nap. But by 7:30 A.M., I roused myself, knowing it was time to get ready for a new day.

I was a member of a health club just a few blocks from the Capitol. I drove over to the gym in my car, which was packed with an overnight bag and clean clothes. I showered, shaved, and dressed. Back at the office before 9:00, others on staff started to arrive. Always in the office early, Charlie greeted me with his typically sunshiny question, "How far do you skip, little pot?"

That day, we started to lose the fight. "Did you hear they arrested Packwood last night?" and "How long do you think the Democrats will force this filibuster?" were the questions on the lips of everyone on the Hill.

Rather than substance, the reform bill was becoming a "Style" section story to the public and other staffers. Besides, it was a "Republican" filibuster that forced the majority supporters to use the arrest motion. Packwood even had a press conference in which Giugni joined him to explain the late night maneuver in entertaining detail. All of a sudden, Packwood was a celebrity, and the arrest was a new topic of discussion.

Aside from the off-the-floor debate, the chamber was filled with acrimony. Senator Hatch called the arrest a "Kafkaesque episode." Specter took the floor to protest "tyranny of the majority leader" and to make a motion to reconsider the vote calling for the arrest. His protest was a legal/constitutional distraction to take the debate off of policy and on to process. (Weeks later he would actually lead a failed effort to change the rules of the Senate on the use of the arrest.)

Byrd later criticized the diversion of attention to the arrest instead of the bill being debated. It was his opinion that senators "are supposed to be grown-up people, not kids. They are the ones who made the calculated decision to run and hide."

In the office that morning, I was downing cup after cup of coffee. After the weekly 9:00 A.M. staff meeting, I tried to return some of the calls coming in. People were anxious to know what private negotiation might be going on and what had happened overnight. I talked to staffers with Senators Kennedy, Levin, Simon, Patrick Leahy (D-Vt.), Bob Graham (D-Fla.) and McConnell. Press calls from the *New York Times* editorial page editor and others came in as well.

But on the floor, the speeches dragged on, and by afternoon, votes on motions to instruct started again. At 2:00, 3:00, and a little before 6:00 P.M., votes occurred. I had been walking between the office to return calls and the floor to help senators during debate. It was an important function for either Bunton or me to be on the floor at all times so that if a senator was caught on a question, we could help out.

On the floor after the third vote of that afternoon—thirty-two hours after that session convened—I got a note from Boren, who was back in the office for a while.

I talked to Mitchell and they [sic] said I won't need to be here until 10 A.M.—there is an agreement on no votes tonight—so go home and get some rest—we'll be responsible from 10 A.M. to noon. DLM

It did not happen that quickly. After all, I still had calls to
return and a responsibility to cover the floor in case another
Democratic senator had questions. Boren had other business to
tend to as well but got out of the office earlier than I did. I did not
get relieved of my duties to the other issue areas as a legislative
assistant. I was still responsible for activities relating to banking,
education, justice, government, and postal legislation. I would
have to catch up on some of those calls and correspondence, too.
But I did manage to go home before midnight, calling the cloakroom staff to check if I was needed before retiring. I managed a
solid six hours of sleep before getting back to the office.

Pending on the Senate floor on day three of the filibuster was
"a motion to table the Specter motion to reconsider the vote" on
the arrest. With much of the day devoted to the secondary issue,
a vote finally came at 3:48 P.M. on February 25. Fortunately, his
effort failed by a narrow 47 to 45 margin. After that point, little
could be said or done. With the public attention diverted and
Republican opposition remaining solid, our chances at shaking
loose a few votes or negotiating on a landmark compromise were
lost. Instead, Boren and Byrd agreed that we would just ask the
Republicans for a final cloture vote to be taken the next day, after
adjourning the Senate. After fifty-seven hours of continuous
debate, the Senate went out of session at 7:24 P.M.

I was physically drained after only sleeping eight of the last
sixty hours. After collecting a few things from the office, like my
razor and toothbrush, I went home for a real night's rest.

The next morning, after my car was disabled by a flat tire on
North Capitol Street, I parked at a service station and walked the
extra mile to my office. There was no time to take care of the tire
problem as I was already running late at 8:00. It was a brisk day
with a sharp sun. This was the first chance I really had to reflect
on what I was doing this week. I had spent what seemed to be
endless hours at the office with telephone calls, briefings, visits
with the senator, strategy sessions with staffers, Common Cause,
and other members, listening to debate, answering questions,
questions, questions.

Although I was disappointed with the results of this "Great Debate," I was still in the storm's eye. I was protected from being exploited by the system I sought to change. I was not the interest group lobbyist being harassed by members looking for contributions. I was not the challenger/candidate seeking to overcome an uneven playing field created by PAC money. I was not a senator worrying about how to raise $3 million to win my next campaign. I was a staffer in the learning dome's shadows, trying to straighten its image and strengthen our democracy.

Having overcome my bad mood and invigorated myself with a mile-and-a-half walk, I was at the office. After going to my desk and settling my things, it was time for the inevitable. Like a death row inmate having made peace with his plight, I walked to the Senate floor for that final vote. The predictable outcome in that February 26 ballot would be the eighth cloture vote, breaking a seventy-one-year record. Never before under the turn-of-the-century cloture rules had the Senate tried so many times to break a filibuster on a single bill.

With the absence of two known supporters of S. 2, we were seven votes short of halting the filibuster that day. Our final tally on S. 2 was 53 to 41.

The Aftermath

The filibuster in the Senate is a frustrating tool of delay. Several senators complained that its frequent use was a signal of the body's failure at compromise and leadership. That particular filibuster and arrest were not carried out with full support from the Democrats either. A day after the final vote, the *Congressional Quarterly* news magazine reported that the posturing for the distant leadership races was connected to this bill's strategy and outcome.

> Every Senate Democrat wants to know for sure about whether Robert C. Byrd will seek another term as Senate majority leader after the 1988 elections. . . . Senate sources say the leading candidates intensified their campaigning significantly in the last two weeks. That activity was part of the background against which Byrd followed a controversial hardball strategy for pushing campaign finance legislation.

Whether or not the result of the strategy and the arrest had an impact on Byrd's ability to be reelected as his party's leader, no one knows. Byrd eventually chose not to run. Instead, he took the position of Senate president pro tempore, replacing the retiring Senator Stennis. In an interview years later, one high-level aide told me that he felt that Byrd "saw it as entirely a parliamentary phenomenon . . . [used to] embarrass the opposition," more than a strategy to force a compromise with Republicans.

In an interview for ABC's "20/20" news program aired in June of that year, Sen. David Pryor (D-Ark.) talked to a reporter during the filibuster. Pryor said, "It doesn't look like either side is going to break on this issue yet." While reflecting on his filmed Senate subway ride to a quorum call vote, Pryor continued his frustrated lament. "I don't know if a vote is ten minutes away or ten hours away. You can't leave to go to dinner because you might get called back for a vote. You can't go home. You're sort of trapped in these walls." With the camera showing the subway's journey through the monotonous white tunnel, Pryor concluded, "Once we come to work in these buildings in the morning, very seldom do we ever see the daylight. We walk through the tunnels. We ride the subways. So in a way, we live like moles, I guess."

For the Republican opponents, the battle could be summed up by a simple statement made by Senator Simpson a week before the filibuster began. In a floor statement on February 17, he said, "There is a reason, a very simple reason, why some of us on this side of the aisle are blocking campaign finance reform. To us, it is a matter of survival."

Where they perceived a fight for partisan survival, we saw obstruction of critical reform. Only hindsight will tell who was right.

As for the process by which the policy might have been enacted, another insight is worth exposing. In the same program for which Pryor was interviewed, a Republican spoke his mind on the breakdown of the process. Sen. Dan Quayle (R-Ind.) got his digs in about those late-night filibuster votes, showing bipartisan disdain for the process. "This legislation, for example, has absolutely no chance of passing this year. . . . It only takes a few people to know the rules and procedures and intricacies of the Senate to thwart what a good majority would like to do."

Quayle, the future vice president, was right on both counts. The legislation would not pass in 1988. And one thing was sure. It would be a long time before the wounds would heal from the anger over the 1988 vote, which was no gentlemen's filibuster. But some words of wisdom did come during the fray.

Perhaps the campaign reform argument during the February filibuster, if not the entire congressional session, came from Sen. George Mitchell, chairman of the Democratic Senatorial Campaign Committee, in the wee hours of February 24. I was among the few persons listening at 4:00 A.M. The point it made to Republican opponents was a telling one.

> The spending limits in this legislation will not protect incumbents. Rather, the legislation will restore a balance to the election process by imposing far tougher limits on the spending of incumbents than on the spending of challengers.
> I would like to make a prediction here: The Republican members of the Senate have repeatedly argued, on and off the Senate floor, that if this bill is passed, they will become a permanent minority. I say that the surest guarantee that they will become a permanent minority is if this bill is *not* passed, because what we are seeing is the Democratic party now with 54 percent of the Senate. After this election, it is likely to be somewhere between 55 percent and 60 percent.
> Increasingly . . . Democratic incumbents have been able to establish themselves and through the enormous fund-raising advantage of the incumbents, have virtually ensured their continued reelection. I predict that if this bill is not passed, there will not be a Republican majority in the U.S. Senate again in this century.

Mitchell's prediction came true with a net gain of a seat for the Democrats in both the 1988 and 1990 elections. The Democrats held their fifty-seven-seat majority in the 1992 elections. Dole made a wish after 1988 that he would again be able to serve his country as the "Senate majority leader." He might have been able to help that happen, if he had only heard the speech that morning by the future majority leader, George Mitchell.

BLACK BOOK

One of the first and most important lessons I learned in politics was to never put anything in writing you wouldn't want printed on the front page of the *Daily Oklahoman*. It was an axiom probed and discussed in depth with my fellow field representative and friend, Paul Gaines, when I worked in Oklahoma City.

Of course, the name of the newspaper can be interchanged with any visible or audible medium of communication, but the point is that your words can come back to haunt you. As a tool to utilize during the CFR deliberations, I constructed a little "black book," filled with statements, op-ed's, letters to constituents, and transcripts from interviews of members of the Senate. Several of them were "on the record" in support of features of S. 2 and our subsequent bill but opposed us when the votes were counted.

Senator Dave Durenberger (R), on March 25, 1987, in a letter to a Minnesota constituent, stated, "Effective campaign finance reform can only be accomplished by examining the entire system, looking at *all* sources of contributions. This includes looking to limit the length of campaigns and the amount spent on them."

Despite this stated concern for campaign spending, Durenberger consistently voted against S. 2. But by the next Congress, Durenberger changed his position and voted for the legislation, which was largely the same bill regarding limits and financing.

The difference was not so much in the language of S. 2 in 1988 or S. 137 in 1990 as it was in the fact that Durenberger was under close, nationally televised scrutiny by the Senate Ethics Committee for financial misdealings. Those indiscretions led to his being indicted in 1993.

Senator Daniel Evans (R), on March 18, 1987, in testimony before the Rules and Administration Committee, stated, "We simply must rein in this cost growth. I believe there is no surer road to a complete breakdown of our electoral process than to ignore burgeoning campaign costs." Evans consistently voted against Boren-Byrd.

Senator Howell Heflin (D), on June 5, 1987, in a letter to an Alabama constituent, wrote, "Something must be done to put an end to the disproportionate role that finances play in politics. . . . action needs to be taken to make ideas, not money, the most important issue in a campaign. . . . We should attack the true culprit in our political system—out-of-control spending."

The true culprit of campaign finance reform were those who denounced excessive spending and then voted against a moderate bill to limit it. Heflin was one of three Democrats who stubbornly opposed S. 2, while supporting an infringement of the First Amendment with a constitutional amendment to limit spending instead.

Senator William Roth (R), on May 15, 1987, in a speech in the *Congressional Record*, said, "Lowering the overall costs of campaigns, reducing the need for astronomical war chests, and shortening campaigns would clearly be a welcome reform in American politics." The Delaware lawmaker had eight chances to give that reform to the American people but chose to vote against S. 2.

Senator Richard Shelby (D), on April 29, 1987, in his "Report from Washington" column appearing in the Jasper, Alabama, *Daily Mountain Eagle* wrote, "Campaign spending is just too high. The stakes are too precious to allow our election process to become a contest between who can raise and spend the most money."

Like Heflin, he never supported S. 2. In fact, he was reluctant to support even the PAC limits. In later efforts, Boren could not have a conversation with him that Shelby did not ask about the aggregate PAC limit and whether its effective date would hamper his fund raising for his 1992 campaign.

Senator Bob Packwood (R), under pressure in his 1986 election campaign, was caused to follow the David Boren model of fund raising by swearing off solicitation of PAC money. Yet his high ideal of representing people instead of special interests wore off in a short six years.

In a trick-or-treat surprise, the *Roll Call* newspaper reported on Halloween 1991 that the Oregon senator reversed "a previous decision not to accept money from political action committees in his quest for a fourth term." Packwood's campaign manager argued that the decision would allow the senator to "fight a battle on four fronts" and that with no self-imposed limit on fund raising, the campaign hoped to raise $5 million.

Packwood was a forceful opponent of campaign reform, devising "one-better" approaches that conveniently fit into his mode of fund raising. In negotiations during the 102nd Congress, he pushed the notion of limiting all individual contributions to focus on the small donor—in the $250 or even $100 range. Packwood knew that Democrats were not at parity with Republicans in terms of small donor fund raising. As the "Crowned Prince" of direct mail solicitation (perhaps only second to Senator Helms), Packwood saw this as the rhetorical high road.

Senator Alfonse M. D'Amato (R) was quoted in the *New York Times* as supporting the congressional limits and public financing that evolved from S. 2. In the midst of his own 1989 ethics problems, the article quoted D'Amato as saying that the questions coming out of the Wedtech scandal "changed my attitude toward public financing of elections; I'm for it now."

I drafted a letter for Boren the next day.

October 6, 1989

Dear Al,

I was interested in your comments published in yesterday's *New York Times* regarding campaign finance.

I have enclosed a summary of my legislation which provides for campaign spending limits and partial public financing, as well as aggregate political action committee limits. I hope you will closely review this bill as it is a careful compromise based on last Congress' Boren-Byrd bill.

Thank you for your interest and comments.

Sincerely,
David L. Boren

No response was ever received.

CHAPTER EIGHT

Puppets and the Press

You are here and life exists and that the powerful play goes on,
you may contribute a verse. What will your verse be?
— *ROBIN WILLIAMS,*
in the 1989 film, Dead Poets Society

I have always strenuously supported the right of every man to
his own opinion however different that opinion might be to
mine. He who denies to another this right makes a slave of
himself to his present opinion because he precludes himself the
right of changing it.
— *THOMAS PAINE*

THERE WAS A GREAT DEAL OF HAND-WRINGING over
the perceived bias of the news media during the 1992 presidential campaign. Vice President Dan Quayle labeled their influence
as part of the "cultural elite." Regardless of any "liberal bias"
the press may have, it unarguably does have a strong impact on
the information the public receives and its perceptions about
issues — governmental, political, business, social, and cultural.

But the actions of players other than the press can create
impressions equally as strong. Some of those individuals, however, are no more than puppets on strings — tied to vices and self-
protection more than the cause of "doing the right thing." Many
players in the campaign finance reform debate had visible halos
that did not match their inner souls. These participants in the

205

political process deserve to have the curtain raised to reveal where the strings of these puppets lead.

But the first line of inquiry into who helps us form our opinions, must be the defenders of the First Amendment right to a free press.

THE PRESS: ACCOUNTS AND EFFECTS

Television

Positive network coverage of a legislative project is considered a trophy for legislators. And for a staff person helping to coordinate the catch, it is a thrill as well.

The press coverage relating to campaign reform over the years was generally favorable to comprehensive reformers like David Boren. The media seems to be skeptical of elected officials whom they oversee and cover. While they often sensationalize stories on Congress or the White House, I respect their responsibility to report to the public. Fairness and balance of reporting is often in the eye of the beholder.

My first experience with helping to set up a major media story came in early 1986. The Boren-Goldwater bill was subject to Senate hearings and expected action later that year. Common Cause had just released a study on PAC contributions to congressional tax-writing committee members, and the tax reform bill of 1986 was being marked up in the Senate Finance Committee. It was a perfect scenario for a hard-hitting story on money, influence, PACs, and my boss—the reformer.

On the afternoon of January 15, I got a call from Ed Hersh, a producer for ABC's "20/20" who had questions about the senator's PAC bill and why it was important. He said the program was interested in doing a story on PACs and reform efforts and he would be back in touch. I went to tell our press secretary the good news.

The next morning, Hersh again called to confirm ABC's interest in the story. He asked more questions about who to talk to and how to go about setting up a taping of Boren. After giving

some names, facts, PAC contribution figures, and my best pitch
on how to tell the story, I asked him to work with Boren's press
secretary to coordinate an interview appointment. In less than
two weeks, a reporter came to tape an interview of Boren, who
gave a line used in the promotional piece for "20/20": "When
special interests control the financing for campaigns, Congress
is verrrry unlikely to act in the *national* interest." Victory! It was
a great sound-bite for a great story. John Stossal gave drama to
the tale needing to be told.

Opening the segment with a predawn shot of the Capitol
building, Stossal's voice intoned, "It's shortly after dawn in
Washington." The picture switches to the corridor outside a
Senate hearing room with business-attired persons standing in a
growing line. "Yet here on Capitol Hill, already a line is forming
in this hallway. Who are these people? Tourists anxious to see
government in action? No! Almost all of them are lobbyists.
Lobbyists waiting to get into the room where the Senate Finance
Committee will discuss tax reform."

Stossal discovers that the lobbyists represent interests like the
American Trucking Association, Atlantic Richfield, and the
distilled spirits industry. While pointing through the hearing
room door, he asks, "Who do these senators represent? You and
me, or the special interests?"

Then comes the graphic showing $6.7 million went from PACs
in 1985 to members of the House and Senate tax-writing committees. The story continued and gave the proper twist to the money-
raising system that we were committed to change.

Coverage like this was always a gamble. ABC could easily
have found that Boren was not worthy of the title "reformer." A
graphic on his large percentage of individual contributions from
oil producers, for instance, could turned the story into a call for
broader reform than the PAC limits we proposed. For our
purposes, it was a home run.

Four months prior to the airing of "20/20," another network
gave a similar slant in our favor after the first vote on our bill. In
reporting on the PAC legislation sponsored by Boren and Gold-

water, Dan Rather gave a strong introduction on his "CBS Evening News" on December 3, 1985, by cynically asking the viewers a question midsentence: "After its first floor debate on PACs in eight years, guess what? The Senate decided it needed more time to study the issue."

That report looked at how PACs decided to direct the $113 million in contributions they gave in the 1984 elections. Correspondent Phil Jones was less than subtle in his indictment and illustration of the system when he stated that, for incumbents, "it's easier raising a quarter of a million dollars at one PAC reception than going door to door back home."

The televised Sunday morning shows are a true inside-the-beltway phenomenon. Growing up, I always felt guests of such shows as "Meet the Press" and "Face the Nation" were atheist politicians who should be in church like I was. But as a legislative aide in Washington, I discovered how important they actually were. Such shows did not offer that much national coverage on the morning they were broadcast. But depending on what provocative pronouncements came out of them, they were sure to make for a prime space story in the Monday morning papers. They are an opportunity to make a big noise and be heard during a quiet time.

Drama such as John Tower reading a statement to personally pledge sobriety on ABC's "This Week with David Brinkley" did not win his confirmation as defense secretary, but it did make headlines and news well beyond that broadcast. While Boren's few appearances did not create such waves on the stagnant sea of campaign reform, they were welcome tools of promotion just the same.

I recall very well the October 9, 1988, appearance Boren made on that same show. It was entitled "The '88 Vote: Incumbency, PACs, and Campaign Reform." With the 1988 elections heating up, reports of more and more money going into them, and an exchange about reform in the vice presidential debate, our issue was ripe for harvest on a big weekend show.

Our press secretary was to meet Boren at his Virginia home. The network would send a car to take them to the studio in downtown Washington, a mile north of the White House. I had gone through the typical routine of preparing a memo for the senator that highlighted statistics and figures he could use to dramatize the growth and influence of PACs. Boren loved to portray things as an "x% increase" over the last election, or "y% of congressmen" got "z% of their money from PACs," and so on. My memo therefore included facts for his use about the current election's spending over previous elections:

PACs have contributed 34 percent more so far in 1988 than they did in 1986;

PAC contributions to Senate candidates has gone from $9 million in 1978 to $45 million in 1986—a 500 percent increase;

The average cost of a winning Senate campaign has gone from $600,000 in 1978 to $3 million in 1986—a 500 percent increase;

And 88 percent of all PAC contributions go to incumbents.

I also reminded Boren of Senator Quayle's publicly stated position in the vice presidential debate. While he said he supported reform, as a cosponsor of the Dole-McConnell bill, I pointed out to Boren why that did not measure up to being a "reform" bill. Of course, Boren already knew much of this as he had fought this fight months earlier. But any senator needs a refresher course on such details.

I arrived shortly after Boren and was escorted to the "green room" near the studio. Boren was in the makeup room, and the press secretary, Kenny Levit, and I sat back to enjoy the corporate fat of ABC. The plush, pretaping room is a waiting and hospitality suite for guests of the show and whomever may accompany them. Outfitted with a brunchlike spread of bagels, lox, danish, and fruit, it could have passed as a $18.95 continental breakfast bar at a five-star hotel restaurant. The beverage selection was also complete. Besides the coffee, decaf, hot tea, and assorted juices, the alcoholic choices included more than the brunch fare of champagne, Bloody Marys, or screwdrivers. While pouring some coffee, I shared a laugh with Levit, who pointed to the bottle of Jack Daniel's black label bourbon whiskey and asked, "How 'bout a belt?"

By this time, Boren and another guest, Rep. Beryl Anthony (D-Ark.) came back from the makeup room. Boren had a few last-minute questions before he was to go to the studio. I later noticed Fred Wertheimer of Common Cause, the first guest to be interviewed, on a monitor from the studio. I joked back at the press secretary that Wertheimer, who looked a little washed out, could have used a belt of that fine vodka from the green room. Hodding Carter and George Will, two of the show's journalist/regulars, popped into the room long enough to shake hands with Boren, grab juice and a muffin, and head for the studio. Separately, Wertheimer, Representative Cheney and Senator Boschwitz, both via satellite, Anthony, and Boren would appear on the hourlong show, followed by fifteen minutes of discussion by Brinkley, Will, Carter, and ABC News correspondent Sam Donaldson.

The introduction to the show was a perfect rundown of the problem Congress has having focusing on reform, as special interest money continued to flow toward incumbents. Jack Smith, the show's reporter, set the stage for the discussion in the opening: "Since incumbents benefit from the status quo, why should they vote against it?" However, like so many times before, the discussion during that show moved from the prospects of reform to a dialogue about the presidential campaign. Another missed opportunity to maintain a focus on the subject at hand.

Another Sunday show I was associated with took place in spring 1990. Boren was to appear on NBC's "Meet the Press." Its panel was Andrea Mitchell as moderator, Elizabeth Drew of the *New Yorker*, and Al Hunt of the *Wall Street Journal*. Boren was the slated guest, as the "point man on campaign finance reform and chairman of the Senate Intelligence Committee."

I met Boren that morning at his home, and we shared a ride in a car sent by the network to carry us to the WRC-TV studios in Northwest Washington where "Meet the Press" is taped. During the ride, in between Boren and Levit's discussion of a new play that opened at the Arena Stage theater, I tried to brief him on facts and figures to use during the three-way interview.

On our arrival, the assistant press secretary, already there and waiting, joined the entourage, which was greeted by one of the show's staff persons, who handed Boren a stack of copied clippings of morning newspaper stories from national news-papers. It was a casual warning that anything in the news on campaign finance reform, intelligence, defense, or foreign poli-cy would be fair game in their questions.

After Boren greeted Mitchell on his way to "makeup," Hunt rounded the corner and gave Andrea a good morning kiss on the cheek, careful not to smudge the makeup. Hunt's affectionate display was chummier than the expected diplomatic formality of weekly co-workers.

This show, in contrast to the Brinkley visit, illustrated for me the coziness between official Washington and the national press. Not only do the players get along socially but they cross over the lines to build personal friendships. (Years earlier, I had a Sunday brunch at my apartment in Northeast Washington for the Boren staff, including the senator. He and his wife attended the gather-ing but left early for a second brunch of the day at the home of CBS correspondent Phil Jones. So I was aware that friendships exist, as they do in any professional setting.)

Mitchell, whose "significant other" is Federal Reserve Chair-man Alan Greenspan, is herself the epitome of the cross-relations in the powerful fields of government, business, and the press. But her upcoming questions would shed more light on how that relation works. The setup for her first question to Boren was slow and innocent.

"Well, you've tried five times out of the last six years. When is Congress going to get its act together? When are you going to get your own party together? And is there any chance this year that it will be any different and you'll actually pass the [campaign finance reform] legislation?"

Boren, after describing himself as "a perennial optimist," discussed the ethics "jolt" in Congress and the renewed public awareness that would add to the momentum in Congress. But Mitchell continued.

"Well, you say there has been a jolt. But your own Democratic party chairman, Ron Brown, is against any limits on soft money. He's out putting the arm on big contributors while you're trying to ban their contributions. How are you going to get anything done, if your own party won't support it?"

Boren responded comfortably, as the struggles with the Democratic National Committee over our soft money language had been public for some time.

"Well, I think our party will support it. And I think, after all, we're not trying to write a bill . . . to get partisan advantage for one party or the other. This has to be an American reform; it's an American problem."

Then Mitchell's bombshell dropped.

"Senator Boren, I don't want to upset you, but just last night I talked to Chairman Brown, and he said he was against any limits on soft money. And he said it's easy for David Boren to be in favor of all this reform because he's never had a tough campaign. He's never had any real opposition back in Oklahoma. But he says that what you're doing would hurt other Democratic candidates."

Boren, ever the cool, never the rattled interviewee and debater, covered Brown's nationally televised hypocrisy by saying, "He has some suggestions about how we change it [the bill] and how we impose the limits."

After the taping, Mitchell told of being at a social gathering with Brown, who told her exactly what her questions implied. Not only were Brown's private comments substantive in terms of news but they were personal in terms of Boren's allegiance to the party. Yet such casual and informal interactions are the stuff that make national television, due to the connectedness within Washington.

Newspapers

Editorials: Support on the editorial pages of newspapers was also incredibly important to us as a tool in the fight for campaign reform. As with any legislative or community effort, a certain aura surrounds the support from a newspaper through their authorless endorsements. The thought-provoking prose from protectors of free speech and a free press give a certain credibility to a cause.

The Boren-Goldwater amendment of 1985–86 brought a considerable level of national editorial support. At my suggestion, Boren proudly boasted of that in his closing speech of the 99th Congress on October 8, 1986: "We have likewise seen widespread support from around the country. Well over 400 editorials in 291 newspapers in 45 states have come out in support of the Boren-Goldwater bill to limit the financial influence of PACs. . . . The news media has shown increasing interest in exposing the correlations between PAC contributions and legislative behavior."

One such editorial came from the *Boston Globe* in an August 10, 1986, piece:

The U.S. Senate is scheduled to vote on the Boren-Goldwater amendment to campaign finance legislation, a first step in freeing congressional politics from the hammerlock of political action committees.

Neither cosponsor is a zealot. Senator David L. Boren (D-Okla.) found out that PACs screened him from his constituents and made him too attentive to lobbyists representing anonymous contributors.

Sen. Barry Goldwater (R-Ariz.), ending a long and distinguished career, is the ideological opposite of another congressional retiree, Speaker [Thomas P. "Tip"] O'Neill. Yet, they agree on the one profound fact. As O'Neill says, "The PACs are destroying this government. Too many guys have big money and no opponent."

This kind of reminder by the press added integrity to the effort. Whether you were in the liberal corner of New England's most popular and powerful politician or whether you voted for Goldwater for president in 1964, you could not deny that their mutual support for limiting PACs was a strong statement.

The next day, as debate on the Boren-Goldwater amendment proceeded, the *New York Times* offered a more demagoguic approach to the issue. It concluded, "A half-empty swamp is healthier than one that's overflowing. The public will soon find out which senators want higher ground and which ones like the muck, slosh, and smell."

One Oklahoma newspaper that jumped ahead of Boren in the fight for true reform was the *Norman Transcript*. I had not been on Boren's Oklahoma staff for two months when I picked up my copy of the July 21, 1983, *Norman Transcript* to read an editorial headline reading "Spending Limits." The piece about "money, the lifeblood of political campaigns," claimed that Senator Boren and Representative Synar's bill proposing a limit on the amount of PAC money a candidate may accept was a good first movement. Yet it claimed that "logical steps would involve spending caps on elections and the public financing of congressional elections." The editorial continued that spending limits and public financing were often criticized because it "would only help incumbents. Obviously, if members of Congress believed that to be true, we would have had the reforms in place many years ago."

The *Philadelphia Inquirer* took an opposite view on the advisability of an aggregate PAC limit bill and the ability to stop the flow of money. At the request of Senator Heinz, a copy of their editorial was placed in the August 12 *Congressional Record*. It stated,

> [The Boren-Goldwater amendment] would not end PACs' purchase of leverage on legislators; indeed it could increase it. . . . The central flaw of this reform stems from its unspoken premise—that somehow rules can dam the flow of money into politics. It can't be done, nor should it be. Rules can only channel the financial flow.

It did, however, endorse the idea of all qualifying candidates getting "a minimum floor of taxpayer-financed funding sufficient to mount a credible campaign, as do presidential candidates." Of course, Heinz did not focus the Senate's attention on this part of the editorial. It would be a struggle to get Heinz or Senator Specter to later accept that advice.

But the *Philadelphia Inquirer's* view of money's inevitable flow was echoed by the *Post's* editorial prior to the first vote on Boren-Goldwater in 1985. Their word on the subject, came under the headline "PAC's Reconsidered."

Senator David Boren (D-Okla.) is one of a handful of national legislators who refuse to accept PAC money. That choice is one that protects him from charges that he is unduly influenced by organized interest groups that have the ability and the resources to make large campaign contributions in order to affect legislation. . . . Believing as we do that the current system is far from perfect, we have come to believe nevertheless that further limitations on campaign spending are not the answer. We no longer believe that current law, which combines the benefits of some regulation and full disclosure, can be significantly improved by further restricting political contributions. . . . We continue to believe that disclosure is the best way to avoid corruption in campaign financing.

This view was a strong perceptual roadblock to us in the cause for reform. I remember cringing that December morning when Senator Heinz picked up a copy of what he called "a very penetrating editorial." Heinz proudly inserted the text into the *Congressional Record*.

News Stories: While the editorial support of the *Washington Post* was important to us, so were the sympathetic news stories that gave ample space and time to build our case. Few, if any, senators are moved to vote for or against a bill based on the editorial views of an inside-the-beltway media corporation like *Post*, but it is the paper that most senators read with their coffee in the morning. Just because it is not their hometown or home state newspaper does not mean it has no impact on the views of their constituents.

The influence of the *Post* or the *New York Times* shows up in the televised media as well. Many stories investigated and broken by these two papers become the subject of national news. While "Watergate" and the "Pentagon Papers" are two obvious examples of how the *Post* and the *New York Times* lead media coverage, many others exist.

The fear of a senator reading his *Post* in the morning is that it will expose the Achilles heel of a legislative issue. One example is the filing for public financing of the Dole for President campaign discussed previously (chap. 5).

Dole was a roadblock to compromise of the Boren-Byrd bill in 1988, at the same time that he was running for the presidency. The key provision of the bill called for spending limits in congressional campaigns. The cornerstone of the presidential system under which Dole ran was a similar system of spending limits. Dole requested to participate in that system in exchange for public matching funds. Yet he could not get his Republican colleagues to stop a filibuster against extending the system to Congress. A July 10, 1987, story in the *Post* cataloged the mess:

> In the *Congressional Record* of June 16, Dole noted: ". . . If there is a groundswell out there, the American people demanding that we pay for our campaigns with their taxes, it has not reached my office yet. . . . I have not gotten any flood of mail saying 'I can hardly wait to pay more taxes so we can fund your campaign for the U.S. Senate.' "

The *Post* went on to report,

> But in a recent fund-raising letter for his presidential campaign, Dole had a different view on the role of federal funds in campaigns: "I will make a formal decision whether to seek the presidency in the next several months. And one of the most important factors in making that decision will be knowing I can count on your support. . . . P.S. Your gift of up to $250 can actually be worth TWICE AS MUCH to me because it will help me qualify for 'Matching Funds.' The federal government will match your gift dollar-to-dollar up to $250."

Later, when Dole filed for public funds, his position was exposed for the fraud it was. While the *Post*'s disclosure never persuaded Dole to engage in the reform debate personally, it did open him up to criticism during his presidential campaign. Groups in support of S. 2 saw the deception and picketed Dole in Iowa and New Hampshire. One such protester was pictured in the January 9, 1988, edition of the *Des Moines Register*. An elderly woman firmly grasped a signed stating, "Sen. Dole—STOP blocking campaign finance reform," with a cut line that read, "Maria Molloy of Des Moines was among picketers outside Friday's debate."

Of course, I cannot make any quantitative or qualitative analysis of whether voters in the crucial Iowa caucuses or New Hampshire primary saw Dole's avoidance of the reform bill as a reason to vote against him. (Social Security was a larger issue in the New Hampshire campaign, for instance.) But I speculate that had the presidential contender publicly maintained his opposition to public financing but proactively come out for some system of congressional spending limits, he might have seen a favorable trade-off in his running the Republican caucus and his running for president. In hindsight, Dole might well have preferred those precious New Hampshire votes in exchange for the temporary angst from Senators Packwood, Helms, and Gramm.

Political/Media Partnerships: The personal, working relationships that develop between these two spheres of influence— government and the media—are important. When a trust and an alliance grows between them, the axis can be quite powerful. A clear example of this was our effort to win the editorial support of the *Washington Post*. In another show of political diplomacy, Boren had a plan to turn the tables in our favor.

In a February 12, 1987, editorial, the *Post* ran a lead editorial entitled "A Paid-For Congress." It decried a scandal that enveloped Sen. Lloyd Bentsen (D-Tex.), who set up a "breakfast club" for lobbyists whose PACs would pay $10,000 for membership. The privilege of membership was attending a weekly breakfast to discuss issues with the Texas senator, who chaired the Finance Committee. In their editorial, the *Post* noted that a reform bill had been introduced by Boren and Byrd (who had his own similar club at the time). The piece reported their bill would provide "for public financing along the line of presidential campaigns." Whether or not that was *the* solution, the editorial only said, "Maybe. Others will have other ideas. But something has to be done. The present system is intolerable."

The *Post*'s previous position during the Boren-Goldwater debate was that disclosure was all that was needed. But the "Eggs McBentsen" affair, as it became known, was the impetus to call for change.

Boren seized on a personal relationship he had with Meg Greenfield, editorial page editor of the *Post*, to discuss the issue at a social gathering. The two decided to have lunch together and discuss the issue in some detail. On Ash Wednesday, March 4, 1987, Greenfield and editorial writer Peter Milius came to the office for a lunch with Boren and me. The way in which Boren received her told me that he and Greenfield had a personal acquaintance, though I never knew how far back their friendship went. As we sat at Boren's small conference table in his office for a lunch of chicken salad and fruit brought in from the Senate dining room, he began to sell his bill.

Greenfield reminded the senator that her newspaper had been supportive of the public financing reforms in the 1970s but that it seemed that money's leakage into the system was inevitable. Even the presidential system, which was supposed to be fixed, "had 'soft money' coming in," said Greenfield.

Boren was relentless in selling his proposal, which he saw as a balance between the demonstrated good of grass-roots financial support and the dire necessity to halt the growth of campaign spending. His arguments were coherent, compelling, and, I thought, falling on fertile soil. That luncheon discussion was brought to a close after pecan pie and coffee, but there was no formal request for editorial support. The request was assumed. Of course, the paper had been barraged not only by studies, press releases, and editorial alerts from Common Cause but by the stories their own reporters kept finding about the system with its premium on fund raising.

The first hint of success came three weeks later in an editorial about PACs guilty of being "switch hitters," of giving to both sides in an election. The editorial, based on a study by Common Cause, called the practice part of "a rotten system." It merely mentioned "a bill now pending in the Senate to reform congressional campaign finance" which "seeks to limit PAC contributions." Stopping well short of any endorsement of the Boren bill, it concluded, "Surely there is a better way."

The next week, their lead editorial—"Backing Down the PACs"—went still further in calling for change. It decried the current system as "the low-grade infection of American politics." The piece mentioned the "Boren-Byrd bill," with its forty-two cosponsors. While it concluded that S. 2 "is not a perfect answer," the *Post* also said that "those who will kill it have the heavy burden of suggesting a credible alternative." Boren and I were pleased at the movement and the honorable mention.

This evolution continued when a strategically timed *Post* editorial entitled "Money Frenzy" was featured. Stating that the Republican resisters to the Boren-Byrd bill had yet to make clear their alternative, the piece said that without overall limits, the "money frenzy would continue. Only in the context of public financing can a sense of proportion be restored." This editorial, just a whisker short of endorsement, appeared on the morning of the Rules Committee markup session to report on S.2.

The final piece of the *Post* puzzle came into place on June 4. Exactly three months after the Boren-Greenfield-Milius-Kubiak luncheon meeting, the newspaper endorsed the bill.

The balloon has gone up on congressional campaign finance. Senate Majority Leader Robert Byrd, facing a Republican filibuster that he lacks the 60 votes to break, has nonetheless called up the public financing bill of which he is a cosponsor. The idea is to force a search for a compromise.

The system now is wrong. The combination of spending limits in the context of public financing is the only way to right it. As both parties reach for compromise, there will be a temptation to rubberize the definition of reform. But there have to be spending limits. Otherwise they're just playing Fool the Voter.

Clearly, our year-and-a-half search for support of Boren's bill from the "campus paper" paid off. Milius even commented to me later that the *Post* had killed a "forest of trees" for all the editorial copy it gave our bill. It would be much later before the support had its desired effect on all of the Congress.

Not-So-Funny Papers: A final and humorous influence of the press that deserves mention are editorial cartoons. With only a minimum of words, an illustrator's drawing can speak volumes. The bias of the cynical press was often in our favor with the editorial page cartoon.

The 1987 filibuster of Boren-Byrd gave the *Post*'s Herblock several opportunities to criticize the opponents of reform. A June 14 cartoon showed a business suit-clad congressman sitting nearly unconscious on a road. With a briefcase marked "Public Financing of Congressional Campaigns" at his side, the man had just been run over by a speeding car with the license tag marked "Senate GOP Filibuster."

That was followed three months later by another drawing set in the Senate chamber. This time, the senator, holding a bill entitled "Campaign Spending Reform," was lying dead, shot full of bullet holes on the Senate floor. In the foreground, barricaded by bags and bags of money marked with dollar signs, Bob Dole blew smoke off a pistol used in the crime. A sign in the background declares, "They shall not pass."

Some cartoons were aimed not only at the appetite of Congress for dollars but at the interest groups willing to give them. Herblock created a masterpiece in October 1988 during debate on a crime bill. A large, pin-striped lobbyist with a National Rifle Association (NRA) button was shown emptying a barrel of cash labeled "political contributions" with a poster in the background reading, "Boost sales of cheap handguns, machine guns, and cop-killer bullets." As a salivating congressman views the money with obvious delight, the NRA lobbyist says, "Remember, power grows from the barrel of a gun lobby."

A four-panel cartoon of Charles Keating by Wasserman of the *Boston Globe* put that scandal in perspective. The late 1989 strip had Keating speaking this monologue: "Sure, we made big contributions to U.S. Senators. . . . But it was standard banking practice. . . . We deposited money in their accounts . . . and they repaid us with LOTS of interest."

One illustration was a favorite of Boren's. He had it framed to hang in his reception room. It first appeared in the *New Yorker*. Set in the Senate chamber, two senators are standing as others sit at their desks. The one senator speaking angrily turns to the other, who interrupts with his hand and finger raised as though seeking recognition. The first senator says, "Listen pal, I didn't spend seven million bucks to get here so I could yield the floor to you."

The freedom of the press, like any other constitutional liberty, comes with responsibility. It should not be seen as an unencroachable domain.

In a speech before the network television affiliates in March 1989, Senator Danforth spoke of that industry's power to "educate and foster the democratic ideal" and appealed to them to "be leaders in reforming political campaigns." Danforth challenged them to support his reform ideas around the advertising rate for political ads, a pocketbook issue for the industry. His appeal for their entry into the debate was strong.

The cost of air time is so high, it distorts the campaign process. It limits the candidate's speech. It makes it much tougher for a candidate to challenge an incumbent. And it has other, more insidious effects. It forces candidates to spend far too little of their time and energy on the issues and far too much on raising money from political action committees. It makes members of Congress reluctant to offend well-financed special interest groups. The need for constant fund-raising raises the specter of undue influence and lessens the public's confidence in its government.

"HOLD THE CHINTZ"

Other detractors from public confidence are politicians exposed to embarrassment. One of the greatest satisfactions the press enjoys is to expose someone — particularly politicians — as something they are not.

Gary Hart begged the attention of press scrutiny when he told the *New York Times* to trail him if they did not believe he was faithful to his wife. Jimmy Swaggert became a household name when the press exposed the holier-than-thou preacher's path, which traveled the same road as prostitutes. And Nancy Reagan got stung when the media found still more designer clothes in her closet, after she promised to be an ethical First Lady and not take such gifts any longer.

More than a few snickers and sighs were heard when *Newsweek* reported in 1991 some of the campaign-related expenses of reformer David Boren. Six years after throwing his bombshell to clean up the congressional campaign finance system, the "Periscope" column had a subhead entitled, "Hold the Chintz." It reported that the Oklahoma senator showed $158,133 in special expenses paid for by campaign contributors after his 1990 reelection. Nothing newsworthy about that. What was interesting was how he used 13 percent of those funds for decorating his Senate office.

Some Boren supporters must have felt betrayed after reading that the senator spent $4,495 for a jumbo, illuminated globe for his office and $522 for a lamp from Gump's. The senator also purchased $15,480 worth of Native American art to decorate his suite of offices, including a conference room that looks like an auxiliary to the Smithsonian Museum of American Art. His spokesman countered the reporter's questions by stating that such purchases would "help the state economy" and would eventually go to a museum.

Constituent concern might have been appeased as American Indian art does promote the cultural richness of Oklahoma's heritage, every Intelligence chairman should have his very own world globe, and despite its rather steep price tag, good light from a good lamp is important to preserve good eyesight. But I would guess that not many donors to Oklahomans for Boren would appreciate a fourth itemized expense from the FEC report of the state's senior senator—$312 for opera tickets for constituents.

Other extravagances of elected candidates were revealed in a book published by two *Los Angeles Times* reporters. Sara Fritz, who covered the campaign finance reform beat during my tenure, and Dwight Morris wrote *Handbook of Campaign Spending* about the 1990 congressional election cycle spending. They estimated that over half of the $446 million candidates spent was not related to voter contact but to overhead, entertainment, and gifts. The book, computer-generated from over 437,000 separate entries from FEC campaign reports, listed spending that sounded more like game show prizes than electioneering items. Such expenditures included wedding gifts, flowers, trips, and cars.

Rep. Dennis Hertel (D-Mich.) took his wife to a Florida resort for a five-day vacation on campaign funds. With a bill of over $1,500 for meals and lodging, Hertel claimed to have been meeting with campaign supporters after a three-day seminar with the electronics industry.

Alaskans were to be treated with special touring privileges on their visits to Washington, D.C., thanks to Senator Stevens. His campaign spent nearly $72,000 on automobile expenses during the six-year election cycle to transport constituents, according to his campaign. Included in that figure was a $23,000 van and a $32,000 Lincoln Continental, bought after the election. After its public disclosure, the Lincoln was sold.

Democrat John Murtha of Pennsylvania got the prize for the most money spent on flowers for constituents in the 1990 House races: $8,306. Texas Republican Bill Archer spent more than any House member for holiday cards, over $22,000. Some salaries could be categorized as jackpots as well. Republican House leader Robert Michel paid a campaign consultant almost $244,000 to manage his campaign. It would appear that the Illinois lawmaker got his money's worth, however, as he took 98 percent of the vote that year.

On the more cerebral end of campaign spending, Sen. Strom Thurmond (R-S.C.) spent nearly $400,000 for a state-run scholarship program bearing his name. He also diverted contributors' funds to endow a professorial chair at the University of South

Carolina and another at Clemson University. Thurmond's campaign gave a total of $733,000 to educational endeavors.

PUBLIC WORDS, PRIVATE ACTIONS

For public figures, the age-old axiom that actions speak louder than words holds especially true. Several have pushed it to its limit, and these puppets of integrity need to be revealed.

In announcing his bid for the 1992 Democratic nomination for the presidency, Edmund G. "Jerry" Brown, former California governor, described our democratic system as having "been the object of a hostile takeover, engineered by a confederacy of corruption, careerism, and campaign consulting. And money has been the lubricant greasing the deal."

His presidential campaign started on October 21, 1991, with a pledge to take no PAC money or any contribution larger than $100. Brown said, "The insatiable appetite for campaign dollars has turned the government into a stop-and-shop for every greedy interest in the country."

Yet *Washington Post* reporter Dan Balz remembered it was former state Democratic Party Chairman Jerry Brown who silently campaigned against the strong "soft money" language in Boren's reform bill in 1989. Balz's story the next morning read, "Among his causes as party chairman was strong opposition to limits on money raised and spent by state parties." While I was never on the receiving end of such lobbying, I was made aware that Brown made contacts with Senate Majority Leader Mitchell and national Democratic officials to argue against our bill's soft money provisions.

Another California Democrat who publicly acted one way but privately operated another was Alan Cranston. Actually, Cranston's AA was a strong private actor for his boss dating back to 1985 (chap. 3). While the senator declared strong support for campaign reform publicly, Roy Greenaway of his staff was maneuvering in quite another direction. While the next chapter will focus on this hypocrisy, it should be noted that Cranston, through Greenaway, was a leader for an ethics seminar to be sponsored by an institute from his home state.

The Josephson Institute for the Advancement of Ethics is a Los Angeles-based "nonprofit, nonpartisan educational organization that specializes in small programs for influential decision makers in government, law, journalism, business, and other fields." Michael Josephson, the president and leader of the seminars, wrote senior Senate staffers on October 1 from a list assembled with the hlep of Cranston's AA. The two-day meeting at a West Virginia resort and conference center was billed as "a provocative and rewarding seminar on 'Politics, Power and Ethics: Effective Decision Making in the Trenches.'" A follow-up letter bearing Greenaway's signature urged my attendance as "ethical considerations are the underpinning of all of the action and decision in our daily routines" as Senate staffers.

Despite previous feelings I had about Greenaway's conduct with campaign reform efforts on his boss's behalf, I thought this new effort would be a most welcome chance to plow new ground with him and other staffers. And since I had never been to the wooded, rustic resort in Berkeley Springs, I accepted the invitation for the November event.

Sessions were devoted to the ethical mine fields of fund raising and campaigning, dealing with lobbyists and PACs, raising and using campaign funds, campaigning on government times, and maintaining independence. Josephson led the discussions with ease and an uncanny familiarity with situations that we faced every day in dealing with lobbyists and moneyed interests.

One of the "discussion cases" involved a hypothetical Senator Whitestone and a fund raiser, Vic Brady, president of Zeno Industries. We were to assume that Brady held a fund raiser for Whitestone that produced over $100,000 for his reelection. The first of two discussion questions for the group of 40 to 50 staffers was, "Was it proper for Whitestone to accept the money and fund-raising assistance from Brady?"

A great deal of discussion resulted in a fairly broad consensus that under our system of campaign finance laws, there was nothing ethically or inherently wrong with this activity. But the discussion strayed from that general agreement with the second question, "What, if any, precautions could Whitestone have taken to avoid the appearance of impropriety?"

Of course, no one knew that a few years later that very issue would be embodied in a Senate Ethics Committee investigation of Senator Cranston that would rock the Senate.

Another member of the Senate who lacked consistency in his arguments on the PAC issue was Mitch McConnell. In the last speech before the vote on the Boren-Goldwater PAC amendment in the previous Congress, McConnell spoke about his opposition to PAC limits.

Any politician who abuses the system of fund raising is subject to judgment where it counts, and that is the voting booth. Any candidate for office can solicit PAC contributions. Any election, I am here to tell you or I would not be here in the Senate, can be won without PAC contributions. There is no reason to impose these restrictions on an individual's right or a group's right to participate.

McConnell was joined by twenty-nine other senators in that vote against aggregate limits on PACs. But he underwent a metamorphosis.

After his defense of PACs in 1986, he supported curbing their influence by seeking to lower their contribution limit in 1987. By the 1989–90 session of Congress, he went further. During floor debate, he applauded Senator Boren for the Democratic support of McConnell's "PAC ban provision we [Republicans] have advocated on this side for some time." He explained this change of heart the next year in more detail in the Minority Views of the April 11 Rules Committee report on the Senate Elections Ethics Act of 1991:

We can reduce special interest influence by banning PACs and special interest soft money. . . . PACs were designed to allow individuals to get together and advance their collective interests in politics. Presumably, that would include supporting challengers. In practice, 80 percent of PAC contributions go to incumbents with little or no regard for ideology or voting records. The apparent goal of PACs is no longer to support candidates of like mind but to buy access to the powers that be.

Banning PACs would reduce special interest influence and increase competition.

The hypocrisy of McConnell and his GOP brethren was exposed at its cynical worst. McConnell and Boschwitz held a meeting with PACs after the 1988 filibuster showdown on the reform bill. A *Washington Post* story by Helen Dewar captured its essence: "Two months ago, Senate Republicans were willing to sacrifice political action committees (PACs) on the altar of campaign finance reform. Now they are passing them the collection plate."

At a "breakfast briefing" for "friends in the PAC community," McConnell, as the NRSC vice chairman for PAC contributions, addressed the session to appeal for their financial support. He told Dewar afterward, "As long as they exist, we'd like them to help us too." He went on to complain, "It's frankly a bit shocking to us the way [Democratic] proponents of labor's agenda have gotten business PAC support."

The story explained that NRSC Chairman Boschwitz wrote to invite PAC leaders to the meeting, explaining that the previously considered Democratic bill "forced us to develop new strategies" and "create opportunities—political opportunities, fundraising opportunities, and opportunities for new friendships and alliances."

The PAC managers must have at least bought McConnell's rhetoric in the upcoming election cycle. FEC records showed that by 1989, McConnell received $1,101,020 from political action committees in two Senate races. McConnell exploited the same perks of office in his 1990 reelection that he condemned as a challenger in 1984. He was one of the heaviest users of the franking privilege in that first term, spending over $2 million in six years, $566,000 between July 1989 and September 1990.

The final note to this discussion of words versus actions

should come back to the Ron Brown/Democratic National Committee (DNC) controversy that was visibly stirred on "Meet the Press." The disagreement between Boren and Brown over soft money had started long before that spring. That provision of the bill language was always a source of contention for the DNC.

The April 24 meeting with Brown in Boren's office was called because of the continued stalemate between DNC officials and Senator Mitchell's staffer, Bob Rozen, and me. Rozen and I would not budge from the central premise that contributions to political parties that affected federal elections should somehow all come under federal contribution limit rules.

A DNC finance official, Paul Tully, in meetings and a March 20 memo urged us to consider a different approach to regulating that money. Stating that his plan was "not the final and complete position of the Democratic National Committee on campaign finance reform," his tone in the memo and in meetings on behalf of the chairman was strong and immovable in opposition to what our Senate leaders were proposing. He opposed our efforts to "federalize nonfederal contributions."

Tully represented Brown with the strongest of images. After Tully's sudden death just six weeks before the 1992 election, Brown referred to him as "the smartest political strategist I ever knew." The quiet, back room master of Democratic politics was described by a *Post* obituary as "a rotund, curly-haired, coffee-drinking chain smoker" who spent half his forty-eight years in politics. But the staunch opposition to disarming the growing DNC arsenal of soft money was Tully's passion. His fast-talking New York accent would chop at Rozen and me in those few meetings in which his anger could be gauged by the reddening of his neck and face.

The DNC's position on soft money came in stark contrast to their platform for 1988. That document stated, "This country's democratic processes must be revitalized by . . . minimizing the domination and distortion of our elections by moneyed interests." In one of the many Senate Democratic caucus luncheons to which I was granted access, I recall a heated debate in which senators were discussing the advisability of the soft money machine that the DNC had finally developed to catch up to the RNC. One senator reminded his colleagues that the DNC was strongly opposed to Boren's approach to dealing wiht soft money.

The broad, general statement of concern in the 1988 platform was improved four years later with a more specific call to "reform the campaign finance system, to get big money out of our politics and let the people back in . . . [by seeking to] limit overall campaign spending and limit the disproportionate and excessive roles of PACs." But still there would be more actions by some Democrats that would not match their call for reform.

"A TOOTHLESS TIGER"

The Federal Election Commission was formed by the enactment of the Federal Election Campaign Act (FECA) of 1971, mainly as the disclosure agency of federal election contributions and expenditures. But as it has evolved through twenty years of operation, it has been charged by one observer as an agency that Congress designed "to fail, building in the propensity for partisan deadlocks, insisting on the appointment of pliant commissioners, and creating a morass of procedural defenses for suspected wrongdoers." In light of a lax interpretation of conflict of interest standards for the commissioners, a federal judge once charged the FEC with having "abdicated its statutory responsibility" with an "impermissible interpretation of the statute."

A journalist who covered election law issues told me he changed his personal views favoring comprehensive reform of and spending limits on congressional races. He feared "the poor regulatory performance of the FEC . . . [because] giving it more control and more detailed law to enforce will go afoul." But perhaps the best charge against the impotent agency came from a frustrated, reform-minded senator from the West. Sen. Harry Reid (D-Nev.), victimized by illegal contributions in his bid for the seat he was to win, summed up the FEC's ineffectiveness by calling it "a toothless tiger."

The most frustrating impasse was also the one that caused the greatest strain on our system of campaign finance. It began with a complaint filed against both the Democratic and Republican national committees in 1984 by the Center for Responsive Politics (see chap. 6). The center took issue with the party committees' channeling of soft money to their state parties in the 1983 special election in Washington state to replace the late Henry "Scoop" Jackson. The center argued for an allocation formula that would reflect political realities as well as for full disclosure for public cleanliness.

On November 7, 1985, the FEC held its first public hearing on a petition filed by Common Cause months before for tough new soft money regulations. By April 17, 1986, it formally rejected the request for centralized reporting and disclosure as well as the staff-developed recommendation to codify its current allocations formula. A *Washington Post* editorial the next week slammed the decision:

The FEC has turned its back on its duty and has approved the single, most glaring loophole in the campaign finance laws. It has seriously undermined two basic principles that have been at the heart of federal campaign finance laws since 1971: First, that contributions should be disclosed, so that all may judge whether undue influences were acquired; second, that contributions should be limited, so as to limit the influence of the very rich and of those who, as custodians of the funds of corporations and unions, can easily spend large sums of other people's money. The commission's shocking and disgraceful action requires Congress to step into the void and take some action. It may not be able to come up with a perfect solution to the problems posed by soft money, but it could hardly do worse.

In their 1988 Annual Report, the FEC finally acknowledged the growing external calls for change:

Somewhat paradoxically, while internal FEC operations ran smoothly, voices outside the agency called for change. In the press and in Congress, attention focused on several campaign finance issues including "soft money," PAC contributions, expenditure limits, bundling of contributions and candidate's personal funds.

. . . The Commission also explored the need for change—particularly concerning the allocation of expenditures between federal and nonfederal accounts and the definition of corporate expenditures within the context of political activity conducted by small nonprofit corporations.

In an unusual move, the year of that report's publication, the FEC also forwarded an extensive listing of "legislative recommendations." Providing the most formal call for help from a partisan-controlled and balanced agency, the FEC sent recommendations concerning independent expenditures by nonprofit corporations, soft money disclosure, elimination of state-by-state limits for publicly financed presidential primary candidates, and more. But despite this token act, the FEC has failed to overcome partisan standoffs to enforce campaign laws just as the Congress has failed to overcome partisanship in revising those laws.

The best-documented indictment of this standoff came from Common Cause. In their September 1989 publication, they suggested a new name for the agency: "The Failure-to-Enforce Commission." The 90-page document highlighted eight case studies of "the FEC's failure as a campaign finance watchdog." Its introduction reads,

In each case the FEC has evaded or rejected enforcement actions recommended by the agency's Office of General Counsel. Many of the cases fall into a pattern in which the Commission's three Republicans and three Democrats voted along partisan lines, canceling out each other's votes and deadlocking the Commission as a result. In these matters, Democratic Commissioners voted affirmatively to support the General Counsel's enforcement advice and Republican Commissioners voted to block such action. Commissioners from both parties have teamed up, however, in decisions that clearly benefit both political parties.

One of the more important loopholes in need of FEC closure was bundling. The practice of PACs or individuals collecting contributions as a "conduit" or "intermediary" and using control over them is against the intent of law in the FECA. Senator Packwood's well-known acceptance of $170,000 from an insurance PAC was only the beginning of abuse of the loophole.

In 1986, a Common Cause complaint to the FEC charged that the National Republican Senatorial Committee sent direct mail solicitation letters "making general references to certain Senate races." After depositing those contributions in their account, the NRSC sent checks to several Senate candidates. Since the FECA law prohibits direct contributions from the senatorial committee to a candidate in excess of $17,500, this was a way around the limits for the NRSC. The NRSC, however, answered that charge by stating that the contributions it received were "earmarked" for the Republican candidates.

The FEC's general counsel ruled that the NRSC's bundling practice was in violation of the law and FEC regulations. However, the FEC voted in a 3–3 partisan split on whether or not to agree and begin action against the Republican committee.

Growing frustrated by the FEC's inaction, Common Cause went one step better and filed suit in federal court in August 1987. Despite a promise to act by the FEC, the District Court had to order the FEC to decide the case by August 1, 1988. Four months later, the "NRSC signed a conciliation agreement regarding the matter — an action which closed the FEC's file on the Common Cause complaint," according to the study. While the FEC found "probable cause to believe that the NRSC" acted illegally in twelve campaigns, Common Cause was forced to file a second suit against the agency for its dismissal and failure to act.

Boren and I grew frustrated well before this public compilation of enforcement gridlock on the FEC. Looking for a radical reform, I convinced Boren, Mitchell, his staff, and Common Cause that S. 137, the bill introduced in January 1989, should include a new idea to reform the FEC. Since stalemate was a certainty with six equally divided partisans, why not add a seventh commission who on a rotating basis could create an odd-numbered panel? Even if the alternating appointments gave Republicans a four-vote bloc one year, proenforcement Democrats would have it the next.

Thanks to the press's ongoing interest in Boren's bills on campaign reform, they published new items about each succeeding bill. One of the changes in our 1989 bill that made limited news in the press was adding a seventh member to the FEC. However, the idea did not survive the Rules Committee markup that year. In fact, the lobbying against it started the night before the bill was actually introduced.

Pete Glavas, Boren's former field representative and chief of staff, was having a reception at his Alexandria, Virginia, home on January 24, 1990, for the Boren office and friends. Glavas, an attorney with the law/lobbying firm of Cassidy and Associates, was having the get-together on the evening before the first day of the 101st Congress, when new bills could be introduced. One of the guests was fellow Oklahoman and FEC member, Danny MacDonald.

I arrived a little late at the party, as I had been busy putting the final touches on Boren's introductory speech for the next day. Yet I saw that MacDonald had buttonholed Boren, and they were engaged deep conversation, right in front of the shrimp bowl—a location Boren did not seem to mind. Judging from the intensity of his expression, MacDonald had obviously read about the changes Boren's bill would make to the FEC.

When I entered that room, Boren, eager to see me, motioned me over to talk to MacDonald.

"Danny seems to have a disagreement with our FEC language," Boren informed me.

Without missing a beat, MacDonald reiterated his pleas to Boren for me.

"Greg, how y'a doin'? You just don't know what that bill will do to us Democrats trying to enforce the law. If you get another Republican on there, it'll just be 'Katy, bar the door!'"

By this time, Boren saw someone else to talk to, so he excused himself by saying, "Danny, this is just our opening bid to show that something needs to be done. A lot of senators are upset about the lack of enforcement, but we want to work with you to find the right ways to get the job done." And Boren was off to the cheese table and another guest.

I continued talking to MacDonald, who I considered a good

friend and fine commissioner. I did respect his opinion but felt he viewed our bill as an insult to him, instead of an indictment of the workability of an agency that was stacked for partisan stalemate.

But the more important stalemate in the fight for reform would not come for the quiet federal commission at 10th and E streets in downtown Washington. The real battle would next come from the governmental entity at 16th and Pennsylvania, the White House.

CHAPTER NINE

"This Is the Year"

Time wounds all heels.
— JANE ACE *(1905–1974)*

A NEW ADMINISTRATION came to the White House in 1989. It brought with it the promise of a new chance at enacting the campaign finance reform legislation. Individual senators would play a key role in negotiating around the impasse that stifled S. 2's passage. And a brewing scandal would be the impetus for forcing the issue forward.

The first bright sign of movement was from the Bush administration. Two of its stated domestic priorities in the first year were to clean up the savings and loan industry mess and to clean up congressional elections. It did not seem that the two could be related initiatives, but eventually their paths would collide, nearly taking down the careers of five senators in the process.

When I constructed the new bill to be introduced in the 101st Congress, it was done with no real confidence of a changed environment. I worked with Boren, the new majority leader, George Mitchell, and his staffer, Bob Rozen, to prepare a revised version of S. 2 for the first day. That bill would not have the same priority that Byrd gave the previous venture, but Mitchell was just as committed to its passage. In fact, not until the second year of the Congress would the subject of campaign finance heat up and give rise to a bill ready for passage.

The introduction of S. 137 came without the fanfare and excitement of its predecessor from the previous Congress. In fact, some would perceive Boren's statement about the bill as a worn out record. "Mr. President, for the past few years, this legislative body has deliberated the need to reform the system of congressional campaign financing. . . . This past election cycle again shows the system is in critical need of fundamental reform. . . . We must bring a renewed focus on the perceptions and realities that excessive money in politics plays."

Although in drafting his speech, I tried not to use the words "again," "refocus," or "redraft," they all made it in. But spring brought a fresh opening for Republican leadership on campaign finance reform from a new source.

A WHITE HOUSE OPENING

Early in the year, President George Bush had forwarded an ethics initiative to Congress and spoke of a forthcoming campaign finance proposal. I interpreted the action as Boren's chance to meet with the president, greet him with the "Skull and Bones" handshake, and talk honestly about joining together in a bipartisan effort.

Boren did not want to expend a chit on meeting with his fellow Yale and secret society alumnus but was quick to agree to sign a draft letter I proposed. The April 17 missive was not only an appropriate appeal to the president but an accurate portrait of the political and financial landscape. It read, in part:

Dear Mr. President,
    I was delighted to see your leadership in forwarding a package of ethics proposals to the Congress last week. For too long, there has been no central leadership in reaffirming the ethical standards of conduct for our government. Your strong personal commitment to the highest standard of conduct for public servants is laudable and appreciated.
    It is my firm belief that no serious, comprehensive approach to address ethics in government can be discussed without a broad and

aggressive attack on our current system of Congressional campaign finance. . . .

There are several factors which make our current campaign finance system flawed. Consider the facts:

- Incumbents hold a 98% return rate in Congress;
- For every $1 of PAC money that a House challenger can attract, an incumbent raised $8.
- Total spending for a winning Senate seat doubled in just one six-year term, from $2 million in 1982 to over $4 million in 1988. . . .

You, like my friend, Senator McConnell, have endorsed the notion of banning all political action committee contributions. While some would argue such a move would simply be unconstitutional, the practical effects could produce a terrible display of unintended consequences. As one who has never accepted PAC contributions, I am somewhat sympathetic to this idea, yet fearful of its impact.

In the 1988 Senate elections, over $49 million was contributed by PACs. It is naive to imagine that all of this money would simply "dry up" assuming we simply banned various groups from joining together to express a political viewpoint with financial contributions. Instead, such a proposal—without an effective voluntary spending limit system as proposed by my legislation, S. 137—would have the effect of pushing such sums into "covert" activities. PACs would still exist under protection of the Constitution but would find other ways to buy influence and access to the Congress. . . .

As you have three times participated in the Presidential system of spending limits and public financing, you are surely aware of its real and intended value in protecting the electoral process for that office. However, what has occurred concurrently with the "soft money" abuses . . . is an uncontrollable arms race for campaign cash which threatens Congressional elections.

While you and I share a disdain for direct public financing of Congressional elections, under the 1976 *Buckley v. Valeo* decision, no system of voluntary spending limits will work without certain practical inducements and protections. . . . As you have signaled your interest and willingness to engage with Congress in discussions of this most vital aspect of the democratic electoral process, I would ask that you work with the Senate leadership on this vital issue.

The complexities of the current system and the temptation of participants to allow personal and partisan concerns to dominate, require us to follow the advice from your February 9 Address to Congress, "Let us not question each other's motives. Let us debate. Let us negotiate. But let us solve the problem."

Again, I applaud your initiative in this area and request your involvement as we grapple for remedies.

Sincerely,
David L. Boren
United States Senator

Boren sent handwritten notes with copies of this letter to Wendell Ford and George Mitchell for their information. He did the same with the Republican leader, Bob Dole, asking that they come together soon to discuss campaign reform "on a bipartisan basis". Dole never responded to Boren's note or letter.

A month later, a presidential aide wrote to Boren thanking him for the letter "on the President's behalf" and assuring him that it "will be conveyed to the President's staff with direct responsibility." Several months after that, I advised Boren again to make a personal contact with the White House. I had appeared on a panel sponsored by the Council of State Governments with an aide to the president. In a discussion after the conference, he indicated an openness in the White House for Democratic negotiations. I wrote a November 1 memo to Boren.

After appearing on a campaign finance reform panel several weeks ago . . . a deputy to the President for legislative affairs . . . mentioned that [White House counsel] Boyden Gray had read *Honest Graft* and the chapter about you and Goldwater and wanted to get a chance to visit with you about the issue of campaign finance reform.

[He] called me back to reiterate the request. Thus, I would suggest that at some time convenient to you — we try to schedule such a casual meeting with Gray.

A meeting did eventually take place, months later, but the ideological bent of Gray was geared to eliminating PACs, the cornerstone of the president's proposal. Gray seemed to feel that spending limits were an unnecessary infringement on free speech and that it would benefit Democrats. He left the conversation with a pledge to consider Boren's well-spelled-out points to the contrary and to keep the dialogue going.

However, months passed without any further indication that

the White House would play a mediating or leadership role to end what the president had called the "permanent Congress." In his staged announcement of a PAC ban bill in June 1989, Bush said, "Incumbents stay in office for decades, amassing huge war chests to scare off strong challenges in election after election. This is not democracy."

Days before Bush took his oath of office in January 1989, former Republican President Gerald Ford appeared in a segment of a four-part PBS program entitled "The Power Game." In its segment devoted to the Congress, Ford stated, "The cost of running for office today is outrageous. And as a consequence, we find good people becoming too dependent on lobbying groups, pressure groups, etc. We ought to put a limit on how much can be spent on a congressional race, a senatorial race."

Bush and his staff ignored that advice. With much of his 1992 reelection campaign devoted to swipes at "the Democrat Congress," I often wondered why Bush could not see that our campaign reform was the way to reorder the system he and Ford both condemned. But neither Bush nor Gray nor any other advisers would go beyond the onetime press event to announce his PAC ban bill. So much for the president's personal concern and leadership on the issue.

MCCAIN CHASE

There was one Republican who was anxious to discuss a bipartisan bill with Boren, Sen. John McCain, an Arizona Republican. The Boren-McCain partnership began with a June 2 telephone call to me from McCain's top aide. The call came before my midmorning meeting with Mitchell's aide and Common Cause, which was to be followed by lunch with Stephen Law of McConnell's staff. But of the three interactions about campaign reform, the telephone call was the most productive.

McCain's AA, Chris Koch, told me that his boss was interested in talking to Boren about a "new bill," one that could be bipartisan. It seems that McCain had grown frustrated with

McConnell portraying himself as speaking on behalf of the Republicans. The staffer asked me if Boren would be open to meeting about a joint bill. I replied cautiously.

"Well, I certainly think he's open to working with anyone to get off high center with this issue. But we need to be sure that they're not wasting their time. Are there any items that are 'off-the-table' for your boss?"

Of course, I wanted it understood right away that if McCain wanted to start a negotiation process over a "new bill," it did not mean that spending limits were not to be discussed. As Boren had said many times during debate, "That's like saying, 'You can go swimming, but don't get wet.'"

"No," was Koch's clear reply.

With that sign of encouragement, I agreed to let Boren know that McCain would be buttonholing him soon to verify this staff conversation and to see if he wanted to set up a meeting. Actually, Boren had already had a brief conversation with McCain, which he shared with me when I told him of the staff contact. Boren's response was a predictable, "Let's set up a meeting."

June 14 was the first day the two senators could work out a mutually convenient time to meet. McCain came in with his AA for the meeting, which lasted no longer than about twenty minutes. They sat, chatted for a while, then discussed the topic of the meeting. They agreed that the current environment was destined for stalemate. They agreed that the only separation was public financing. They agreed that there may be "creative ways around" that issue. Despite my misgivings, they agreed to write a bill that would ban PACs, following the president's recommendation. They agreed that such a joint bill could attract strong bipartisan support. They agreed that it could realign the borders of partisan separation on this issue. And they agreed to let staff work it out.

My biggest fear and growing realization from such summits as this was that the principals come together and agree to concepts of a bill, only to let staff disagree on the specifics. But, there *seemed* to be a genuineness in McCain's desire to be on *the* bill to break the gridlock. He spoke of his willingness to take a position out front of his party. And furthermore, he spoke with urgency. He seemed to want the bill drafted and put in within days. Boren picked up on that enthusiasm and encouraged me to meet with McCain's staffer right away.

Two days later, I went to McCain's office for the first negotiating meeting. Koch and I covered a number of areas of agreement right away. My notes reflected the issues we discussed and the decision or separation of positions:

```
Indiv.'s—index from present
PACs—0—contingent on total package
"soft money"—agents provision
              —disclosure: state, nat'l, labor, corp.
              —redefine—personal contrib. limit
Spending limits—limits?
                  enforcements—tax
Bundling—
Membership—leadership PACs, grandfather clause, franking,
              roll-over
```

Interpreted, my notes reflected that the individual contribution limit would be left at $1,000 but increased by the Consumer Price Index (CPI) for the future. PACs would be banned, but sensing how hard this would be for Democrats to swallow, I stipulated we should come back to it, to see what the whole package looked like.

In the soft money area, we agreed to prohibit the "agents" of presidential candidates from soliciting money not regulated by federal limits (a provision from S. 137) as well as "full" disclosure. I also brought up limiting contributions to state parties who spend those funds directly or indirectly on federal elections. This was the crux of our soft money clamp in S. 137, and at first blush, Koch agreed that it was an avenue for abuse of contribution limits.

Our only discussion under the heading of spending limits was that McCain could live with actual limits—much like those contained in Boren's bill. While he was not as enthusiastic as McCain was two days earlier, they were clearly on the table. I pressed the point that to make such voluntary limits meaningful, there had to be inducements to comply, thus the reason for our support of public financing for the last two and a half years. I mentioned that some of those could come in the form of "tax" incentives and disincentives.

There was also discussion and agreement on a number of other issues. We agreed our bill would close the bundling loophole. We agreed that leadership PACs, those political sluch funds to help members of Congress dole out contributions in return for leadership votes, be abolished. We agreed to limit the franking privilege that allowed Congress to spend taxpayers' dollars on clearly political newsletters and mass mailings before elections. We agreed to abolish the "grandfather clause," which allowed members elected before 1980 to convert leftover campaign funds to personal use. And finally, we agreed to somehow limit the rollover of campaign funds, to discourage the building of war chests that were common to incumbents.

Considering the brevity of the meeting, we made fairly good progress. We realized which issues needed discussion and which issues were agreeable.

I zipped together a memo to Boren declaring the first meeting "productive." I did warn him that Koch wanted to wait to see the White House's official proposal and language, which was to be presented soon. And I advised Boren to tell Mitchell that McCain had approached him about doing a bill together.

It would be a good while before Koch and I could have the next discussion. I was to be in Oklahoma for the next week mixing business with a family reunion. A two-week Senate recess was to begin the following week, and Koch and I were both scheduled to be out of town part of the time. So we scheduled our next meeting for July 17, more then a month after the original Boren-McCain summit.

But a separate occurrence before that date would put a new light on that meeting and the entire effort. The July 13 edition of

Roll Call carried a story that blew the lid off the quiet attempt by Boren and McCain to construct a compromise bill. A leak in late June, most assuredly from McCain's office, caused the reporter to call me to ask, "What's going to be in the new Boren-McCain package on campaign finance reform?"

Stunned that the secret meetings were made public, I tried to downplay the story, characterizing the talks as just preliminary and routine, the kind of discussions we have "all the time with Republicans" to find a way out of the impasse.

But the reporter persisted with information about the bill that was to be introduced before the August recess, a point never discussed between Boren and McCain but curiously brought out in the story. The reporter pressed me about how we could overcome the spending limit issue. Feeling that if a story came out, it would be better to have fuzzy facts instead of sensationalized speculation, I finally gave her some information. The paragraph was still a bit too revealing:

The package, if successfully pulled together, is likely to retain spending limits based on the voter-age population of a state but drop the controversial public financing that has been an integral part of Boren's past legislation. Instead, the bill would use incentives for compliance other than federal funding, such as broadcast discount rates, according to Greg Kubiak, Boren's chief legislative aide. It would also incorporate some of President Bush's campaign finance recommendations offered earlier this month.

Needless to say, my telephone was ringing after that edition of *Roll Call* was delivered. The first call was from my friend and fellow campaign finance reform staffer in Senator DeConcini's office, Laurie Sedlmayr. Despite our frequent conversations and occasional lunch dates, I had never told Sedlmayer about the effort with her boss's state colleague. I got the strong impression from our conversation that she felt McCain was just using the opportunity to work with Boren to relieve some pressure over upcoming ethics questions that faced McCain. She knew, of course, that I had to honor what I thought was the confidential nature of our meetings. I merely recall a warning from her about McCain's real motivation.

Koch called as well. He sounded vaguely upset about the public disclosure, hiding what I later realized was relief. His voice suggested a "let's just move on" attitude and confirmed a meeting we had set for the following Monday.

Press calls came in, too, from *Congressional Quarterly* and Gannett News, seeking more information about the Boren-McCain meetings. I put them off, giving them no more insight than what was revealed to the *Roll Call* reporter.

The last wave of reaction came from Stephen Law, McConnell's LA. He delicately questioned what issues had been resolved, doing his best to hide his surprise and embarrassment over the secret meetings. Law was a constant defender of his boss's expertise and mantle of leadership on campaign finance reform. Such a covert effort by the Arizona Republican was an airing of intraparty laundry he would rather I had not seen. But I assured my staff colleague that discussions were preliminary, taking pride and comfort and a sadistic pleasure in saying to him, "Well, Stephen, McCain came to us, we didn't go to him."

With that last deed done, I just wanted to leave the office. My biggest fear was that I would receive calls from Democratic staff asking, "Why is Boren selling out public financing in this back-room negotiation with the Republicans?" A strong dose of jet lag hit me around 2:30 P.M. (I had returned from Taiwan just three days earlier.) So I left the office to sleep away what I hoped would not be a public setback to the private negotiations.

Monday morning's meeting was set for 10:00 A.M. Again, out of courtesy to the prospective cosponsor, I walked down to McCain's office to meet with Koch. On this trip, though, I took a slower approach. It happened that McConnell's office was located in the same corridor of the first floor of the Russell Senate Office Building as McCain's. Though it sounds overly paranoid, I did not want to run into Law, or for that matter, his senator, on my way to help displace or upstage McConnell's leadership on campaign reform.

This second meeting with Koch was still productive but slower than the first. We discussed combining the president's language to ban corporate and labor PACs and lowering the limit for ideological PACs to $1,000. We discussed details of the soft money language I was trying to sell him. After some more dialogue on rollover of funds and franking privileges, Koch threw out a real curveball. "Why should we have absolute spending limits that could stifle in-state contributions?" he asked. He went on to explain that the real concern was "bad" money from PACs and interested lobbyists. Why not encourage in-state contributions?

At that point, I suggested a 50 percent tax credit up to $100 for in-state candidates complying with spending limits. In that way, candidates would rely more on those funds, and participation of in-state voters would be enhanced.

Koch was likewise concerned about the costs. But I asked him, "What's the difference between reduced postal rates or broadcast discounts for those complying with limits?" It was our position that someone has to pay the price to encourage living by those limits. I must have looked a little perturbed by his constant opposition to a concept our bosses said was a given. He persisted.

"I just don't see how limits are going to work. You're going to stifle competition."

"Well," I said, "if you think we've got competition with a 98 percent reelection rate in the House, an 8 or 12 to 1 ratio of PAC contributions to incumbents over challengers, and challengers getting outspent by incumbents by 2 or 3 to 1 in *close* races, then I'd hate to see your definition of a tight race! How are your Republican challengers going to be hurt by our limits?" I demanded to know.

We both smiled at my impromptu soapbox speech. "We're both looking for a way to get bipartisan support, aren't we?" I asked. "I just made your [Republican] argument for some kind of a spending limits bill."

The AA agreed but countered, "Yes, we want a bipartisan bill, but that means McCain's got to sell it to Republicans."

I was still growing angry at this new stone wall I had hit with Koch. What could have been a compromise bill ready for drafting had just turned into a semester-long term paper at Senate U. Koch was more interested in research, rhetoric, and reflection than drafting a bill. He had thrown a monkey wrench into the machinery, obviously because of pressure he was getting from Republicans—staff, party officials, and members of Congress.

I suggested he get his ideas for a bill firmed up and in writing. I would do the same, and we could meet again in two days.

Our third meetings was on July 19. I had hoped it would be the meeting to dot i's and cross t's on a Boren-McCain bill. Instead, our discussion was more of the same. I came prepared to show Koch proof positive that the S. 137 limits did nothing to harm challengers. The limits were high enough to allow a competitive level of spending. The limits were set low enough to force incumbents to scale back. That is where the burden of reform was placed—on the backs of incumbents, not challengers. I wanted to talk limits.

Koch was unimpressed and quick to change the subject. He came with charts and computer runs of his own to counter my arguments. Rather than debate my logic for limits, though, he shifted to the subject of soft money. His question was, why should state parties have to abide by federal limits for "mixed activities"? That was an "imposition on states' rights by the feds" to regulate the states, he claimed. He saw the S. 137 soft money language as a federalization of state laws.

I countered with examples of Democratic and Republican presidential campaign practices. I was none too polite in using the example of ambassadorships being given in exchange for $100,000 contributions to the GOP as a reason to limit the practice. My point was that under a revised congressional sys-tem, complete with spending limits, it was necessary to plug the other loopholes through which illegal money would flow.

I had hoped this would bring Koch back to the spending limit issue, but it was clear we were at an impasse without more direction from the principals. Figuring I could prove that he was not accurately representing of his senator's wishes, I suggested that the four of us meet again. Koch picked up the telephone then and there to see what McCain's schedule was for the next day. The senator could meet in the afternoon. I replied that I would go back to my office and have our scheduler call McCain's. I did not even bother to wait to ask Boren.

I angrily rushed back to the office to get a meeting set up and prepare an uncharacteristically long memo for Boren. While writing it, a meeting had been confirmed for the two, with staff, at 1:30 the next day. My memo laid out the situation for Boren.

I have noted a stronger opposition to spending limits by McCain staff than the senator indicated in our meeting last month. Part of this must be due to the fact that word has gotten out that McCain is working with us on a bill with spending limits . . . even before the [leaked] *Roll Call* article was published. . . .

McCain will accept our [soft money] provisions on national, state party and corporate and labor disclosure. He will accept our provision on certifying that no agent of a presidential candidate will raise illegal money. But they so far will not accept limiting federal activities funneled thru state parties or setting the 100% allocation rule [limiting "mixed activities"].

Only McCain himself can decide if he wants spending limits. And if he does not, I would suggest that we find another Republican with whom to work—Rudman or Kassebaum—because a limitless bill will be a waste of time.

In the afternoon meeting on July 20, McCain was obviously well briefed by Koch on how strongly Boren would push to get a bill together that included a McCain-favored PAC ban and a Boren-favored spending limit provision, with no direct public financing as they previously agreed. McCain was much less enthusiastic this time around. He still wanted a bill but did not want to pay for enforcement of spending limits. He hoped that inducements could be found to encourage compliance that were not a direct hit on the treasury. He also, for the first time, voiced a concern for the historical party imbalances in some states, where spending limits might harm a Republican challenger.

This was a charge mentioned in debate before, by both McConnell and Dole. The worry was that in states where Republicans were at a historical party registration disadvantage, such as in the South, a challenger would need more spending ability than the Democratic incumbent. It would be a hard equation to formulate, but I remained silent throughout that part of the meeting, just hoping for McCain's statement of intent for a joint bill.

The meeting ended with yet another charge to the two staffers to work out details and come back with a recommendation to break the impasse. The next day, I returned to meet with Koch. And again the following week. What I experienced were new tactics for delay again and again and again.

The only new development in my understanding of McCain's desire to be on a reform bill was from a column published on July 23. Jack Anderson and Dale Van Atta wrote an op-ed piece highlighting details of the ethics mess brewing for McCain and four other senators. Part of the piece described McCain's position:

> McCain is embroiled in a political dogfight that, by his own admission, has caused him to lose sleep. . . . At issue is McCain's attendance at two meetings where he saw other senators browbeat federal thrift regulators who were perceived as being too tough on a savings and loan.
> The [details of those 1987 meetings] . . . are only now coming to the surface, much to the distress of some of those involved.

The article discussed the efforts by the five senators to intercede on behalf of Lincoln Savings owner Charles H. Keating, Jr., who contributed over "$300,000 in campaign contributions from the Lincoln empire" to those lawmakers. Still, the piece portrayed McCain as a good guy in the cause on behalf of Lincoln because he had "stayed awake worrying about the appearance of impropriety."

It was now clear to me that McCain's only interest in being on a Boren bill was to further distance himself from the upcoming explosion from the "Keating 5" bombshell. But the pressure on McCain from his constituents was no stronger than the pressure on McCain and Koch from GOP party officials, senators, and staff. In my last meeting with Koch on July 28, he admitted to his fear of again being confronted by Senator McConnell, who had personally badgered him for negotiating with Boren's office.

My understanding of the game being played came as my patience wore out. Further meetings with Koch would be futile. He would negotiate a bill no quicker than his boss would force him to, and this did not seem to be imminent. And since McCain needed Republican friends as much as he needed home state popularity three years away from a reelection campaign, the effort was not worth the energy.

Three days after my last meeting with Koch and with the long August recess about to begin, I wrote a final McCain memo to Boren.

I know you had expected that we could have at least announced a bill by you and Senator McCain before the August recess. However, it will obviously not come about and I wanted you to know what the problems have been.

Basically, as you know from the two meetings in which you and McCain have discussed a bill, McCain appears committed to doing a bill that includes spending limits. . . . At least that had been my impression from everything McCain has said. . . .

However, it has become blatantly obvious that he [Koch] is seeking to slow our efforts thru delays and by bringing in completely new concepts to our negotiations. I am 99.9% sure that he has consulted in-depth with Republican party officials in an attempt to arm himself with ammunition to kill spending limits from this plan. He has computer charts that were custom-run based on our discussions from other than Senate computers—only the RNC could produce these; and one of his counterproposals to our "spending limits" was the same as was privately negotiated by House Republicans in the CFR Task Force, so I have learned. . . .

My purpose is to let you know this so you can be equipped to prod McCain—so that perhaps he will take an interest in directing his AA to stop delaying. It would be counterproductive for you to actually accuse McCain's AA of intentional delay—as I hope to continue working with [him]. However, I wanted you to know that I have been diligent in trying to produce a bill.

What I earlier thought was Koch's relief at the public disclosure of this joint effort seemed to me now to be a more sophisticated plot. In fact, my realization about the two-month episode would suggest that Koch, without the knowledge of his boss, leaked the story to *Roll Call*. By remaining unnamed for the story, he suggested that the reporter get details of progress from Boren's office. Since I had talked several times before to that reporter, she was quick to call. After getting me to provide information and to be named in the story, McCain's aide could remain blameless in the eyes of his senator for the disclosure to the press. The leak appeared to be staged as a way for conservative Republican senators to halt the treasonous efforts by McCain. Another theory was that it was a delaying tactic of the Republicans all along.

McCain was anxious to get on legislation with Boren that would be introduced quickly, due to brewing questions of his involvement with Charles Keating. While McCain seemed sincere in his desire to be associated with a bipartisan, "good government" reform bill, it was not without reason. McCain foresaw the questions that would be raised with regard to his ethics in an official investigation into his intervening for the savings and loan figure. This legislative preemptive strike might provide him with goodwill and cover for an Arizona electorate whose approval rating of him would slide.

McCain and Koch's delay in action was a direct result of partisan pressure. The outcome, like the filibuster months before, was stalemate.

THE "KEATING 100"

In fall 1989, long after the dust had settled on the bitter 1988 presidential campaign and well after the heated emotions cooled from the filibuster on S. 2, a new campaign was about to grip the closed club of the U.S. Senate. Earlier that year, the Congress acted on the Bush administration's first major domestic policy initiative, the bailout of the savings and loan deposit insurance fund. But its aftermath left a series of questions about decisions made by the old Federal Home Loan Bank Board (FHLBB). Those questions would be asked by blood-hungry public interest groups before an anxious and waiting working press with an angry electorate looking on.

October 13 was a most unlucky Friday for five senators who were linked to Charles Keating. On that day, Common Cause made public a request to the Senate Select Committee on Ethics to investigate activities of the five with respect to a southern California savings and loan known as Lincoln.

In a letter to Sen. Howell Heflin, chairman of the Senate Ethics Committee, Fred Wertheimer, president of Common Cause, urged the committee to conduct an investigation with an outside counsel to determine if the five senators "violated Senate ethics rules and standards." The Resolution Trust Corporation, a government agency that grew out of the savings and loan legislation had one month earlier filed a $1.1 billion fraud and racketeering civil lawsuit against Keating. Common Cause was not alone in its accusation that severe wrongdoing was tied to this case. Yet missing from the Common Cause press release and Wertheimer statement were the typical rhetorical slams of "influence buying" and public service "on the auction block." Instead, the words were measured, formal, and legalistic.

The central issue was how this savings and loan in southern California could have been allowed to remain open despite technical insolvency to the point of costing the taxpayers in excess of $1.3 billion. The answer assumed by Common Cause was the inappropriate actions of five senators who received large campaign contributions from Keating and his empire.

Also in on the act at this point was House Banking Committee Chairman Henry Gonzales. In an unusual move against four senators of his own party, Gonzales began hearings in October on the Lincoln Savings and Loan affair and the political influence of its overseer, Keating. The move might have been seen by some as the jealous House trying to embarrass the "upper" body or as stupid strategy by others. At any rate, all of a sudden, the term "the Keating Five" took on a scandalous tone similar to "Water-gate," "Teapot Dome," and "Abscam."

Reflective of this mood surrounding the Keating Five was the conduct displayed by each. Two, McCain and Glenn, fearing the least from the attention, eventually went on the Sunday shows to tell their story. On ABC's "This Week with David Brinkley," the two did a surprisingly good job of defending their actions, at least with respect to meetings with FHLBB officials. McCain had much more to answer for, as he accepted from Keating $13,000 worth of personal hospitality and travel to, among other places, the Bahamas. Another, Senator DeConcini, went on a public relations blitz by putting paid political advertisements on television in Arizona to tell his side of the story.

Senator Cranston was perhaps the most affected by the scandal. His popularity in California polls at one point saw the percentage ratio of those approving of his job performance versus those *not* wanting him to run for another term drop to 20 to 69. As he was the indirect recipient of $850,000 in soft money/voter registration contributions from Keating, he was seen as the major player in the influence-peddling scandal.

A December 6, 1989, page 1 *New York Times* headline de-clared, "Cranston Inquiry Widens to Include Signing of Voters." This report, unlike previous ones, focused not on an ethics committee investigation but on a federal law-enforcement investigation to examine "whether employees of two of the [voter registration] organizations were instructed to register more Democrats than Republicans . . . in violation of the tax-exempt status that the groups enjoyed based on their nonparti-sanship."

But with respect to the ethics charges, a former staffer to the senator told me two years later that "what Senator Cranston did was no different from what other members do. It's the system that's corrupt, not Senator Cranston." In fact, I sat in on more than one meeting during this period in which Boren would discuss the Keating "scandal" as not totally dissimilar to what all senators do. He related that he and other senators would often say, "There but for the grace of God go I." It could as easily have been called the "Keating 100 Scandal."

With responsibilities as Boren's banking aide as well, I encountered a number of people who could have been bankers in Keating's clothing. One financier/banker from Ardmore, Oklahoma, came to see me repeatedly about a "master limited partnership plan" he had developed to infuse capital into failing savings and loans under a consolidation plan. His interest was in getting the FHLBB to approve of the plan as a way to consolidate failing Oklahoma savings and loans. In a matter of a couple days after first meeting with this man, I drafted a letter for Boren to a deputy director of the FHLBB. In it I wrote, "With the severe need for capital infusion and disposition of problem real estate portfolios, to help relieve the burden from the Federal Savings and Loan Insurance Corporation, I am hopeful that this and other plans can be met as being constructive and positive." We were basically asking the FHLBB to review and approve of his plan and give him the responsibility and profits for devalued assets (real estate) from the thrifts. Any inheritor of such assets would over the long term be a bit wealthier than before.

Had the banker been a large contributor/fund raiser for Boren and had the FHLBB official felt the letter too strong a push for a potential buyer of failing savings and loans, Boren could have been seen as equally as guilty as the other five senators in the Keating case. But guilty of what? Guilty of helping a constituent who had money to keep state savings and loans locally owned and operated? Guilty of calling the banker's interest to the attention of the slow-moving FHLBB? Guilty of lawfully accepting a contribution from a constituent?

But there was a difference between letters, meetings, and contributions in the Keating case, as there was for Boren in his actions for state investors and bankers. It was a matter of degree. That level was defined when the Senate Ethics Committee issued a formal reprimand to Cranston but not the other four.

The Senate did eventually "strongly and severely reprimand" Cranston for an "impermissible pattern of conduct" that was "improper and repugnant." Citing his "poor health" and his announced "intention not to seek reelection," the Senate Ethics Committee fell short of recommending censure or expulsion.

The dramatic events, disclosures, and hearings leading up to this action seemed at the time an unfortunate blessing. Even if it was the media that characterized it as a scandal, the Keating affair would create an environment in which campaign finance reform got a real boost in public attention and discussion. Boren told me after the Senate Ethics Committee's decision to investigate that our bill was ripe for passage.

His public comments bore that out as well. In a press interview, Boren was asked when Congress would pass campaign reform.

I really think it's going to happen this year. Sometimes it takes a jolt—and I think the number of ethics cases that are now pending in Congress is the kind of jolt that it has taken to cause people to wake up to this problem around the country. We now have about 80 percent of the American people, according to the latest polling data, that see this as a serious problem. They want limits put on the runaway spending of campaign funds to get elected. So I think the people are now demanding action. I think the Congress knows it. The people in Congress know that the institution is in trouble. And I think *this is the year* in which we have the best chance by far that we've ever had to get something done.

BOUT WITH A SENATOR

Senator Cranston never impressed me as being very sincere about campaign finance reform. His main interest had always seemed to be protection of the fund-raising strengths he had developed from several years in public office.

It was a top Cranston aide who in 1985 angrily confronted me in the Democratic AA's luncheon I attended to explain the Boren-Goldwater amendment. Likewise, Cranston was the last Democratic holdout we sought to support us in that first vote. His floor speech minutes before that vote was indicative of his struggle and desire not to be a lone and obvious opponent to Boren-

Goldwater: "Mr. President, a vote to table the Boren amendment is not a vote against campaign reform. A vote not to table the Boren amendment is not a vote for campaign reform. I am for campaign reform, but until a few moments ago it was my intention to vote to table the Boren amendment."

In the next round, it was Cranston who covertly tried to work with Senators Mitchell, Kennedy, and Kerry after Boren introduced S. 2. Those secret efforts in 1987 caused a crucial delay in Democratic unity that ultimately led to Republican suspicion and distrust. Had Boren been freed from watching out for Cranston's efforts to divide Democrats, he might have had more time to appeal for bipartisan support from key Republicans.

And now, two years later, Cranston would again instigate an effort to alter Boren's bill and sabotage his leadership. Cranston would put together another undercover attempt, this time to gut the Boren-Mitchell bill of its strong language against soft money. As the subject of an ethics scandal, Cranston was getting desperate.

On February 2, 1990, a year and eight days after we had introduced S. 137 with its strong provisions against the soft money abuses characteristic of the Keating episode, Cranstone called a secret meeting of senators. It was attended by about five of his colleagues and several staff persons associated with the Democratic Policy Committee (DPC) for the purpose of discussing changes in the soft money approach in the Boren-Mitchell bill.

Soon thereafter, I was contacted by three offices, questioning what "Boren thought about Cranston trying to garner forces to take out his 'soft money' provisions." I immediately talked over the reports of secret meetings with Susan Manes of Common Cause and Bob Rozen of Mitchell's staff. Both were aware of the meeting and of its danger. A second meeting of the group was scheduled for February 6. It was apparently rescheduled, however, as the weekly Democratic caucus luncheon was the same day. A written agenda of that meeting prepared by Cranston's office proved that he "questioned" whether the bill's prohibitions on state party soft money were good policy.

The war was waged. At the Democratic conference/caucus luncheon that afternoon, aware of the secret struggle that Cranston was trying to engage in for power over the process, Mitchell gave a verbal "ordination" of Boren as *the* leader of campaign reform for the Democrats. Mitchell thought this approach would discourage senators from going along with Cranston's effort under the guise of the DPC.

In a meeting with Common Cause the next day, Boren felt comfortable that with Mitchell's public proclamation to the caucus, Cranston would back down with this DPC "study group." I recall that he was feeling comfortable that Cranston would no longer be a threat, because Mitchell was standing strongly by Boren's side as the joint leaders on the issue.

Yet on Friday, February 9, the battle still raged. A one-paragraph "Washington Wire" piece on the front page of the *Wall Street Journal* stated that Mitchell "has prioritized campaign finance reform with restrictions on 'soft money' for early March," despite efforts by Democratic party activists and Cranston to water down provisions of the Democratic leadership bill.

After reading that piece, I intercepted a written memo from Cranston to Boren, dated that day. It stated that Boren was invited to participate in a Cranston "task force" on campaign finance reform. Boren was on his way to Oklahoma for the week-long Senate recess that just started, so I conferred again with Rozen in Mitchell's office on this continued struggle. I felt the majority leader needed to take action. Rozen agreed, and within hours he called me to say tht Boren was "officially appointed" by Mitchell to head a Democratic task force—a move right out of the Byrd playbook from years past.

The letter from Mitchell to Boren came with the same speed as the other events of that morning, the *Wall Street Journal* piece and the Cranston memo. It read, in part:

One of our top legislative priorities for this Congress is passage of meaningful campaign finance reform legislation. . . . In Conference this week, I asked you to coordinate suggestions on campaign finance reform. I would like you to serve as Chairman of the Democratic Task Force on campaign finance reform.

After listing the nine other senators in the group, Mitchell informed Boren that he would be "sending a letter to all Democratic senators asking them to be in touch with you and the other members of the task force."

Most people would have gotten the hint to stop such private efforts as Cranston's. He was told in the company of his colleagues by the majority leader that Boren was to coordinate the party's efforts in the Senate. Further, Mitchell formalized that role for Boren with the chairmanship of this new task force. Yet Cranston still had scheduled a February 20 meeting of senators to discuss changes in soft money provisions. While Boren was invited, along with "other senators" with an interest in the issue, the point still did not seem to get through to Cranston that his efforts were divisive and not welcome. Everyone seemed to understand that except Cranston.

The *New York Times* picked up on the troubles within the Democratic camp after the leak to the *Wall Street Journal*. I assumed that the original leak to that paper was fed by a senator or staffer other than those associated with Mitchell or Boren. Another bet on the origin could have been Wertheimer, who had a good relationship with the *New York Times* and its reporter, Rick Berke, who covered the money in politics beat out of the newspaper's Washington bureau. He saw the ethics questions surrounding Cranston and was onto his secret efforts to protect his money-raising talents.

I became aware of Berke's lead on a story after Lincoln's birthday, when he called me with lots of questions. I had no hesitation in sharing with Berke my knowledge of Cranston's efforts, all off the record. However, over the weekend, Berke called me at my Silver Spring, Maryland, home at least three times. He had questions about Cranston's efforts that he wanted answered for the story. I gave him all the dirt I had, facts, telephone calls, meetings, and other sources to question and quote. But the last call, around 6:30 P.M. Saturday, was to say that he could not get a named source for some of the charges. Without one, he did not feel he could legitimately run the story. His question was, would I go on the record with a quote that would give backbone to his story?

I knew the risks of even a calculated statement. Even a statement that did not indict Cranston directly could point to me as the "unnamed Democratic source" for some other comment.

But my patience with Cranston had grown too strained. The story could expose his efforts and put him out of commission as a troublemaker for good. With the ethics trouble surrounding him, he would surely not ever try to unseat Boren again as the bona fide leader of the issue. And besides, it was the truth. Why was I being shy about telling the truth? I gave Berke a slow, deliberate quote and told him to run with it.

The next morning, I rushed to the 7-Eleven a mile from the house to pick up a Sunday *New York Times*. There was the story, "Dispute in Senate on Finance Reform," headlined on page 1.

Supporters of the Democrat's leading campaign finance proposal say Senator Alan Cranston, the California Democrat whose fund-raising techniques are under the scrutiny of Federal law-enforcement authorities, is quietly maneuvering to dilute the measure.

I was named as Cranston's first accuser after the article looked at his connections to Charles Keating and after his top aide, Roy Greenaway, defended his boss by claiming that the bill's language would "preempt money raised by the state party."

"Senator Cranston appeared to be interested in undermining the bill's protections against what we regard as illegal contributions to influence Federal elections," said Greg D. Kubiak, chief aide on campaign finance to Mr. Boren. He described the provisions involving state parties as "central to getting a good bill," adding, "Any weakening of these provisions would be a serious mistake."

After saying that Mitchell's office had no comment, Berke quoted Wertheimer, who took a dual and more direct hit at

Cranston: "Without this key provision, Charles Keating would still be able to make the kind of huge contributions that helped Senator Cranston in 1986 and the $100,000 contribution that helped President Bush in 1988."

Also quoted was an unnamed Senate aide who attended the first meeting who "characterized the session as an informal discussion of campaign finance matters," according to the story. Yet Berke's piece indicated that "other staff members said privately that the Senator and his aides have made clear in other conversations that they wanted to delete provisions that would curb spending on Federal races by state parties."

The story pointed out that in 1986, "Charles H. Keating, Jr., who owned the Lincoln Savings and Loan Association in California, gave $85,000 to the Democratic Party in California for a voter drive that the Senate has said was critical to his reelection." It went on to explain that S. 137 "would have sharply restricted the California Democratic Party's ability to use the $85,000 to help Mr. Cranston."

When Berke told me that his story would mention the other staffers at the meeting who were lobbied by Cranston and Greenaway on this provision, I reluctantly but deliberately agreed to give him a quote for use in the article. I knew the risks but had grown impatient at this backstabbing attempt by the Democratic whip. In the angry confines of my home office that Saturday evening, I wrote out my quote and then read it to Berke. It came out the next morning in the *New York Times* looking like this:

> The meeting apparently angered Mr. Boren and his staff, who accused Mr. Cranston of undermining their efforts on the issue. "While Senator Boren invites the input of any senator on this issue," Kubiak of Mr. Boren's staff said, "it is disturbing that another senator has called a covert meeting in an apparent effort to gut the bill of its strongest protections against special interest money."

The article reported Mitchell's appointment of Boren to head a Democratic task force "on the day Mr. Cranston announced the second meeting." It closed with Greenaway's defense of his boss: "Alan is one of the best fund-raisers in the party and probably knows the most about it. . . . Why should he be touchy about that?"

Boren, still in Oklahoma on the day of the article's publication, was tracked down by Cranston with a flurry of telephone calls over the President's Day holiday weekend. Knowing that I put Boren in an embarrassing spot with his colleague, who was also a member of his Intelligence Committee, I arranged to meet Boren's plane at National Airport.

Before that, however, I received a call from Cranston's staffer (who helped lead that "ethics seminar" two and a half years earlier). Greenaway asked that I come meet him and another Cranston aide in the whip's office in the Capitol at 1:00 P.M. on February 20.

I had John Deeken, former LC, former assistant press secretary, future legislative director, and consistent friend, attend the session with me. Greenaway and the attorney/staffer were cordial and careful in the meeting. I did not want to rehash the circumstances of the story with Greenaway, but I was prepared to do so if he got as embittered as he did in the 1985 encounter over the bundling and PAC provision of Boren-Goldwater. But Greenaway forced a compassionate voice and said, "We didn't want to displace Boren as the leader of this, Greg. It's just that Alan was asked to lead a study group by [Senator Tom] Daschle."

Daschle was the co-chair with Mitchell of the Democratic Policy Committee at the time, but no mention of his active involvement had been mentioned before now. I remember replying simply, "Roy, it's not important now who did what. What we have to focus on is how to be united in getting this bill ready for debate in the Senate, since Mitchell wants to push it soon."

Greenaway agreed and let the other staffer begin to discuss flaws they felt existed in our soft money language. After listening to her espouse the uniqueness of California with its volatile "initiative/referendum campaigns," I excused myself for a trip across the river. I met Boren at National Airport, and we talked about the circumstances that led to my decision to go public. He was understanding about my motivation but seemed to want to see how things would settle down before he passed judgment. I gave Boren a detailed memo that afternoon entitled "Cranston Episode."

I wanted to give you a fuller account of my actions with respect to the *New York Times* article so you would know the story and what misunderstandings took place.

First, you should know that I am sorry for any embarrassment I have caused you and that I do know how I should have handled the situation differently. However, as has been the case in dealing with this bill and effort over several years, I have had to make several important judgments and risks based on my personal knowledge of the issue, on your perceived wishes and best interests, and my own practical and political instincts. Perhaps my pointing out other factors may give partial explanation for how the matter transpired.

After a chronological detailing of events to refresh Boren's memory on the calculated tactics of Cranston, I concluded the memo,

While I needn't go into further exhaustive detail about this, you should know I was aware of the risk once I went public. . . . However, I merely wish to state part of my motives in going public were to protect the bill and your leadership position on it. I feared that if Cranston was left unbridled without timely constraint, it would not be in your or the bill's best interests. Even if it meant a "good cop/bad cop" scenario, my judgment at the time indicated it was necessary.

Boren's response could not have been more supportive. He scribbled back,

Greg, I understand completely. No sleep should be lost over this. We'll just do a little strategizing in the future because I'm afraid that more efforts will be made to sabotage the bill. . . . Next time, we can all talk over how to handle a report and use it as an opportunity to get out a common message. Sometimes it's useful for staff to be quoted instead of me. . . . Thanks, I understand the situation—DLB

TIME TO LEAVE

My hardball tactics to control the Cranston episode were merely symptomatic of my growing disgust for the game-playing and throat-cutting around me. I had seen a very dark side of the legislative process in five years of work on campaign finance reform.

It had troubled me for some time that the 1988 filibuster had left deep scars on relationships in the Senate and the willingness to work out a compromise. I certainly had other activities on Boren's staff to keep me occupied with education and banking legislation as well as my duties as his chief LA. But the nightmare of failure on this effort kept haunting me. I worried that if we got a bill to pass the Senate, if the House passed one, too, and even if a joint conference produced a measure for the president, he still might not sign it. Despite the ethics revelations surrounding Speaker Jim Wright, Senators Durenberger and D'Amato, and the Keating Five, there was no guarantee that this bill could become law.

As I mentioned before, one of the greatest honors I had as a Senate staffer was the opportunity to address a class at the Kennedy School of Government at Harvard. Earlier that day, October 11, 1989, I attended a White House arrival ceremony for the president of Italy. A ticket to such pageantry is seldom shared with Senate staffers of the opposite party, but that day I was on the White House list. I figured at the time it was due to my role in helping get Boren to be the first Democratic Senate cosponsor of the president's education bill that year. But for whatever reason, I was honored to be on the South Lawn that morning for the traditional, diplomatic welcome.

I had little time to spend at the office after the event before I would catch the 1:05 P.M. flight to Boston for my appearance at former Governor Askew's class. After a rewarding experience with enlightened and enlightening students, not much younger than me, I was shuttled back to Logan Airport for my flight back to Washington.

The stress, excitement, and transitional autumn temperatures caused me to come up with a bit of a cold that next day at the office, so I left early. The rest of that day and the next, I sat at home, nursing a sore throat and the sniffles. But the rest and time alone caused me to reflect on what I was doing and where I was going. The strains of the Senate office were beginning to set in. They were physical, psychological, and trivial.

My near-sightedness had worsened by nine grades in a two-year span during the intense Boren-Goldwater, Boren-Byrd office hours. The 12- to 14-hour workdays had taken a large toll on my overweight, cocktail reception-fed body. At age twenty-eight, I had even sprouted a gray hair on my temple.

My generally good demeanor toward summer interns—of whose rank I once had been—had soured. At times I was unapproachable to staffers because of my impatience with endless CFR meetings. Whereas my early years in Washington were marked by my being the "Social Chairman/Morale Officer," the waning years brought a short fuse caused by tunnel vision for one bill. Other pressures had led me to consider going to graduate school to work on a master's degree. Maybe now was the time to do it.

Finally, in contemplating my professional life and work on "the bill," more than anything, I did not believe that it would be enacted into law during this Congress.

That next day, October 13, as Common Cause was polishing their rhetoric for a request that the Senate investigate the Keating Five, I decided to resign. I planned to leave at year's end—giving Boren ample notice and me the time to find another, less time-intensive occupation. But I would keep the plan to myself.

I kept up my work and started to organize the timing of my resignation and postdeparture plans, including a trip to Europe. Since the Congress would adjourn late in a nonelection year, I decided to wait until Oklahoma Statehood Day, November 16, to break the news to Boren. As expected, the senator was shocked at my letter of resignation. I slipped it to his executive assistant and warned her, "Let me know when he gets it." She knew by the look on my face that its contents were serious.

Of all the personal and professional reasons Boren could have mentioned in our hour-long visit after he got my letter, he only chose one. After asking me to reconsider, he said those familiar words, "This is the year for campaign reform. You have to be here for that. I need you." Boren asked that I sleep on the matter and have lunch with him the next day to talk about it again. Even though he would try to talk me out of it, my mind was made up. To help Boren through the transition of my departure, I gave him an assurance that if the bill was to move, "I'd return." But I did not think it likely.

The next day, we constructed a press release about my departure. The reference to my work on campaign finance reform read, "He's shown immense intellectual and political capabilities in his work on my campaign finance and PAC reform legislation over the past 4 years. I believe that Greg's initiative and persistence have helped set the stage for future reforms."

I would leave my position with a great deal of satisfaction about my service. One test of my impact on Boren's career came when the University of Oklahoma awarded him their Distinguished Service Citation, a tribute equivalent to an honorary degree. Boren's award mentioned five accomplishments from his twelve years in the Senate. Three of those distinctions were ones I helped craft: the establishment of the Oklahoma Foundation for Excellence, a nonprofit educational trust recognizing outstanding teachers and students; his efforts to bring the "best and brightest" into the classrooms with a teacher scholarship bill; and, of course, his tireless efforts for campaign finance reform.

Nineteen-hundred eighty-nine started out as the year in which campaign reform would be passed and enacted. It ended as a year of frustration as I said I would leave Capitol Hill. The decade of the nineties began with constant news analysis of the daily, almost hourly changes occurring in Eastern Europe. That first year of the decade was the prelude to peace "breaking out" in Communist countries and the eventual fall of the Berlin Wall. From the lone student in Tiananmen Square in Beijing who seemingly stopped that rolling tank to the Christmas day execution of the Rumanian Communist dictator, Nicolae Ceausescu, our international memory became rich with visions of the strength of democracy. These scenes and stories will forever stand as video images, etched in the American mind, of the people of the world becoming free.

But the year drew to an end, leaving me with a sense of emptiness. Just as the world was changing in response to people's demand for free elections, political choice, and true democracy, collectively, the U.S. Congress stood strongly resistant to reforming their own electoral process. United leadership against the addiction to money's link to power could not be found.

CHAPTER TEN

A Report from the Field

*Even though most Americans view government as a "public
trust," many senators regard their office as an "earned asset."*
— GREG D. KUBIAK (1960–)

*Our responsibility is not discharged by the announcement
of virtuous ends.*
— JOHN F. KENNEDY (1917–1963)

AFTER OFFICIALLY RESIGNING as Boren's chief legislative
assistant, I made an agreement with the senator that should there be
some indication of movement on campaign reform in 1990, I would
return part-time to consult and see through the effort to passage.
Otherwise, my November 16 announcement put me on an easy path
of transition from legislative adviser to graduate student.

I spent part of the holidays in Oklahoma, explaining why I
decided to leave Boren's staff for graduate school and "other
opportunities," and part in Crested Butte, Colorado, on a ski
trip. But I returned to the office on January 5 with one week
before my January 12 departure date. The week was primarily
made up of two-hour lobbyist lunches and packing. I had files
and papers to hand over to Cody Graves, who was named to
replace me.

The two weeks following my departure, I came into the office a couple of times to introduce John Deeken as Boren's new campaign finance reform czar. We met with Chris Koch, Susan Manes, Bob Rozen, and Jack Sousa of the Rules Committee. I also held a quick briefing session with Boren during that time, at which he reminded me of my pledge to return if the situation warranted. I agreed then to return for a meeting with Boren and Mitchell on February 1.

The 11:00 A.M. meeting was arranged for Boren to discuss with Mitchell a strategy on how to force an honest negotiation of the issue between Republicans and Democrats. Mitchell had Rozen attend the meeting, and Boren had Deeken and me at his side. The conventional wisdom coming out of the discussion was that only with the threat of votes on the floor would Republicans be willing to negotiate. But one signal came from the GOP that gave us a sign of hope. The substantive sign of a changed environment—or at least an open door—was a news story published in mid-December during the Senate adjournment. The Associated Press story concerned comments by Bob Dole.

After years of stalemate on how to revamp the campaign finance system, faint sounds of possible compromise are coming from congressional leaders, including Senate Republican Leader Bob Dole [who said] he would be willing to consider spending limits on congressional campaigns if a workable proposal can be developed, and if Democrats would drop their past suggestions for partial public financing.

The story related that Dole was urging Mitchell to establish a bipartisan panel to explore the spending limit issue in particular and campaign reform in general. Dole told the reporter that such a panel should be composed of "experts in campaign finance reform, the academic types," instead of Republicans and Democrats in Congress or political party insiders.

Mitchell told Boren that he felt he must follow up on Dole's virtuous announcement but that regardless of its result, he would put the bill on the floor in the spring to force the Republicans' hand. Boren took great delight in this sign of Mitchell's commitment as well as his statement, "This is the year for campaign reform." But then, I had heard that before.

After the meeting, Deeken saw that Boren wanted to talk to me privately, so he made some excuse to hurry back to the office via subway car while Boren and I walked through the Russell–Capitol tunnel.

"Well, Greg, you heard Mitchell. He really is going to push this bill. It looks like with the Keating stuff brewing and Dole's comments for a panel, we've got our opening to make it happen," Boren said.

"I know, Senator, but since I've started classes, I really can't afford more than a half-time position to consult. I have every bit of confidence that John can work this issue," I replied.

"You can do it any way you want. It's just I need your help, and you deserve to see this bill passed. I don't think the Republicans will filibuster again. That would just be too foolish. I think it'll pass this year. And you should be there."

He did not have to say more. I agreed to stay on as a "special assistant" and see the bill through.

PANEL OF SIX, GROUP OF TEN

The Dole notion of a bipartisan panel of experts to study and recommend a reform package could be seen as one of two things: an effort by Dole to get a quick remedy to the nagging issue that would provide him cover from his coleagues, or yet another device for delay and the appearance of goodwill.

Realizing, after consultation with Boren and Ford, that he had no alternative but to try it, Mitchell agreed to the panel and joined Dole in a February 8 letter appointing the six members.

During the past several years, Congress has grappled with the issue of campaign finance reform. Despite the good faith efforts . . . Democrats and Republicans have simply been unable to come together and fashion a bipartisan reform package that reflects the concerns of both parties.

Slyly speaking to the ethics troubles of the Keating 5, the letter continued,

> Needless to say, recent events have made the argument for meaningful campaign finance reform even more compelling. As a result, we are looking for some new and innovative ideas that will stimulate discussion and perhaps even help break the legislative logjam in Congress. To accomplish these goals, we thought it would be useful to establish a Campaign Finance Reform Panel.

After instructing the appointees that "the panel will work independently of us and any other member of the Senate," the letter charged the group to "complete its work no later than Tuesday, March 6, 1990."

On February 22, the Senate approved Senate Resolution 248, "Establishing an Advisory Panel on Campaign Finance Reform." The action, to assist in the formulation of policy relating to campaign finance reform, authorized this official panel to receive funds for their expenses from the Senate contingency fund but, of course, no salary for the few weeks of work.

The six invited experts did agree to join in the task and included experienced and knowledgeable persons. Dole's appointees were Herb Alexander, a University of Southern California professor, head of the Citizen's Research Foundation, author, and election law academic; Jan Baran, partner in a D.C. law firm, former counsel to the Republican National Committee, and former executive assistant to an FEC commissioner; and Larry Sabato, a professor and author from the University of Virginia. Mitchell's appointee were Robert Bauer, like Baran, a partner in a D.C. law firm and counsel to congressional candidates and Democratic campaign committees; David Magleby, a Brigham Young University professor, American Political Science Association congressional fellow in the office of Senator Byrd during S. 2, and author; and Richard Moe, yet another D.C. law firm partner, veteran of several Democratic campaigns, and former chief of staff to Vice President Walter Mondale. Moe was also a

member of the 1987 Lobbyists and Lawyers for Campaign
Finance Reform (chap. 6).

This panel of three lawyers and three scholars was also
balanced by political ideology. Despite their supposed political
nonallegiance in this effort, they each had partisan baggage to
carry along in the venture, just as the FEC did and does. But the
recommendations did breathe new life into the debate. Beside the
agreements on contribution rates for individuals, disclosure for
soft money, limits on PACs, and improvements in the FEC, they
forwarded two ideas that broke new ground.

The panel bought an idea pushed by Sabato to provide free
broadcast time to parties for the use of candidates in elections.
The National Association of Broadcasters, angered at the Boren
proposals that for four years called on reform of the expensive
venture of televised campaigning, now had a bipartisan foe in the
panel. The report of the panel stated,

> At least forty cents of every dollar raised in Senate elections is
> devoted to purchasing time for media advertising, and in some recent
> elections, well over half. . . . The rising price of broadcast time,
> which has increased at a rate several times the Consumer Price Index in
> recent years, is clearly a major factor in the skyrocketing cost of
> campaigning. This is especially significant because the United States
> is the only major democracy in the industrialized world that does not
> provide some free broadcast time.

The recommendation called on broadcasters, "as a condition of
license renewal, . . . to provide eight hours of free time for
political advertising every year" to be controlled by the major
political parties.

The second idea, a more sweeping breakthrough in the current
debate, was to establish a system of "flexible spending limits."
Such spending caps were to be "reasonably high" and would not
displace party and small in-state donors. In return for abiding by
such a program, candidates would receive "preferential broadcast advertising rates, reduced postal rates or a free mailing, and
tax credits for small in-state contributors."

In an interview after the panel's release of the report, panel member Larry Sabato told NBC News the rationale for the recommendation. "The good money is in-state, individual money. And the bad money is out-of-state money and political action committee money. And so we say, take the bad money and put a limit on it. And keep the good money to the side and put no limit on it."

With cautious and calculated words the day after the panel's report, Dole and Mitchell issued a statement to the press:

We have not had an opportunity to study the entire report thoroughly and do not endorse or reject every proposal. . . . It is significant, however, that these experts on election finance law have been able to reach an agreement. It shows the issue is capable of being resolved despite the strong differences between Republicans and Democrats.

The press conference was packed with reporters, cameras, video crews, and CFR staff like me, who barely squeezed into the ornate Lyndon Baines Johnson Room off the Senate floor for the event. Mitchell, knowing of the breakthrough for some sort of spending ceilings, appeared to be optimistic, but one reporter's question was directed to Dole.

"Mr. Dole, does this report mean that Republicans are willing to accept some sort of system of spending limits?"

With his usual biting charm, the minority leader avoided the question until he could feel out the report's impact with his caucus.

The Democratic caucus went through repeated closed sessions to discuss the issue, strategy, and, of course, the panel's report. One such session was held on March 22. One of the topics confronting Boren was how to deal with soft money. Out of concern for the constant war with the GOP over raising party funds, Democrats were concerned about shutting down fund-raising strengths. As discussed previously, Cranston's efforts to thwart this issue, which were going on in early 1990, were starting to have an effect as more senators questioned the advisability of stopping the flow of soft money.

In preparation for the caucus, I wrote a memo to Boren reminding him of the typical "party building" functions of most soft money transactions.

> With your colleagues, you can always use the example of how the DNC "Victory '88" fund treated Oklahoma in the election. They let [Vice Presidential nominee Lloyd] Bentsen be scheduled to visit the state but only if in conjunction with a fund raiser thru the Oklahoma State Demo. Party "Victory '88." After the goal was met, most of the money was shipped upstream to [Dukakis/DNC fund raiser] Bob Farmer in D.C. for allocation to swing states since they already wrote off Dukakis in Oklahoma. THE POINT BEING THAT "STATE PARTY" BUILDING ACTIVITY DID LITTLE IF ANYTHING FOR OKLAHOMA DEMOCRATS (especially since you had to help host a fund raiser for them here last year so they could keep their doors open).

This reminder to Boren was a helpful device in talking to other senators. Many knew that soft money was nothing more than a slick loophole to avoid federal limits, by using state party funds to affect the presidential elections. The point in this bill was that a spending limit system for Senate races would create the same incentive for abuse through the conduit of state parties.

During the discussion on soft money, one senator mentioned that Ron Brown, chairman of the Democratic National Committee, had strong concerns about going too far in closing down state party soft money. Out of frustration, one prominent southern senator asked, "What the hell's the DNC ever done for us?"

The discussions on the panel's recommendations would continue to be viable, insofar as the "flexible" spending limit issue was concerned. Other products of their work faded almost as quickly as the study group endured. But discussion between senators and staffs did heat up. One group was informal, one structured.

The day after the Mitchell-Dole press conference announcing the panel's recommendation, Boren had a 5:15 P.M. meeting with his good friend and colleague, Senator Danforth, the ranking Republican on the Senate Commerce, Science, and Transportation Committee. While on that committee, he was very involved with legislation affecting the broadcasting industry, with a renewed focus on the "lowest unit rate"—a discount price supposedly guaranteed to political advertising. Further, it was Danforth who wrote the language on "response time" to combat independent expenditures which Boren used in the 1985 legislation. So there was a history of Danforth's interest in reform.

Common Cause, as with McCain the year before, did a great deal to cultivate Danforth's desire to work with Boren on a compromise. It paid off. The effort brought Danforth to Boren's office, where they talked candidly about the concern for the rising costs of campaigning, mainly because of television advertising costs. Danforth indicated an interest in working with us.

The following day, March 9, Boren met with Senator Stevens, another moderate whose voice of reason was often drowned out by McConnell. Stevens expressed a similar interest in joining with Boren in a renewed effort at compromise now that a bipartisan panel had provided a blueprint for reform. Boren suggested that the two of them join with Danforth in a joint venture. Boren was eager and enthusiastic but needed another Democrat to balance the threesome. Without hestiation, the duty fell to Wendell Ford.

In the course of several meetings, staff progress was made toward a common agenda. However, the same fears that scared off John McCain months before gripped these two Republicans as well. Goodwill was eroded when details became solid.

While the public cry was that Republicans were backing away from the only bipartisan solution to be offered as a logjam breaker, Democrats were not sole owners of the high ground. Our private and partisan negotiating sessions of staff for Mitchell, Boren, and Ford had explicit instructions to interpret "flexible" limits as "flexibly fixed" above the previously fixed limits of S. 137. This was the philosophical gridlock. I saw it as more a position of Democratic protection than responsible legislating. Here was our chance, if ever there was one, to find a common device for compromise. But ideological purity won out over pragmatic policymaking.

I was not alone in my view that Mitchell was finessing the flexible spending limits issue. A journalist for Gannett News told me long after the 101st Congress that "a compromise could have been worked out on the flexible spending limit plan without sacrificing principle, but as long as the Democrats insist on a strict spending limit, I don't think a workable compromise is possible."

Mitchell wanted to pressure Dole on the flexible limits issue. However, he agreed to a final and formal bipartisan effort at compromise before forcing the issue to the floor. The two leaders would appoint a group of ten to a negotiating team.

Having met a few times in a summit-style confrontation, stalwarts on both sides would not budge. Instead, McConnell was working to head us off at the pass. He did so with a formal commitment from White House Chief of Staff John Sununu that the president would veto S. 137. The Republicans had all the cover they needed. They could let the bill pass without the pain of blame. There would be no need to filibuster. They could rest comfortably that the bill would never become law as long as Bush was in the White House.

Seeing that my prediction of failure was correct when I originally resigned my Chief LA position, I was ready to depart the scene. My six-month extended stay on the Hill cost me a planned trip to Europe, a certain academic work load in graduate school, and a great deal of patience. I wrote Boren my final memo prior to the scheduling of floor consideration of S. 137 to tell him that since our bill had no chance of ultimate passage, it was time to leave his staff for good.

As I already had been given a going-away, gold Senate seal watch by Boren and the staff in December, there would be no good-bye party or bill-signing ceremonies. So my departure from the scene was a depressing withdrawal. Like the "old soldier," General MacArthur, I too would just fade away, disappointed that years of effort were drowned in partisan stalemate.

Perhaps one of the most satisfying acknowledgments for my work on Capitol Hill in the battles for campaign finance reform came from a paragraph in *Roll Call* on July 9, 1990, which mentioned my departure. The paragraph in the "Heard on the Hill" column was entitled "Bad Omen."

The Democrats' top dog on campaign finance reform—Sen. David Boren (D-Okla.)—is once again losing his top aide for the issue, Greg Kubiak, . . . [who] returned as a special consultant in January when it looked as though campaign reform would be a hot issue in 1990. Now, in the wake of a failed bipartisan reform summit, Kubiak is going back to the books part-time at American University. . . . HOH interpretation: Campaign reform is fading fast.

I departed the staff by the Fourth of July 1990—my own Independence Day—available only by telephone for conversations with Boren or his staffers who now carried the ball. My last appearance in the Senate would come on August 1, when the Senate was due to vote on S. 137, which was inroduced some nineteen months earlier. The debate was much like the S. 2 script of the previous Congress. There was only one change in the plot. Republicans let the bill go through based on their assurance that even if the House passed a bill, the White House would veto anything the Democratic Congress might produce. A filibuster was not necessary.

Boren asked me to come sit on the floor with him during the final roll call vote, saying that I "deserve to be there when it passes." My eligibility for floor privileges was intact as I remained on the payroll through that week to compensate for my extra hours on the job. However, I respectfully declined.

Instead, I watched that final debate in the family gallery of the Senate chamber, next to Boren's wife, Molly, and AA David Cox. That bittersweet decision came as the clerk called out the results: "59 yeas and 40 nays. The measure is agreed to."

For the first time ever, I was publicly thanked by Boren, who spoke on the floor of the Senate after that vote.

I would especially mention the work of Greg Kubiak who joined my staff in 1983, coming with me to Washington in 1984, and has been here and worked with me for all action on the legislation since Senator Goldwater and I first introduced that piece of legislation. . . . He is young in years . . . [but] has devoted approximately one-fourth of his own lifetime to this issue.

This was something of an exaggeration but appreciated nonetheless.

The House passed a similar version of our bill by a 255 to 155 margin two days later, on August 3. Despite the rush for the August recess and adjournment for the elections, there was a purposeful delay in setting up a conference committee to meld the two together for final passage and the president. As I predicted, the 101st Congress ended without passage of campaign finance reform.

THE BREWING STORM

Over a period of several months, the public witnessed the Keating Five ethics investigation, the rancor over the House and Senate pay raise votes in 1989 and 1991, and the unrest over the bounced checks in the "House Bank." It was enough to worry any incumbent who felt the slippage of public tolerance of Congress, much less support. You could begin to see that slippage with the drive for term limitation referendums on ballots in states like Colorado, Oklahoma, California, and Washington.

After the awful episode of the Senate's consideration and hearings on Clarence Thomas's nomination to the Supreme Court, a new low was reached. As the insensitivity to a charge of sexual harassment forced the Judiciary Committee to oversee an extraordinary second round of public, television hearings, one news commentator asked a central question, "Can't they do *anything* right?"

After Thomas was sworn in and armchair analysts discussed the nature of sexual harassment, the chauvinism of the Senate, and impropriety of leaks of classified FBI reports, one Senate member gave his own spin on how the Senate "Club" should change its rules. He connected Senate political fears as the sad, underlying motivator for most of their official deeds. In the Sunday, October 20, 1991, *Washington Post* opinion section, Texas Sen. Lloyd Bentsen (D) stated,

> Negative advertising is the campaign weapon of choice. Thirty-second spots with slick images often down out thoughtful discussions of genuine issues. Modern campaigns are not only too negative but they last too long and cost too much, and the money chase is a time-consuming diversion from legislative duties. Campaign finance reform is long overdue.

Even though the focus of Bentsen's op-ed piece was the outdated rules of the Senate, his point on modern campaigns was important. Underneath their behavior as aggressive advocates or timid interviewers, senators were afraid of reprisal from powerful, constituency interest groups and their campaign resources. The systemic reform needed after the debacle of the sordid Thomas nomination was not punishment for leaks to the press or a requirement for closed executive sessions of the committee but rather a more level field of competition between fearful incumbents and soon-to-be challengers. Still, those "reforms" would be written by the "reformed."

Keith White, a seasoned reporter for the Gannett News organization, summed up the plight of congressional reform efforts by quoting cartoon character Pogo: "We have met the enemy, and he is us." The journalist said, "I think individual members of Congress are too close to the issue to view it with detachment, and everybody inevitably thinks about how the rules would apply to their own campaigns. I don't think incumbents are ever going to give challengers the benefit of the doubt."

But somehow, the Senate and House acted to remove the shroud that darkened their institutional honor. The Senate moved first at lightning pace to set the tone for House action. On April 11, 1991, early in the calendar of the 102nd Congress, the Senate Rules and Administration Committee reported on Boren's fifth bill on campaign finance reform. The evolution of Boren's legislation traveled the date line from 1983 to 1991 with S. 1443, S. 1806, S. 2, and S. 137. But not until 1991 would his measure move with such speed and ease. In the short period of thirteen days, Wendell Ford's committee held three days of hearings and one markup session to report, by a 7 to 2 vote, the latest of Boren's installments, S. 3.

Boren's final appeal for the bill on the floor was put simply:

> What are we talking about when we talk about campaign finance reform? What is the real issue? We are talking about whether we ought to do something to stop unlimited spending of money on political campaigns. Those of us who are supporting S. 3 say yes, this is what is wrong with the political system. . . . How long are we going to wait to stop the money chase in American politics and return this government back to the people? . . . Do we want to limit spending, or do we not? That is the issue.

The Senate agreed that it was the issue. On May 23, the bill passed by a 56 to 42 margin, with five Democratic senators joining Republican opponents of the bill while five Republicans joined the Democrats.

The House passed its bill after a great internal and intraparty struggle. Rep. Sam Gejdenson (D-Conn.), as chair of the House Task Force on Campaign Finance Reform, helped develop the Campaign Spending Limit and Election Reform Act of 1991. Its goal, by Gejdenson's measure, was to "control the escalating costs of campaigns, reduce the time spent fund raising, and remove the public perception that special interests and wealth dominate campaigns." That bill was reported out of the House Administration Committee in November 1991 and passed soon thereafter.

Unlike the 1990 legislation I watched pass, these two bills had time to be reconciled in a joint conference committee of the House and Senate. Thus the normal legislative process we all learned in high school could come into play. They did pass a conference report, with the House taking the first crack at it on April 9, 1992, in the midst of the House Bank check scandal. In a

speech on the floor, longtime reform leader Oklahoma Rep. Mike
Synar appealed to the House:

It would be ironic, indeed, as the emerging nations of Eastern
Europe slowly return power to their citizens, that this Congress, which
for the dark days of Communist rule was the bright beacon of hope for
those behind the Iron Curtain, is seen as moving away in the opposite
direction. . . .
If we truly are committed to beginning to rebuild the public
confidence which is so necessary to the fabric of this democracy, let us
accept this challenge today and pass this legislation. Then we can say
that we have made this democracy more competitive, we have improved the access of its citizens to the democracy, and we have
enhanced this democracy the way our Founding Fathers would have
wanted it.

The conference report on S. 3 was then adopted by a vote of 259
to 165. The Senate followed suit, passing the bill on April 30 by a
vote of 58 to 42.

THE BUSH VETO

History will remember great presidents for an ability to work
within the rugged boundaries of a democratic government on
issues important to the country. Despite the unilateral powers of
a president to engage troops in war or dispatch aid to flood-
ravaged areas of the nation, the more difficult task and test
of leadership is success in working with the legislative branch
of government. A president must convert those powers of electoral persuasion that earns his occupancy of the Oval Office to
powers of congressional persuasion in fulfilling the duties of that
office.

But history will also remember the failure to persuade and
lead. In the absence of his ability to influence Congress and lead
for his own agenda, a president can yield, compromise, or utilize
a tool of failure, the veto. Pres. George Herbert Walker Bush
often—and successfully—resorted to the veto. And his disin-
terest in campaign finance reform, beyond as a device to blame

Congress for the failures of government, led him to use his twenty-eighth consecutive successful veto on S. 3.

After the evening news on a quiet spring Saturday night, May 9, 1992, I continued work on this manuscript pouring over various documents to review for inclusion in the saga of campaign finance reform. Taking a break around 9:20 P.M., I thought I would check the Prodigy news service on my home computer to see if I had received any electronic mail and what headlines were making the news. There, on the blue and gray screen came the bold headline that would surely be front page news for the Sunday newspapers being printed that night: "Bush Deep Sixes Campaign Reform Bill."

For the first time since Gerald Ford signed the 1974 Federal Election Campaign Act, a president was given a fundamental reform measure of our most basic instrument of democracy. And George Bush vetoed it. The text of the president's veto message to Congress outlined his three goals of reform: "For three years I have called on the Congress to overhaul our campaign finance system in order to reduce the influence of special interests, to restore the influence of individuals and political parties, and to reduce the unfair advantages of incumbency. S. 3 would not accomplish any of these objectives."

Probably no statement about the reform legislation that eventually passed both houses of Congress in 1992 better epitomizes the lack of engagement between the opponents and supporters of campaign finance reform. Bush contended that S. 3 would not reduce the power of PACs. In fact, the bill, since its inception a decade earlier by bipartisan House sponsors David Obey and Thomas Railsback, would do plenty to reduce the influence of PACs. The debate wore down to two devices to do so.

The Democratic way to reduce PACs was through an aggregate limit. Rather than ban the legal—if not constitutionally protected—participation of PACs by disallowing their contributions, supporters of the bill argued for an aggregate limit. Some Republicans and opponents argued the evils of PACs in support of a total ban. Yet sensing the Free Speech thicket of such a change, the president's legislation allowed for their continued existence in case the Supreme Court overruled the ban. Then their contribution limit would be lowered to $1,000.

So here is the result. Under the Democratic bill, a House member would be limited to $200,000 in PAC money under an aggregate limit. Under the president's bill, with well over 4,000 PACs in existence, the same House member could theoretically get over $4,000,000 from PACs. So who wants to lower PAC influence?

The President's veto declared a desire to return the "influence of individuals and political parties" in the electoral process. His concern was that individuals might be foreclosed from conributing to the candidate of their choice if spending limits shut them out. He also cared that political parties—particularly the Republican party, then flush with funds to share with candidates—be able to give more to their candidates.

What is so noble about a wealthy businessman giving $100,000 to the Republican National Committee, which then divides it between several state party committees who cannot excite enough in-state voters to contribute to it. This is a common soft money practice. The Democratic bill respected individuals by encouraging their direct involvement with campaigns and candidates. Is an elected candidate going to be more responsive to voters whom he or she has no time for, or big money contributors who keep his or her campaign afloat in a never-ending sea of money.

The Republican philosophy on money, espoused indirectly in the president's veto message, was one spoken privately by McConnell in a negotiating session I attended in 1988: "The average Republican is a small business person who doesn't have time to get involved for a candidate. He doesn't have time like a labor union worker does to go door to door for a Democrat. He runs a business and wants to participate by writing a check to the candidate who is going to protect the way he does business." McConnell spoke passionately for his constituency that values money as a sign of political commitment.

House Speaker Tip O'Neill, before he left office, decried the current finance system in Congress when he told a journalist in 1986 that incumbents should not be able to build such big war chests. With no limits and no competition, we have seen incumbency take on more a royal blessing than a public responsibility.

The biggest incumbent advantage—more valuable than staff and franking privileges—is that they are in power, now. Money from special interests will follow that power. You can be a challenger who wins a congressional seat with 51 percent of the vote and is deep in campaign debt today and have your committee assignment and a debt-retirement PAC fund-raiser tomorrow. If Bush was serious about curtailing incumbent advantages, he would have signed S. 3.

So it was. Through the entirety of the Bush administration, campaign finance reform was dead. The irony in his veto was deep indeed. Despite the president's adamant opposition to public financing schemes for congressional elections, the Bushes consistently checked "yes" on the earmarking of $1 to the Presidential Election Fund on their federal tax returns. A system good enough for him but not for the Congress.

REMEDY FOR REFORM

The saddest lesson I learned through the eyes of a Senate staffer was that even though most Americans view government as a public trust, many senators regard their office as an earned asset. As noble as many may be who hold those cherished offices, after a certain point in time, many forget how they got there, who they work for, or what their job is.

I saw it when a conservative Republican senator stormed out of the Russell Senate Office Building with two aides in tow, looking desperately for his car and driver, which were supposed to be waiting, then berating the aides and even a Capitol police officer for not knowing where they were. Too many of these men expect to be waited on hand and foot, forgetting that "Senator" is not a title of royalty but one of service.

I saw it when a liberal Senate Democrat impatiently questioned why Senator Boren and I were not open to the idea of exempting "fund-raising costs" and "flower funds" from the spending limits of the campaign finance bill. This proreform senator who swore off PAC money in his first Senate campaign and was a national champion for liberal organizations like Public Citizen felt passionately about carving loopholes that would render impotent an otherwise strong spending limit bill.

And I saw it when Sen. Bob Dole of Kansas physically avoided Boren on the Senate floor at key times in the debate on campaign reform, knowing he was charged with representing the selfish interests of his party and the conservative faction of his Senate caucus rather than his own or his state's interests on an important national issue.

Despite my personal dislike for the darker side of politics, I am reminded that such actions are not lost in time. The corresponding political axiom is, "What goes around, comes around."

Minnesota Republican Rudy Boschwitz, leader of the opposition to the Boren-Goldwater PAC amendment, lost his seat in the Senate after a campaign four years later that focused on his reliance on special interest, PAC money. It is widely believed that how the late former Sen. John Tower treated his colleagues while a senator was the real reason for the defeat of his nomination as secretary of defense. Charges of drinking and womanizing were merely complementary and public reasons. And the excesses of Alan Cranston's thirst for campaign dollars were evident in the Keating Five ethics investigation that forced his decision to retire and the official reprimand from the Senate. Despite members of Congress who tarnish the image of the institution, publicly or privately, most serve with honesty and honor.

Those in Congress who are serious about changing our campaign finance laws should be mindful of two central objectives of equal importance. They go back to the dual reform considerations mentioned in the first chapter: ethical and competitive. Not only should the influence of narrow-interest money be checked, balanced, and diminished but true competition must be restored and promoted in our electoral process.

In the wake of the visibly painful Keating Five Senate ethics hearings, all one hundred senators should be frightened by potential links between their exponentially growing pool of contributors and the need to do background checks on those potential donors. Further, the growing wall of incumbency advantage is fortified by those monied special interests — and the public knows it.

I accept the political and human reality that no sitting incumbent wants to help enact a law that will make it potentially more difficult for him or her to seek reelection to Congress. But the hidden truth for Congress to realize is the underlying disgust and disdain the public is increasingly feeling toward its government. My own theory makes a clear progression from the cozy relationship between monied interests and public officials to the inaccessibility of those officials to the public to general cynicism about government.

A Kettering Foundation-sponsored survey from spring 1991 dispels the conventional wisdom that Americans are apathetic about politics, in favor of a more sophisticated belief that "they no longer believe they can have an effect." It goes on to proclaim that citizens are reacting to negative, expensive, sound-bite campaigns by turning away from politics on one level, while getting involved in "community action" on another.

Bill Moyers, former top aide to President Johnson and respected journalist, seems to agree with the state of the politics, media, and the citizenry. In a *Washington Post* magazine interview he said, "The purpose of politics in the media age is to make people feel good, not to think critically about what we need to do to solve our problems."

Congress has started to feel the energy that exists in their states and districts, where political vigilantism is seen in the form of everything from tame neighborhood drug watches to state referendums on congressional term limits. America's clearest distrust of Washington as the place to find answers to their problems is concluded in the Kettering summary statement: "Citizens believe there has been a hostile takeover of politics by special interests and lobbyists." The winds of citizen unease could be diagnosed as the logical plea to put competition back into elections, bring into balance the inordinate power of special interests, and thus raise their own respect in the process.

Through seven years of fruitless toil to reach a bipartisan agreement on campaign finance reform, one lesson was taught over and over and over: Everyone protects his or her own interest. PAC managers espouse the virtues of collective, disclosed giving as a sign of healthy political involvement. Party officials, despite verbiage to the contrary, prefer the status quo of evading the spirit or letter of the law. Elected officials individually work to produce 535 potential reform bills that will ensure collective stalemate. And citizens are left cynical, confused, and without recourse. The recipe for comprehensive reform at this point in the debate consists of three basic ingredients: A little *time*, a little *heat*, and a lot of *leadership*.

As the ethics clouds that have darkened Congress in recent months and years are still boiling, public "heat" continues to grow hotter. "Leadership," the most important ingredient, however, is the biggest question mark. Are Congress and the administration willing to act beyond their own or their party's interests? Despite the usually pessimistic state of affairs for action on the perennial issue of campaign finance reform, goodwill and leadership could see real reform enacted.

If agreement on principles can be made on the two basic objectives of true competition and cleaner campaign money, then what follows is a broad outline for a bipartisan bill:

1. Voluntary, Flexible Spending Limits. The 1990 Senate Campaign Finance Reform Panel issued a breakthrough outline for a way to overcome Republican opposition to spending limits. Distinguish between good and bad money. Limit the bad (PAC, out-of-state, and large contributions), not the good (small, in-state). Set limits by state and district that are high enough for challengers, but exempt from that limit the first $250 of an in-state contribution.

The equal number of Senate Democrats and Republicans who still balk at this are being partisan. All the more reason to pass it now. The last three years of opposition to spending limits by Republican incuments have ill-served many a Republican challenger.

2. Public Resources. Even with flexible limits, challengers and open seat nominees are at a disadvantage in getting early "seed" money to get name recognition. A public grant or broadcast voucher of high value would be the ticket for those who agreed to the spending limit. As with the Senate bill passed in 1990 and 1991, a threshold amount of private fund raising must be accomplished to prove viability and protect the public funds, which could come from a better publicized tax checkoff. (Just as an aside, I would repeal the state-by-state spending limits and coverage of convention costs in the presidential system today. They encourage cheating and drain the fund unnecessarily.)

3. Broadcast Rates. It is time for broadcasters, who have gouged political advertisers in front of a blinded FCC, to provide a true "lowest unit rate." Coupled with vouchers for air time, candidates would have two great incentives to comply with flexible spending limits. Further, the persistent problem of setting limits to distinguish varying costs of campaigning might be addressed with a biennial task force to derive a "campaign cost index" (CCI). Such a committee structured within the FEC—made up of five representatives from the FEC, FCC, and national party committees—could meet each off-election year to issue the CCI by congressional district and state. The CCI, a legislated factor of cost-per-gross-rating point in state or district media markets, inflation, postal rates, and perhaps other campaign sensitive costs, could then be multiplied by the base spending limit in each race. Such a system would ensure that true campaign costs in a television age could be reflected in the spending limits while still slowing the money chase.

4. Limit on PACs. Despite a background of bashing PACs, beginning with Senators Boren and Goldwater in 1985, I have never believed it wise to write them out of existence. Aside from being constitutionally "risky" (opening the door for a Supreme Court decision that could give back direct corporate and labor union political/financial influence), it is not necessary. An aggregate limit on candidate receipt of PAC money will put the right rein on a de facto incumbent advantage. Also, it will cut in half the individual PAC contribution rate, to $2,500.

Some contributors prefer to dilute or define their money through PACs. The risks are not worth taking away that ability.

5. Parties. Even though I do not think we will ever change from a candidate-centered electoral system to a party-centered system, I agree with every self-respecting observer of campaign financing that parties should be strengthened. The greatest role they can play is to be a resource for challengers, rather than the incumbent service organizations they have grown to be.

But rather than blindly open the coffers as potential conduits for money that gets squeezed out from other places in the system, I would no more than double their "coordinated expenses" allowance to candidates. And even though incumbents would not go for it, I would increase that allowance by a penny per voter for challengers only as an extra benefit. Incumbents get plenty of public perks that would not begin to be offset by such a modest challenger bonus.

Democrats should not ignore this issue any longer. The "party of the people" cannot be seen as philosophically consistent by proudly issuing press releases boasting of $100,000 "soft money" contributors, on one hand, and opposing hard-earned money contributed by hardworking citizens being channeled to financially hard-up challengers, on the other.

6. Federal Election Commission. The weakest link in our curent system has been the FEC. Commonly called the "toothless tiger" of enforcement, the six-commissioner stalemate seems a hopeless fate. I would recommend adding to the mix a presidentially appointed, Senate-confirmed general counsel as a voting member of the commission. This commissioner/counsel could be empowered to engage in more timely investigations and begin enforcement actions unless halted by a majority vote of the commission. If political goodwill prevailed, such appointments would be individuals with the same judicial temperament and nonpartisan background as any Supreme Court justice nominee. Even though some would see it as the creation of an election czar, it retains a check on the counsel's power while improving lax enforcement of the law.

7. Soft Money. Any reform will be rendered useless if money that affects federal elections is not brought under the same contribution limits as federal law. Otherwise, the financial growth industry of the 1990s will continue to be soft money.

I would stipulate that no candidate or federal officeholder could raise money for *any* party or other 501(c) committee which does not meet federal contribution limit requirements. Otherwise, the Keating/Cranston story could be retold again and again. We should end the days of fat cat contributors for good.

Congress has mistakenly taken everyone — PACs, party officials, contributors, political consultants, broadcasters, academics, and themselves — into consideration when addressing campaign finance reform. Everyone but the disillusioned voter. Citizens vote only when they feel they have a stake in the system. They feel no stake in the system when power brokers with money control it. And special, monied interests control the system when the sky is the limit on their financial influence.

Our Capitol building remains a vivid symbol of democratic governance. The beauty of the dome can give even the most cynical critic a sense of pride. However, the Congress that works underneath that dome has become gilded with gold given by factional interests.

But we can return to the day when the quality of debate is more important than the quantity of money to influence it. With the right care and real reform, the gilded dome could be more reflective of the intended beauty — and less deceptive of the inherent faults — of our democracy.

Index